Hypocrisy

Hypocrisy

The Tales and Realities of Drug Detainees in China

Vincent Shing Cheng

Hong Kong University Press
The University of Hong Kong
Pokfulam Road
Hong Kong
www.hkupress.hku.hk

© 2019 Hong Kong University Press

ISBN 978-988-8455-68-3 (*Hardback*)

All rights reserved. No portion of this publication may be reproduced or transmitted in any form or by any means, electronic or mechanical, including photocopying, recording, or any information storage or retrieval system, without prior permission in writing from the publisher.

British Library Cataloguing-in-Publication Data
A catalogue record for this book is available from the British Library.

10 9 8 7 6 5 4 3 2 1

Printed and bound by Paramount Printing Co. Ltd., Hong Kong, China

Contents

Acknowledgements — vi

1. Introduction — 1
2. Tales of 'Heroes' and 'Saviours' — 16
3. Police and the 'Hooks' — 30
4. Initiation Ceremony in Drug Detention — 47
5. Prison Authority and the 'Inmate Elites' — 79
6. Post-discharge Reintegration and Surveillance — 103
7. Conclusion — 118

Appendix: Basic Information of the Former Drug Detainees — 127

Chinese Glossary — 129
References — 140
Index — 157

Acknowledgements

This book would never have been completed without the encouragement, advice, and support of many people.

First and foremost, I wish to thank the former drug detainees who trusted me and shared their stories with me. I also want to show my deepest gratitude to Professor Børge Bakken, my mentor, supervisor, and friend. I have benefited enormously from his encouragement, guidance, insight, and wisdom, without which this project would not have been accomplished. My sincere thanks also go to the examiners of my PhD thesis: Professor David Palmer, Professor Cheris Chan, and Professor Sue Trevaskes. Their comments and advice showed me how I could improve my research. Special thanks go to Professor James Seymour and Professor Saskia Hufnagel who provided extensive and insightful comments on this manuscript.

I also owe thanks to many academics who offered stimulation and encouragement along the way. These include professors I met at the University of Hong Kong: Karen Laidler, Maggy Lee, Travis Kong, Eric Chui, Lui Tai Lok, Thomas Wong, Chu Yiu Kong, Michael Adorjan, Alistair Fraser, Jeff Martin, Li Cho, Wang Peng, Peter Cunich, and Bert Becker; scholars I met through the East Asian Policing Studies Forum: Lawrence Ho, Peter Manning, Jessica Li, Nicole Cheung, Sara Zhong, Melissa Bull, Michael Siu, and Bo Jiang; and academics I met through different academic conferences: Ivan Sun, Liqun Cao, Dennis Wong, Xiong Moulin, Spenser Li, Doris Chu, Enshan Li, Liu Liu, Lennon Zhang. My apologies to anyone I have omitted.

I would also like to thank 'Børge's army'—Dr Jianhua Xu, Dr Trent Bax, Dr Yujing Fun, Dr Tiffany Ip, and Xi Zhang. Their knowledge and support have helped me through many difficult times during this research. Special thanks go to Dr Xu, my *shixiong*. Without his encouragement and guidance, I would still be 'thinking' about writing a PhD proposal. He has been my role model since a dozen years ago when I met him at the University of Hong Kong.

The Centre for Criminology at the University of Hong Kong had also provided valuable resources for the preparation of this manuscript. I would like to thank Professor Karen Laidler and Leona Li for their kind support.

Acknowledgements

My gratitude also goes to the academics I met at the Open University of Hong Kong for their support when this manuscript was under preparation: Garland Liu, Charles Kwong, Wai-leung, Beatrice Lam, Michael Ng, Percy Lui, Tess Pak, Raymond Lau, Samson Yuen, Kaby Kung, Eden Li, Walter Lee, Arbitor Ma, Carol Tsang, Chi Hung Wong, Jonathan Ngai, Yuxing Yu, Yuka Chan, Kosaku Yoshino, and Michael Keane.

I have also enjoyed intellectual discussions and leisure time with old and new sociology graduate students from the University of Hong Kong, many of whom are now promising young scholars in the field: Sandy To, Sun Jue, Au Yeung Shing, Kent Lee, Nazrul Islam, Walter Yuan, Zening Yao, Connie Yan, Han Zhang, Yang Chen, Lu Chen, Qing Liu, Marius Wamsiedel, Yanran Yao, Corrina Leung, Leona Li, Grace Au, Allison Tsui, Dorothy Wong, Heather Xie, Tianchi Lue, Owen Fung, Kent Deng, Ayumu Kobayashi, Tony Lin, Albert Yau, Cherie Yan, Carmen Tong, and Zhao Liu. Special thanks go to Kin Tsang; we cheered each other up during some of our most frustrating times.

The support staffs at the University of Hong Kong and the Open University of Hong Kong have been very helpful and I would like to thank them for their administrative support: Davy Lau, Kelly Lee, Connie Ko, Tina Wu, Vincent Chau, Rachel Lo, Fandy Li, Eagle Wong, Dolores He, Charlie Kwok, Cathy Wong, Mary Chue, Ling Chan, Kathy Koo, Mary Lok, Jingjing Hu, Billy Wong, Terry Lee, and Candy Leung.

I have also benefited greatly from the guidance of my editors, Susie Han and Clara Ho of Hong Kong University Press. They guided me through the whole process of manuscript publication. Two reviewers also offered valuable suggestions that helped me improve this book.

I also want to thank my family and especially my grandfather, who encouraged me to pursue an academic career but passed away the day before I received my PhD offer from the graduate school.

1
Introduction

This book tells the story of Chinese drug detainees who have been incarcerated for illicit drug use. It documents their experiences of being arrested and imprisoned as well as their lives after release. Behind their painful experiences is a fundamental contradiction between the unrealistically ideal party propaganda, which is made according to 'exemplary norms' (Bakken 2000), and the actual everyday practices of police officers and detention facility and prison officers, which are based on a variety of practical norms guided by different bureaucratic rules and regulations. This book is first and foremost about a failed system of rehabilitation, but also bears on a more general system that drug detainees perceive as hypocritical in contemporary China.

All former drug detainees depicted in this book had been arrested and incarcerated in different detention facilities, 're-education-through-labour' camps or centres because of using illicit drugs.[1] They were all discharged and claimed to have been able to abstain from drugs[2] when I met them in two Chinese cities—Zhiyang and Motai.[3] These detention facilities are all prison-like, although they are not legally classified as 'prison'. In this book, I use the term 'former prisoners' interchangeably with the term 'former drug detainees' and 'former drug users'. By 'prison', I am not referring to the legal definition of prison in China. According to Chinese law, 'prison' (*jianyu* 監獄) refers to what was previously called a 'reform through labour camp' (*laodong gaizao* 勞動改造) where court-sentenced criminals are incarcerated. However, in this study, I do not limit my definition of prison to the Chinese official use of the term. Instead, I refer to the former drug detainees' colloquial use of the term, which includes 're-education through labour' (*laodong jiaoyang* 勞動教養), 'compulsory isolation for drug rehabilitation centre' (*qiangzhi geli jiedu suo* 強制隔離戒毒所), 'compulsory drug rehabilitation centre' (*qiangzhi jiedu suo* 強制戒毒所), and 'detention centre' (*kanshou suo* 看守所). These institutions are also

---

1. These drugs include heroin (n=40), amphetamines (n=18), ecstasy (n=6), ketamine (n=5), dolantin (n=3), marijuana (n=3), cocaine (n=3), magu (n=3), and morphine (n=1).
2. One former prisoner, Jim, however was using a pill called 'happy pill' (*kaixin wan* 開心丸) when I met him in 2013. Jim claimed that it was not an 'illicit drug' but a prescription medicine he obtained from Japan. However, according to one of Jim's friend, his behaviour after taking the 'happy pill' was very similar to his behaviour after taking amphetamine.
3. Both Zhiyang and Motai are pseudonyms.

sometimes referred to colloquially as the 'great wall' (*daqiang* 大牆), the 'palace' (*gong* 宮), or merely the 'inside' (*limian* 裡面). All the former prisoners had been incarcerated in at least one of the above institutions. Among the forty-six former prisoners, thirty-three had been incarcerated in 're-education through labour'. Forty had been incarcerated in 'compulsory drug rehabilitation centres', and eight had been incarcerated in 'compulsory isolation for drug rehabilitation centres'.

Since one of the main parts of this book concerns the condition in the 're-education-through-labour' (*laojiao*) institutions in China, some clarification of this system must be made at the start of the book. This is particularly important since the system was officially terminated in 2013 (Liu 2017), in the midst of my fieldwork on the project. *Laojiao* is not a legal but an administrative system of punishments. It enables police officers to sentence anyone for as many as three years of detention in a re-education-through-labour camp, with a possible one-year extension—in some cases, this is even stretched to much longer periods (State Council 1982). The police may decide on this without the participation of courts, lawyers, prosecutors, or legal interference at any level. The re-education camps or 'centres' were in all practical ways totally dependent on police discretion. Subsequently, the inmates were not seen as 'criminals' but as offenders of administrative orders and regulations only.

The mainstay of the camps' inmates are drug users, and the official propaganda surrounding these detainees (or 'former inmates' and 'prisoners' as I freely call them here) is that of 'helping', 'educating', and 'saving' them from their drug habits and the 'evil drug dealers' who lure them into drug abuse. The final aim—so goes the official narrative—is rehabilitating them for a future normal life in society. The system is clearly a prison in all but name. This book will focus on the conditions in these institutions and the daily life of their inmates. I will also focus on how the ideals of the official propaganda run counter to the reality and experiences of the inmates, creating an ethic and structure based on hypocrisy rather than 'help' and 'education'.

After the termination of the *laojiao*, 'compulsory isolation for drug rehabilitation centres' (*qiangzhi geli jiedu suo*) were established all over China to take over drug users from *laojiao*. Much like the *laojiao*, the new centres are also prison-like institutions. Arrested drug users are still sent to an institution of incarceration rather than a court after the official termination of the *laojiao* system. In other words, the change is more one in name rather than in substance for the type of inmates I describe in this book. Some of my interviewees, as well as the steady stream of new people recruited into the system, might well find themselves in different forms of 'treatment' or 'legal education centres', or other types of 'community correction' units in the future. They will still be detained over long periods of time under more or less the same prison-like conditions described in this book. Discretion will still be the reality of the system, and there is reason to believe that the system I describe here will continue in one form or another. There may be some added humane traits like better food and living conditions, but the basics of the system will most probably be upheld in the forms I describe here. The discrepancies between the ideals of rosy party propaganda and the realities of humiliation and pain in detention will also most probably be upheld in forms similar to those described in this book. We may hope that some of the system of 'hypocrisy' discussed in this book will wane and finally disappear, but for that to happen there needs to be much more reform of the system than a merely formal 'termination' of the system. This change will continue, but there is no 'abolishment' on the books whatsoever in terms of the reality of inmates' suffering under prison-like conditions during detention.

Many studies exist that examine the factors that contribute to former prisoners reoffending and factors that make them withdraw from offending (Adorjan and Chui 2014; Das 2008; Farrall et al. 2011; Gao 2008; Maruna 2001, 2004; Maruna et al. 2004; Maruna and Roy 2007; Mauer 2005; Meachum 2000; Mulder et al. 2011; Paternoster and Bushway 2009; Sampson and Laub 1993; Sinha 2001; Spohn and Holleran 2002; Visher, La Vigne, and Farrell 2003). One common factor that contributes to recidivism, according to these studies, is ironically the interventions from the criminal justice system (Farrall et al. 2011; Mathiesen 1990). The prison, among other criminal justice agents, has been regarded as a breeding ground of subculture, hate, and recidivism (Meachum 2000; Spohn and Holleran 2002; H. Yao 2012). Instead of being rehabilitated, inmates very often go through a process called 'prisonization', in which they take on the prison culture (Clemmer 1966), which is usually seen as 'deviant' and counterproductive to rehabilitation. Moreover, instead of learning from the 'education' provided in the prison, prison inmates tend to 'reject the rejectors', which further reduces the chances of rehabilitation (Mathiesen 1990; McCorkle and Korn 1954). Beside the criminal justice system, other risk factors like individual personality and psychopathic traits (Das 2008), employment opportunities (Mauer 2005), drug use (Visher et al. 2003), neighbourhood environment (Kubrin and Stewart 2006), and dysfunctional families (Mulder et al. 2011) were suggested to be related to discharged prisoners' recidivism.

Beyond what makes offenders reoffend, another major question in the existing literature is what makes some other offenders withdraw from offending (Adorjan and Chui 2014; Gao 2008; Maruna 2001, 2004; Maruna et al. 2004; Maruna and Roy 2007; Paternoster and Bushway 2009; Sampson and Laub 1993). One of the earliest criminological discussions of desistance from crime can be found in Quetelet's (1984) discussion of the relationship between age and desistance. Some scholars have suggested that this age invariance theory conforms to the 'law of nature', which suggests that criminals 'age out' of crime when they grow up and get old (Gottfredson and Hirschi 1990, 124). Similarly, Matza suggests that adolescents would leave delinquency behind after their 'maturational reform' (1964, 22). Other than ageing factors, criminologists also examine psychological and social factors that help former criminals withdraw from crime. Braithwaite (1989), in his treatment of traditional Japanese society, suggests that reintegrative shaming is useful for the prevention of recidivism. By shaming the criminal act instead of the criminal, and by having a 'ceremony' of reintegration with words or gestures of forgiving,

Braithwaite suggests that the criminal can be more effectively deterred from reoffending. Other social factors like successful job placement and marriage are also shown to be beneficial to former offenders' desistance from crime (Sampson and Laub 1993).

In addition to looking at how social factors can affect former offenders' withdrawal from crime, some criminologists also examine how former offenders can desist from crime through cognitive process (Maruna 2001, 2004; Paternoster and Bushway 2009). By comparing persistent criminals and former criminals who desist from crime, Maruna (2001) suggests that the key for former criminals to 'go straight' is their ability to 'make good'—that is, to reinterpret their past failings or criminal acts in a positive way. Instead of seeing their previous criminal acts simply as shameful or as a failure, those who desist from crime can actually 'distort' their criminal past and positively 're-biograph' their life stories. One common story is that previous criminal history does not determine future failure but instead can operate as a necessary prelude for a new life. Other than self-biography, criminologists have also found that former criminals who have the will to acquire a more desirable non-criminal identity (the positive possible self) and are anxious about what they might become (the feared self) are more likely to desist from crime (Paternoster and Bushway 2009). To them, it is the *intention* of change that makes them change.

While important in explaining why certain former prisoners withdraw from crime and others continue to commit crime, such theories are less helpful in explaining the feelings and the narratives of the former prisoners I encountered. In traditional criminology, former prisoners' perceptions, especially their complaints against law enforcers, are very often seen as a neutralization technique which is used to rationalize or downplay their own wrongdoings (Sykes and Matza 1957). The neutralization argument suggests that delinquents develop different justifications so as to rationalize their criminal acts. Such rationalizations are used to protect the delinquents from self-blame and to more effectively lay the blame on others. Though the neutralization thesis explains the psychological mechanism behind former prisoners' complaints, it very often fails to take the full extent of the former prisoners' experiences seriously. This study attempts to fill this gap by examining and explaining Chinese former prisoners' subjective experiences and exploring the wider socio-political structure that might have contributed to their experiences.

Play-Acting and Hypocrisy

Former prisoners in this study have various complaints against police officers and prison officers. This study discusses issues surrounding two of their grievances: 'They are self-interested' and 'They say things in one way and do things in another' (*shuo yitao zuo yitao* 說一套, 做一套). By 'they', the former prisoners were referring to police officers, prison officers, and the party-state itself. When I dug deeper into what they actually meant when they said this, they were criticizing the fact that 'what they say' was far better than 'what they do'. To the former prisoners, they had seen a 'system of hypocrisy' in which the official propaganda glorifying the unrealistically 'selfless' 'models' (*mofan* 模範) of law enforcers or 'educators' contrasted sharply with the practical reality of the 'self-interested' individuals and the daily pain and humiliation of prison life. Since 'hypocrisy' is the main theme of this book, it is important to explain this concept in more detail before going deeper into the former prisoners' narratives.

The English word 'hypocrisy' derives from the Ancient Greek *hypokrisis* (ὑπόκρισις), meaning a 'public or theatrical performance', or simply 'play-acting' in the negative connotation of insincerity (Morwood and Taylor 2002). In moral psychology, the term is often defined as the failure to follow one's own expressed moral rules and principles. While psychologists have often seen the act of hypocrisy as the dark side of human nature, the concept has also had political connotations of deceit and manipulation. Niccolò Machiavelli, the master interpreter of political intrigue and the cynicism of power, once remarked: 'the mass of mankind accept what *seems* as what *is*; nay, are often touched more nearly by appearances than by realities' (Machiavelli 2006). This analysis of the discrepancies between ideals and realities can be applied to the rationalities of propaganda in today's China—to what *seems* and what *is* real—a theme I will return to later in this book.

Former prisoners frequently used the Chinese term for hypocrisy, *xuwei* (虛偽)—connoting falseness, emptiness, and ill intent—when referring to the way authorities had treated them. They often talked about the hypocrisy of the authorities that promised them help and education but in the end only provided pain, shame, and humiliation. Many former inmates confessed that they felt conned or manipulated. A recurring theme in my interviews and talks with the former inmates was distrust towards police and prison officers, a feeling that developed into resistance and scepticism towards official propaganda and official intent in general.

Building on my interactions with former inmates, this book attempts to visualize the very phenomenon of 'hypocrisy' as they experience it. I will take the original *etymological* meaning of hypocrisy as 'play-acting' and apply that original meaning to Erwin Goffman's *sociological* analysis of how such 'play-acting' takes place on different stages: one on the 'front-stage' and one on the 'back-stage' (Goffman 1958). According to this dramaturgical approach, individuals perform in specific ways on the front stage of 'impression management' that do not carry over to the backstage.

By rewinding this observation to the original Greek roots of 'hypocrisy', I hope to use that term as a lens through which we can see the lives of the former inmates from a clearer perspective. I will attempt to explain that in our context 'hypocrisy' is not only a personal, psychological, or ethical issue. While many of the roots and connotations of hypocrisy are anchored at the micro level, hypocrisy can also be understood from a larger macro perspective. Hypocrisy has to do both with structural and psychological factors. We may talk of more structural 'ways of lying' that are not only the fault of indecent or unethical men in uniforms, or the mere 'evil intent' of individuals (Bakken 2000). The system has its own logic of political and corrective philosophy, survival strategies, managerial rationality, and forced implementation. In a more concrete context, the official promises of 'help and education' to 'erring' individuals have been replaced with 'pain, shame, and humiliation' for alleged 'criminals' destined to suffer such negative treatment.

While I am far from suggesting a 'theory' about hypocrisy and its link to the prison system, I will propose a way to describe and understand the discrepancy between the 'ideals' and the 'realities' experienced by former inmates in the Chinese system of incarceration. We can perhaps see the contours of an even larger social 'system' in my description of the experiences of the former prisoners. While former prisoners very often criticized individual police and prison officers for the system of hypocrisy, this study can also be seen as an attempt to address the structure behind this 'system'. C. Wright Mills (1959) in his celebrated book *The Sociological Imagination* reminds us of the importance of understanding 'personal troubles' through 'public issues of social structure'. This book attempts to follow this wisdom and locates the former prisoners' grievances in a wider 'system of hypocrisy'.

Similarly, I understand the party propaganda as the party-state's self-presentation and strategy of 'impression management'. The actual day-to-day practices, especially those that involve the direct confrontation between former prisoners and the police and prison officers, can be seen as the 'backstage'—as practices which are usually not seen by the general public. From the vantage of the former prisoners, this is hypocritical—the front-stage ideal presentation is far better than the backstage 'reality'. For the 'system of hypocrisy', as I try to develop in more detail in this book, I am referring to this simultaneous occurrence of both the front-stage propaganda and the backstage reality not presented to the front-stage audiences, but exposed to the insiders of the backstage only.

The main research objectives of this book are to (1) document the discrepancy between the ideals of propaganda and the realities of the former prisoners' lives, with a particular focus on their experiences of arrest, imprisonment, and life after release; and (2) to examine a 'system of hypocrisy' as it is reflected in the experiences of the former prisoners.

More specifically, I first explore how the party-propaganda presents the model police officers and the model prison officers. I also examine the logic behind such presentations. Second, I examine former prisoners' narratives about their experiences with the police and prison officers when they were being arrested. I put particular focus on one of the police practices—the use of informers—and explore the police officers' concerns behind such practices. Third, I uncover former prisoners' interpretations to their experiences of imprisonment. With the example of what I call the 'initiation ceremony' in the prison and the example of the cooperation between the prison officers and the powerful inmates, I examine the practical norms that govern the day-to-day practices in the prisons. Finally, I explore former prisoners' encounters with police officers in their current post-release life. With the example of a surveillance system targeting former prisoners, I study the administrative concerns behind the police officers' practices. All these issues may reflect more specifically the Chinese former prisoners' personal experiences, but I would argue that they also possibly reflect a broader 'system' that is sometimes seen as hypocritical in contemporary China in general.

Heroes in the Propaganda and the Criminal Justice System in Reality

Mass media have been used as tools to propagandize political ideology in China at least since the early Maoist time (Brady 2008). In this propaganda, different 'model figures' (*mofan renwu* 模範人物) are made to educate the public, to enhance the party's moral legitimacy, and to maintain social order (Bakken 2000; Jiang 2001; B. Xu 2012; R. Yan 2004). Among other 'model figures', 'police officers' and 'prison officers' are very often presented in a way that highlights their 'exemplary' moral qualities, which are usually unrealistically 'ideal'. The specially tailored image of the model police and prison officers has, however, led to a specific form of hypocrisy. Former prisoners, with their experiences of direct contact with police and prison officers, can see the 'reality' behind the propaganda by comparing the model figures with those whom they meet and experience in their daily lives. While the propaganda very often propagates the idea that the law enforcers strive to save and rehabilitate drug users, the reality experienced by the former inmates was very different. We might say that the propaganda seems to somehow still work in the beginning, since the former prisoners did expect the police and prison officers to be possessed with at least some of the propagated moral qualities. It was not until the former prisoners had experienced real-life contact with the police and prison officers that they witnessed the system of hypocrisy.

Former prisoners might have had different types of personal contact with police officers even before they started to use drugs. However, their first arrest usually marks the inauguration of their experiences to the system of hypocrisy. While police officers are very often depicted as 'selfless', 'brave', or 'wise' in the party propaganda, the former prisoners saw the backstage of reality. Through their new experiences they began to see the police officers who arrested them as immoral, cunning, and self-interested. Most former prisoners would relate one specific police practice when they talked about the police officers—the use of drug dealers or drug users as informers. Former prisoners saw the police use of informers as a self-interested and immoral act. Although the Communist Party has a long tradition of using informers (Dutton 2005b), the police use of informers also seems to be grounded in the bureaucratic pressure which requires the individual police officer to meet a certain arrest quota (Han 2009; G. Wu 2009). Similarly, the individual police officers are required to maintain a close surveillance of former prisoners and former drug addicts upon their release from the prisons. The surveillance tactics, however, very often expose former prisoners' stigmatized identity and thereby put them in humiliating and degrading situations. From the former prisoners' point of view, all these practices show that the police officers are only concerned about their own self-interests and not in saving or rehabilitating drug users. This kind of hypocrisy can also be found in their experiences of imprisonment.

Prison, according to the propaganda, is a place for offenders' education and rehabilitation. Prison officers are supposed to be the people who help the inmates in their rehabilitation. The propaganda is all about helping and rehabilitating the drug users to get back to society, and the former prisoners also expected to see such efforts before they were incarcerated. The prison officers did provide some type of 'education' to the inmates by forcing the inmates to memorize classical Chinese moral texts and legal documents. The former prisoners' memories about imprisonment, however, are overwhelmed with different types of physical and mental pain. Upon the arrival of the new inmates to the prison cell, the prison officers and powerful prison inmates organized different 'initiation ceremonies' to socialize the new inmates into the prison environment. They were painful and humiliating ceremonies in which the new inmates were physically tortured and mentally degraded. Similar pain and degradation can be found throughout the whole process of incarceration. In the daily life of the prison, inmates were forced to obey different degrading rules and regulations in the name of 'education' or 'rehabilitation'. To many former prisoners, these rules are nothing more than tools of the prison officers to maintain power and prison order. Similarly, compulsory labour was enforced in the re-education-through-labour centres in the name of 'rehabilitation' and 'vocational training'. However, to the former prisoners, compulsory labour was more about generating profit for the prison authority. While the former prisoners recognized the 'pretence of rehabilitation', they had also learned to survive the prison by pretending that they were rehabilitated. While they saw the discrepancy between propaganda and reality, they also had learned to be hypocritical in order to survive the prison system.

Another important dimension of prison life is the formal and informal control system in the prisons. In order to maintain control and ensure the efficiency of the prison factory, prison officers appointed and cooperated with various powerful prison inmates in the daily operation of the prisons (Feng 2012; Y. Lu 2009). In order to maintain the control of these powerful prison inmates, the prison officers very often would provide them with legitimate and illegitimate benefits and privileges. In order to maintain these inmates' power, the prison officers invested them with the power to discipline and punish other inmates, which not only encouraged the heightened level of violence in the prison but also exposed another nasty backstage reality of the prison system to the inmates.

Breaking into the Social World of Former Drug Detainees

The journey of this research can be traced back to 2007. I met three former prisoners when I was doing fieldwork for my MPhil thesis in a coastal Chinese city—Zhiyang (not the real name). After my graduation from the MPhil programme, I travelled to Zhiyang again in 2009. The original purpose of this trip was to express my gratitude to the former prisoners who had provided me with enormous help during my fieldwork. In a banquet a former prisoner told me a story about one of her friends—also a former prisoner—who was humiliated by police officers during a raid at a hotel. This story triggered me to explore this topic further. I did not at first plan to develop my explorations into a book; at most, I planned to develop my thoughts into a paper. The more stories I heard from them, however, the more I got interested in their experiences.

Between 2007 and 2013 I met forty-six former prisoners who were willing to share their stories with me. I have conducted semi-structured interviews with forty-three of them and participated in their formal and informal social gatherings. In these interviews, I adopt a life-history approach. The former prisoners were invited to talk about previous experiences that they found important to their identity as a 'former prisoner' or 'former drug user'. I was also invited to join two Internet-based online chat groups counting over fifty members, who are all either former or current drug users. In this chat group, I had access to a database that contained daily conversations between the members.

Gaining access to the social world of former drug detainees is not an easy task. I was clearly an outsider when I first met the former prisoners. First, I was not born there and did not grow up in their city. I cannot speak their local dialect. Second, and probably more importantly, I have never been jailed, nor have I ever taken any illicit drugs. Similar to the situation in most other countries, people who have been incarcerated and taken illicit drugs are discriminated against, labelled, and stigmatized in China (Y. Chen 2008). Former prisoners do not want to expose their stigmatized identity and experiences to any outsiders.

This fact made part of my data collection difficult. When I first met Kaopu, a former prisoner in his early twenties, he refused to talk to me about any issues related to his previous experiences in the criminal justice system. He said, 'Why should I talk about it? I am now "normal" [*zhengchang* 正常]. There is nothing much else I want to say.' Similarly, Hui refused to see me in person when I contacted him through another former prisoner.

Goffman (1968b) has pointed out that once the stigmatized identity is exposed, stigmatized persons might not only face discrimination and reduced life opportunities but also blackmail from anyone who knows their secret identity. Therefore, stigmatized persons, especially those whose stigma is not immediately visible, usually manage their image and hide their stigmatized past very carefully. They only share their 'secret' information to those 'sympathetic others' who can adopt their world view and standpoints. Goffman points out two types of the 'sympathetic others': they are the 'own' and the 'wise' (1968b, 20). The 'own' are those who share the same stigma. Spending time with their 'own' people, stigmatized persons can feel at ease and be accepted as normal persons. For the former prisoners whom I met, their 'own' are other former prisoners who have been incarcerated for using drugs. Being a person who has never been incarcerated nor taken any drugs, I had no chance to be counted among their 'own' people.

The 'wise' are 'normal' persons, but 'whose special situation has made them intimately privy to the secret life of the stigmatized individual and sympathetic with it, and who find themselves accorded a measure of acceptance, a measure of courtesy membership in the clan' (Goffman 1968b, 28). According to Goffman, facing the 'wise', the stigmatized person can feel easy and knows that he would be seen and treated as a normal person. There are two types of the 'wise'. The first type is people who work in agencies that allow them to have close contact with stigmatized people. For example, social workers who serve former prisoners would be one type of the 'wise' in their conception. The second type of 'wise' people is those who are personally related to the stigmatized persons and who somehow share their stigma. They can be family members or close friends of the stigmatized person. I am neither the first nor the second type of the 'wise'. However, what I learned from Goffman is that stigmatized persons trust those whom they see as different from other people who might discriminate against them, threaten them, or blackmail them. The problem I faced in the beginning of the fieldwork is how to present myself as different from the dangerous 'others'.

A little bit about me and the winning of trust

Almost every former prisoner has said to me, 'You won't understand us, because you do not have our experience.' However, as some of the former prisoners said, I am somehow different from the 'ordinary people' (*yiban ren* 一般人). Some of my personal characteristics and habits might have made me 'different'. I have also consciously managed my image to make me 'different' from the others. Some of my personal characteristics and (bad) habits have turned out to be surprisingly helpful in kick-starting me to mingle with the former prisoners, and later winning their trust. I had spent a few years in a youth gang at a lower-class public housing estate when I was a kid. 'Deviant' acts like swearing usually bring me excitement rather than disgust. I had once been quite a heavy party drinker, and I am still a cigarette addict. I enjoyed the moments when I smoked and drank with the former prisoners. These little deviant acts became effective social lubricants and icebreakers for me during my fieldwork. During my research, I talked with them, listened to them, dined with them, sang with them, danced with them, smoked with them, and got drunk with them. To many former prisoners, the 'ordinary people' would never do these kinds of things together with them.

Many of the former prisoners had the experiences of being discriminated against. From their point of view, the 'ordinary people' do not want to talk to them, do not care about them, are afraid of them, or even hate them. A former prisoner, Shufang, said:

> In the ordinary people's eyes, we—those who take drugs—are not human beings [*bu shi ren* 不是人]. [In their eyes] we are 'inhuman' [*mei renxing* 沒人性]. (Shufang, interview 67, 2012)

Paradoxically, the social stigma, which was supposed to be a barrier for me to win the trust of the former prisoners, has instead made my fieldwork easier than I thought. Willingness to talk, eat, smoke, drink, and dance with them became evidence to many former prisoners that I was different from the 'ordinary people'. During these occasions my image as an 'outsider' gradually faded away—at least I felt so. Three of the former prisoners had asked me similar questions on different occasions: 'Are you really studying for a PhD? You look more like a "little gangster" [*xiao hunhun* 小混混].'

I was very aware of my self-presentations during the research. However, my membership role is not totally under my control. My membership role in the field was in between what Adler and Adler (1987) called peripheral and active membership. In the very beginning my role among the former prisoners was quite detached and they saw me as a 'student'. In 2007 when I was doing my fieldwork, in order to minimize the power relationship between the 'researcher' and the 'informants', I presented myself as a 'university student' (*daxue sheng* 大學生) who came to 'understand' (*liaojie* 了解) them. From 2009 to 2013 I was gradually referred to as 'the boy from Hong Kong' and 'the one who cares about us' (*guanxin women qunti deren* 關心我們群體的人). I saw it as a good sign that they increasingly trusted me while I could maintain a more detached role. I was physically with them, but without being seen as one of them.

However, starting from 2010, more and more former prisoners actively found me for 'heart-to-heart talk' (*tanxin* 談心) and consulted me on different issues like their relationships with their boyfriends, girlfriends, or partners, issues related to their studies and their work. Some of them started to refer to me as 'Teacher Cheng' (*Zheng laoshi* 鄭老師). I have told all of them that I am studying sociology and criminology instead of psychology. However, no matter how many times I explained the difference, some of them still referred to me as 'PhD in psychology' (*xinli xue boshi* 心理學博士), vaguely implying that I was a kind of counsellor or even clinical psychologist. I was seen as someone who could give them consultations. Moreover, since I had become one part of some of the former prisoners' lives—their 'counsellor'—I was no longer just a 'researcher'. Instead, I played a more functional role in their social community. The good side of it was that more and more former prisoners started to tell me their 'secrets'. The bad side was that it was increasingly difficult for me to 'play dumb'. As inspired by previous research (Becker 1954), I employed a 'playing-dumb' strategy in the beginning of my fieldwork so that I could ask some 'stupid questions' which might otherwise seem too naive to raise. By using this strategy, I was also able to make the former prisoners elaborate on some of their points of view that they had taken for granted. Playing dumb worked very well in the very beginning of my journey. However, the more the former prisoners treated me as a 'teacher', the less I could 'play dumb', especially in the last stage of my research during my revisit. When I asked them questions like 'Do you think the police officers arrested you so as to help you to be rehabilitated from using drugs?', many of them responded to me as if I were asking them a very stupid question. They assumed that I should have known the answer that they had taken for granted—the answer is no.

In this study, I recruited all my informants through inmates' referral, or what social scientists called 'snowball sampling'. Through recruiting a small number of informants, the researcher can get access to a larger number of similar informants through their social networks (Neuman 2004; Ritchie and Lewis 2003). Without the aid of government officers or social workers, former prisoners in China would be hidden populations to me. The most obvious way for me to recruit them was to go through the former inmates whom I already knew from my MPhil project. The former prisoners I had met in 2007 were also the first snowflakes, and they again introduced me gradually to some of their friends. Their friends further introduced me to more friends and so on.

Besides interviews, I joined the former prisoners in different social activities like attending banquets, drinking and singing in karaoke bars, and making short trips to nearby cities. These activities served several purposes. First, they provided me with chances to observe and participate in their usual daily interactions. By listening to their conversations, I had the chance to triangulate the data I had collected during the interviews. It was especially the case when I sometimes heard them talking about their experiences. I could cross-check what they had said with their friends and what they had told me during the interviews. The content of both was generally consistent. However, doing data collection during these social activities was sometimes difficult. Sometimes the former prisoners talked to each other in their own dialects, of which I could understand less than half of the content. Many times they would speak at the same time, which made it even more difficult for me to grasp what was being said, especially when someone was talking to me at the same time. I had to turn on my 'research radar', so to speak, all the time—to be very alert of conversations and words that were related to my research.

Recording these data was even more difficult. Whenever the situation allowed, I excused myself to the lavatory to write down short notes. When that was impossible, I wrote notes on my way back to my living place. Only on very rare occasions would I take notes in front of the former prisoners. There was one time when I attended a birthday party of a former prisoner, Ying, in a karaoke bar. I had drunk more beer than I should have and felt quite tipsy. Suddenly, she started to hold my hand and started talking with me about her experiences of using drugs and about her incarcerations. My 'radar' was turned on by what she had said, and I started to listen very carefully. After she had finished, knowing that my impending hangover might totally blot out any memory of what she had said, I drew out a paper from my pocket and started writing them down. Below is an excerpt from my notes:

> Two guys came at about 1 a.m. She told me that one of them did not know her past and said, 'Do not talk about those things.' However, after she got drunk, she started to talk about her old life again. I said, 'Hey, the guy is there.' Ying's face turned pale and stared at me. After a while Ying started talking about those things again. She was very drunk by that time. She said, 'I told you the truth. I do not like those people. They are giving you "courtesy" [*ketao hua* 客套話], "lip service" [*menmian* 門面], and "official languages" [*guanfang de hua* 官方的話]. I do not need those things. I do not want to hear those things. They are working for the government. I wouldn't take drugs if I hadn't decided to do so.'

The process of taking such notes is both awkward and physically demanding. Ying and her friends saw me half-lying and half-sitting on the sofa, struggling to get hold of the ballpoint pen and take notes in English on a paper. Since liquor was spilled on the table, and I was so drunk that I could not sit up straight, I had to put the paper on my own chest when I wrote the notes. Ying and others were laughing and teasing me when I was struggling to concentrate and write down what Ying had told me. I only had two things in mind: I had to make my handwriting readable, and I had to keep the notes safe. It took me more than ten minutes to write this small paragraph.

During my fieldwork, sometimes I obtained important information when my informants and I were under the effect of alcohol. Alcohol is an effective social lubricant; however, it might also obscure the reliability of the information that I had collected. In our conversations, Ying had mentioned things that were closely related to my research—'lip services' and 'official language'. However, what she had said might have been affected by the fact that she was drunk. So I found her a few days later and talked to her again about this topic, and she confirmed what she had said. Similarly, when I interviewed Jim he vaguely confessed to me that he had recently used 'happy pills'. Since I could not use information obtained from informants who were under the influence of psychotropic substances, alcohol, or illicit drugs directly, instead I used it as a conversation starter for later interviews.

During the course of this study in 2012, three former prisoners invited me to join three QQ online chat groups of former drug users. Each of these chat groups had several hundred members. The first group was organized by social workers. In this chat group there were former or current drug users who had or had not been incarcerated and their family members, social workers, and some prison officers. The second chat group was for former or current drug users and their family members. The final one was exclusively for former or current drug users who had been incarcerated for using drugs. Since then, I have followed up these chat groups very closely and use the content of the chat groups as a source for new inspiration and triangulations.

The Researcher Self

I started analysing the data from the very beginning of my fieldwork. I was more able to maintain an 'objective' self when I had just started my research. However, the more time I spent with the former prisoners, the more empathetic, and sometimes sympathetic I was to them. Each of these former prisoners had told me some of their sad stories. Some of them had offered me important advice not only to my research but also to me as a friend. Many of them had offered me different types of help during my research. In 2012 I was suffering from a stomach ulcer when I was doing my fieldwork. I was running out of pills one week after I left Hong Kong. There was a thunderstorm that day, and my stomach started severely cramping while I was in a former prisoner's house during one of their social gatherings. The house was somewhat rural and quite far away from any pharmacy. Several of them rode downtown with their electro bikes under the heavy rain to help me find the pills I needed. One of them had even saved me from a potential street fight during my visit to a karaoke bar. My experiences with some of the former prisoners had made me no longer able to maintain a completely 'objective' or 'distanced' self when I was doing my fieldwork.

Nevertheless, the longer I left the field, the more I felt able to retain my role as a researcher. I am fully aware of the need to present the former prisoners in an unbiased way. In this book I do not attempt to misrepresent or distort any of the data for the purpose of presenting a 'good image' of the former prisoners. Nor do I attempt to present those they dislike—the police officers, prison officers, and some local cadres in a negative way. This study is not solely about the former prisoners' suffering, nor about the police, the prison staff, or the local cadres as individuals. Following Mill's (1959) wisdom of sociological imagination, I seek to examine the problematic system behind the 'personal trouble' suffered by all these individuals. In order to explain the experiences of the forty-six former prisoners and the 'system of hypocrisy' behind it, the core chapters of this book will be divided as follows.

In Chapter 2 I critically discuss examples of model police officers and model prison officers. I examine how the 'models' were portrayed in the party propaganda and why they were portrayed in this way. I also examine how the party propaganda might affect former prisoners' expectations of the police and prison officers in real life. Chapter 3 focuses on former drug detainees' experiences of being arrested, and Chapters 4 and 5 look into the former prisoners' stories about their real day-to-day experiences in prison. Chapter 6 relates former drug detainees' experiences after they were released from prison. From Chapters 3 to 6 I highlight the law enforcers' practical concerns, like the need to maintain efficiency in making arrests, the necessity to maintain order in the prison, the pressure in the management of the prison factories, and the obligation to control and manage the former prisoners. In the final chapter, I revisit the characteristics of the failing rehabilitation system and also argue that the experiences of the former prisoners could possibly mirror a larger social system in which people in different arenas can possibly see through the official propaganda when the experienced reality becomes very different from the officially propagated narrative.

2
Tales of 'Heroes' and 'Saviours'

Since Mao's era different means of communication like electronic media, print media, and school education have been used to propagandize political ideological 'lines' (Brady 2008). 'Model figures' (*mofan renwu* 模範人物) play an important role in such propaganda. While all types of models play the role of propagating the strength of and faith in the party in some way or another, one type of model figures represents the 'party' or the 'government' more directly, being a direct part of that structure. Government officials, police officers, and prison officers are some of the usual characters representing this type of propaganda. As I will demonstrate in this chapter, the images of these 'model figures' are carefully tailored according to what Bakken (2000) has called the 'exemplary norm'. Police officers and prison officers are very often presented as either 'heroic evil fighters' or 'benevolent saviours'. The purposes of constructing these model figures can be both educational and political (C. Jiang 2001). However, as Scott (1990) reminds us, in practice the government's favourable portrayal of its own image can backfire and endanger its own rules and legitimacy. The unrealistically 'perfect' image of the model figures has unavoidably led to a specific form of hypocrisy. Instead of being convinced or fooled by the propaganda, the hypocrisy can be easily seen by people who can compare these figures with those whom they meet and experience in their daily lives. In the case of the former prisoners discussed here, instead of blindly accepting the front stage of fake propaganda images, to use a term coined by Goffman (1958), they see the 'backstage' of reality behind those fake images. They interpret the exemplary images of police and prison officers as how things *should be* instead of how they actually *are* in real life. The former prisoners clearly distinguish between what these officers have *said* and what they have *done*.

In this chapter, selected examples of 'model' police and prison officers in the media will illustrate how such party propaganda is being created and based on 'exemplary norms', and how this has again created expectations among the former prisoners about how the police and prison officers *should* act.

Media, Propaganda, 'Model Figures', and Moral Legitimacy in China

In China the mass media has been acting as 'the mouthpiece of the party' (*dang de houshe* 黨的喉舌) and as a tool of propaganda. In a speech given at the Secretariat of the Central Committee, Hu Yaobang (1985) outlined the criteria of 'proper' journalism in socialist China. He stated that in newspapers more should be reported on the 'bright side' (*guangming mian* 光明面) of society, while less should be reported on the 'dark side' (*yin'an mian* 陰暗面). The proper proportion of news reports on the 'bright side' and the 'dark side' of society should be, according to Hu, '80 per cent [of the reports should be] used to praise the "achievements" (*chengji* 成績) and the "bright side", only 20 per cent [of the reports should be] used to criticize the "shortcomings" (*quedian* 缺點) and the "dark side"' (Y. Hu 1985, 18).

Explicitly, Hu was trying to say that the news reporters should be conscious about how they report different news. However, his instructions also implied that the news media in China should serve the party as a tool of propaganda. The news reporters should, according to Hu, propagate more stories that reflect the 'good' side of society instead of the 'bad'. While 20 per cent of the space in newspapers should be a place where 'bad news' could be reported, thirty years after Hu's speech, 'freedom of the press' (*xinwen ziyou* 新聞自由) is said to have become one of the 'seven things that are not to be talked about' (*qi bujiang* 七不講) (Deutsche Welle [Chinese version] 2013). If the rumour of the 'seven nos' is real, Hu's speech was actually more liberal than the prevalent political opinion today.

While different heroic model figures had been widely propagated in Maoist China, nowadays they are still one of the central themes in party propaganda. In Contemporary China, various old and new 'model figures' are created and recreated in government propaganda. Throughout the 1990s old model figures like Lei Feng 雷鋒, Jiao Yulu 焦裕祿, and Kong Fansen 孔繁森 reappeared to promote the values of self-sacrifice and serving the party. In 2005, at least a hundred new model figures appeared in the mass media (Brady 2008). While I was in China in 2012 every day I would witness several model figures propagated on different television programmes, including dramas, documentaries, reality shows, and news.

Chinese scholars in the field of 'government public relations' (*zhengfu gongguan xue* 政府公關學) like C. Jiang (2001) suggest that presenting model figures' deeds in the mass media basically serves two important purposes. The first purpose is that through publicizing these 'outstanding' people and their heroic deeds, the public may be encouraged to pursue 'truth, good, and beauty' (*zhen shan mei* 真善美). In other words, the audiences can be educated through learning from these models. Bakken (2000) has pointed out that in China the idea of model emulation can even be traced back to the ancient philosophies of Confucius, Legalism, and Mozi. In contemporary China, model learning is still the main method of moral education.

Other than education, the second purpose of promoting model figures is to win people's support to the government through 'integrating the righteous image of the government with the righteous images of these good and heroic people' (C. Jiang 2001, 12). In other words, model figures enhance the 'moral legitimacy' of the party-state (B. Xu 2012). That means that by promoting the images of the model figures, the propaganda is also promoting the positive image of the party. This is clearly a type of 'impression management' (Goffman 1958) on the state level and an attempt to create a favourable 'public transcript' (Scott 1990). It seems to be common for government leaders to construct positive images for themselves and the party. R. Yan (2004), another Chinese scholar in the field of 'government public relations', suggests that by constructing positive images the government leadership can be equipped with 'authority and credibility' (*weixin* 威信) and the 'power to secure people's submission' (*zhefu de liliang* 折服的力量). B. Xu (2012), in his studies of Chinese government leaders' performance during natural disasters gave a vivid example of this phenomenon:

> Wen arrived in Yushu the day after the earthquake. He went to an orphanage, hugging and kissing a tearful little girl. 'The disaster you suffered is our disaster. Your suffering is our suffering. Your loss of loved ones is our loss. We mourn as you do. It breaks our hearts,' Wen Jiabao said to the local residents. (B. Xu 2012, 125)

Wen Jiabao was the premier of the State Council at the time of the disaster; his performance for sure was supposed to represent the image of the government. His acts can be seen not only as his own impression management but also a 'political performance' that attempts to enhance the party's 'moral legitimacy' (B. Xu 2012). The same argument can be applied to understanding the presentation of model police officers and model prison officers. The 'good deeds' of these model figures, through publication on newspapers or airing on television, became a wide range of 'political performances' that are re-created and re-presented to the public. The party-state is glorified right along with the model figures. This becomes abundantly clear when news reports announce that these model police officers and prison officers are not just laymen but 'Communist Party members' (*gongchandang yuan* 共產黨員) (J. Chen 2007; *People's Daily* 2007, 31; 2010).

Scott (1990) has pointed out that the phenomenon of a dominant power presenting itself in positive ways so as to enhance its own power is nearly universal. However, what has been considered 'positive' is very much contextual. In contemporary China the 'positive' quality is governed by the 'exemplary norms', which are rooted in both historical and political contexts.

'Exemplary Norms' and the Construction of Model Figures

The Chinese 'exemplary norms', according to Bakken (2000), are a set of carefully selected traditional norms which the Chinese party leadership used as a binding force to control the potential uncertainties and chaos brought by modernization. Instead of a repetition of traditional norms, Chinese authorities consciously reconstruct and revive those norms and cultural traits that are seen to represent a binding and stabilizing force. In the 1990s, under Jiang Zemin's call to return to 'traditional' socialist and 'Chinese' values, Chinese scholars were commanded to examine how 'traditional values' could be incorporated into domestic propaganda (Brady 2012b, 62–63). In this propaganda, one of the most important norms that was revived and propagated was the heroic spirit of 'self-sacrifice' (*ziwo xisheng* 自我牺牲), or the spirit to sacrifice, even one's life, for the collective benefit. As we will see later, 'self-sacrifice' and 'selflessness' play a very important role in how police officers and prison officers are portrayed in the media.

Police and Prison Officers in the Media

In China different tales and stories about model police and model prison officers are spread through newspapers, television news, documentaries, and entertainment shows. The examples I discuss below are closely related to the former prisoners' expectations on how the police officers and prison officers should perform. However, I should make it clear that former prisoners never specifically mentioned the cases that I am going to present below. Their expectations fit so naturally into how the model police and model prison officers are represented in these cases that it is reasonable to suggest that the style of such propaganda played an important role in shaping the former prisoners' expectations. Some of the following examples come from the annual anti-drug campaign organized all over China in June and some from more general news reports and television shows.

In these stories, there are two main types of plots or storylines: 'the hero fighting the evil forces' and 'the saviour rescuing the victim'. In these stories there are generally four types of characters. The first type is the 'heroic evil fighter' represented by the model police officers. The second type is the 'benevolent saviours' who are usually represented by both the model police officers and model prison officers. The third type is the negative character—the 'evil'—represented by the cunning drug dealers. The final type is the 'victim' represented by the drug addicts and the prison inmates.

The 'heroic police' fighting the 'evil drug dealers'

In the first typical plot ('the hero fighting the evil forces'), standard storylines very often go along with the depiction of the brave hero represented by police officers who sacrifice their own well-being and even their lives to fight the cunning and dangerous dealers. In these stories the police officers have faced and overcome different difficulties and barriers to finally successfully bust the drug dealers. The images of both the model police officers and what might be ironically called the 'model drug dealers' matter here. In these stories, drug dealers are usually depicted as evil criminals who seek self-interest by any means. They are said to be people who are 'extremely fierce and vicious' (*qiongxiong ji e* 窮凶極惡) (J. Chen 2007; L. Lin 2011; *People's Daily* 2007; Y. Zhang 2012), 'mad' (*fengkuang* 瘋狂) (Tian 2012), 'tricky' (*guiji duoduan* 詭計多端) (*People's Daily* 2010), 'shrewd and crafty' (*laojian juhua* 老奸巨猾) (*Guangming Daily* 2009; Liu, Wang, and Zeng 2014), and individuals who would 'desperately fight against the police' (*fuyu wankang* 負隅頑抗) (*Qianjiang Evening News* 2009). The images of the model police officers and the evil drug dealers are matched: the more evil the drug user seems to be, the more heroic the model police officer.

Slaying the drug devil

One typical narrative can be seen in a news report titled 'The Southern Sword Slaying the Drug Devil' ('Nanmen lijian zhan dumo' 南門利劍斬毒魔) in the *People's Daily* in 2012 during a drug campaign on the 'international anti-drug day' (Y. Zhang 2012). This report is, on the surface, the story of an anti-narcotic squad in Yunnan but in reality describes a whole set of exemplary moral qualities attributed to individual police officers. The report starts by talking about the difficult situation the police officers faced when they started their work in the early 1980s:

> Yunnan anti-narcotic police officer He Qingwen has devoted thirty years to anti-narcotic operations: 'In 1982 when I first joined the anti-narcotic squad, the conditions were really bad. Each officer was equipped with only one pair of handcuffs, a briefcase, and a pistol,' he said. (Y. Zhang 2012, 9)

Then the report goes on to tell two stories about police officers who died in drug raids. In the story of Ke Zhanjun, the author wrote:

> On 23 February 2012 at six in the afternoon, Ke Zhanjun and his team encountered the drug dealers in the corridor. Facing the drug dealers who opened fire at the police, he [Ke] risked his life [*fenbugushen* 奮不顧身] and charged towards the battle [*chongfeng xianzhen* 衝鋒陷陣]. In the life-and-death battle [*shusi bodou* 殊死搏鬥] with the drug dealer, he was shot and sacrificed his life. He was only 30 years old. (Y. Zhang 2012, 9)

In this story Officer Ke is described as a fearless warrior who sacrificed his life in a battle. The story is romantically sensationalized. Readers can almost imagine exactly what had happened at that moment. The key moral quality of the police officer portrayed above is the spirit of self-sacrifice. The second story, through the narrative of a widow, continues to tell how these fearless police officers sacrifice their own good in the battle with evil drug dealers. In the story about Shi Xiangning, the author wrote:

Tales of 'Heroes' and 'Saviours'

Shi Xiangning was among the first cohort of narcotic squad officers in 'new China'. 'He was also the first who sacrificed [his life in this squad],' said Sun Jie, Shi's wife, who is also working as a local police officer. On 27 September 1986 Shi Xiangning risked his life and jumped into a strong current in the Liusha River when he was chasing a drug dealer. Unfortunately, he was swept away by the strong current. He was only 24 years old, and it was the third day after his marriage with Sun Jie. (Y. Zhang 2012, 9)

In this report, the heroic deed of Shi is presented as a tragic love story. Through the words of Sun, the sacrificed police officer's widow, the image of a selfless police officer is vividly described. One can almost imagine that in the morning of the third day after Shi and Sun's marriage, Shi, the brave warrior, loaded his gun and went to the merciless battlefield, never to make it back home. Shi went from being a newly-wed wife to a widow in only three days. The story aims to increase our respect for Officer Shi and our sympathy for his widow, Sun, and at the same time increase our hatred towards the evil villain who caused Shi's death. The author also wants to make it clear that Ke's and Shi's deaths were only the tip of the iceberg:

This is not an exceptional case; facing the extremely fierce and vicious drug dealers, anti-narcotic police officers disregard their lives [in their fight against the drug dealers]. Over the last thirty years, forty police officers sacrificed their lives, and three hundred and sixty police officers were injured. (Y. Zhang 2012, 9)

This report shows, on the one hand, the evil character of the drug dealers. On the other hand, it underlines the bravery and noble character of the police. The heroic police officers in the report are not only brave but also wise. The police officers use both their bravery and wisdom when they fight the drug dealers. In the same report, a story about how the police managed to outwit the drug dealer is also told:

He had disguised as a buyer when he was investigating a drug case. 'Considering that I might be searched, I did not bring any weapon,' said He. After meeting the drug dealers, He was locked in a room for 'investigation' [*kaocha* 考察]. During the process, he found two grenades in a cabinet. After a whole day of 'investigation', the drug dealers decided to trust He, and had agreed to trade with him that same night. He informed his 'comrades-in-arms' [*zhanyou* 戰友] when he went out to get the drug money. During the time of exchange, He found the grenades on the bed next to him. When the drug dealers were counting the money, He grabbed the grenades and threw them out the room. He then fired a warning shot and shouted, 'I am a police officer. Freeze!' The police officers outside then moved in and arrested the drug dealers. (China Network Television 2012)

In the battle of wit, He overtrumped the cunning and suspicious drug dealers. In this story, He is described as wise and tactful, and the police officers Ke, He, and Shi represent the state. The righteous image of the model police officers is used to glorify not only the police but also the image of the state, and consequently the party. In the next case, this connection is shown much more explicitly. The story is taken from a talk show broadcast on the CCTV news channel and was shown repeatedly during the anti-drug campaign.

The model police officers and the party-state

The talk show *One-to-One* (*Mian dui mian* 面對面) interviewed an anti-narcotic squad police chief, Xie Jiaqiao. Again, the spirit of sacrifice and the bravery and wisdom of the anti-narcotics police are described:

> Host: Can you describe your job?
> Officer: If our police officers didn't risk their lives [*sheshen wangsi* 捨身忘死] and hadn't been working days and nights almost without sleeping and eating [*feiqin wangshi* 廢寢忘食], if we hadn't stopped those drugs on the boarder, I cannot imagine how many families and teenagers would have been victimized. . . . One of my mottos is that a police chief in the narcotics team is either a hero or a sinner [*zuiren* 罪人] . . . If you successfully combat [the drug dealer], if you rescue the drug users, you are definitely a hero. If you fail to do that, drugs will inundate [*fanlan chengzai* 泛濫成災], endanger, and erode [*weihai qinshi* 危害侵蝕] many families. Then are you not a sinner? (China Network Television 2012)

The documentary shows that these model police officers are willing to sacrifice their lives when they are on the spot fighting with the drug users. It goes on to tell the audiences that these police heroes are actually risking their lives on a day-to-day basis, because the 'evil' drug dealers desperately want to kill these heroes.

> From Xie's point of view, being an anti-narcotics police officer, he is ready to sacrifice his own life [*ba shengsi zhizhi duwai* 把生死置之度外]. Because of his strikes against the drug dealers, they had even put a bounty of three million [yuan] on his head. (China Network Television, 24 June 2012)

This documentary programme also highlights the police officers' wisdom by describing how they have outwitted the drug dealers:

> Military police: Many of them use the front wheels of the truck [to hide the drugs]. They use magnets to stick it up there.
> Host: Magnets?
> Military police: Yes, they used stockings to wrap the magnets.
> Host: But it is so dark. Can you still see it?
> Military police: [I] can still see it. It's a rectangle, but it is difficult to find it.
> Host: How many cases have you cracked so far at this checkpoint?
> Military police: So far we have had 360 cases. It means that we have one case per day on average.
> Xie: These drug dealers, they thought they were clever, they thought that the police would not find them out, but the fact is, a lot of our police officers have successfully arrested many of them. (China Network Television, 24 June 2012)

Again, the relationship between the police officers and the drug dealers is described as a battle of wits and courage. One of the most interesting segments in this television show is when, in the middle of the talk show, the camera pans to a close-up shot of a poetic couplet printed on a white paper stuck to the wall next to the police chief's desk: 'Be upright as a person, be clean as an officer' (*zuoren yishen zhengqi, weiguan yichen bu ran* 做人一身正氣，為官一塵不染).

In the talk show police officers are depicted as selfless heroic warriors who devote themselves to combating drug dealers in order to rescue the drug users and their families. This image is cleverly combined with the image of the party-government as a whole with the content of the poetic couplet. The word *guan* (官) in the poetic couplet plays a very important function in this documentary. The ancient pictograph of *guan* (𠨎) is composed of a 'bow' (𠃌) which symbolized the 'army' inside a 'house' (宀) (Gu 2003). The character 官 (*guan*) originally stood for an army barrack. It was later used to refer to the state government as a whole. The term *guan* in this poetic couplet has subtly connected the image of the heroic police officers to the image of the party-state. In another news report in 2007, the parallel between the model officers and the party was made even more clearly. It is a report about Luo Jinyong, a Yunnan police officer who died in an operation. The report goes:

> Facing the fierce drug dealers, he risked his life and fought heroically [*yingyong bodou* 英勇搏鬥]. He was, however, outnumbered and badly wounded. . . . Luo did all this because of . . . his 'boundless loyalty' [*wuxian zhongcheng* 無限忠誠] to the party and to the people, because of his hatred for evil [*ji'e ru chou* 嫉惡如仇], and because of his 'fearless revolutionary spirit' [*yingyong wuwei de geming jingshen* 英勇無畏的革命精神]. . . . With his youth and blood, he demonstrated the noble quality [*chonggao qinghuai* 崇高情懷] and the awe-inspiring righteousness [*haoran zhengqi* 浩然正氣] of a Communist Party member, and of a People's Police [*renmin jingcha* 人民警察]. (J. Chen 2007)

All the descriptions about the 'heroic' deeds and 'noble quality' are attributed not only to the police officer Luo Jinyong but also to the Communist Party member in general. Through the story of Luo, this piece created and promoted a perfect image of a 'Communist Party member' and the 'party' that he represents.

Saving the drug addicts

Drug users, in contrast to drug dealers, are usually described as poor people who somehow deserve sympathy. They are either said to be people who were originally good, but have turned evil because of using drugs, or they are described as people who were originally healthy, but turn sick because of using drugs. These two narratives somehow both describe drug users as people who are by nature 'good'. These good people turn 'bad' or get 'sick' only because they are corrupted by drugs. One common way for the news report to describe drug users in China is to say that they were 'seduced' (*yinyou* 引誘) (Liu and Li 2014, A08; Tang 2014, A8) to take drugs and have therefore 'gone astray' (*wuru qitu* 誤入歧途).

If the reports on drug dealers highlight the masculine and tough side of the goodness of the police, the news on pathetic drug users draw audiences' attentions to the feminine and caring dimension of the goodness of the police. In these kinds of reports, police officers are described as caring, sympathetic, and benevolent 'parents' who educate and rescue the pathetic drug addicts and their families. One typical example can be seen in a report about a female police officer who had saved a drug addict (J. Lu 2012).

Sister police: Qing

The title of the news is 'Treat the People [*lao baixing* 老百姓] as Family Members [*qinren* 親人]' and the subtitle of the story is 'Saving a drug addict, she sees the girl who commits suicide as her sister'. The story goes as follows:

> Six years ago, Wang Qing, a new police officer in a local police station received an emergency call. She was told that someone was trying to commit suicide by jumping from a building. Wang immediately went to the site and saw a middle-aged woman sitting dangerously on a balcony. The woman had one of her legs hanging in the air and looked as if she were in much pain. Wang kept persuading her [not to jump] with her kind-heartedness. The woman finally put her leg back on the balcony. Wang immediately held on to her and brought her back from the balcony.
>
> A helpful old lady told Wang, 'Officer, she squandered all her family's fortune on drugs. She cannot live on any more.' That night, Wang went to the woman's home to 'straighten her out' (*kaidao ta* 開導她) and said, 'Do not be that pessimistic. You will be fine. Let me help you.' (J. Lu 2012, 8)

Instead of being described as an evil person, this woman is described as a miserable person whose life was ruined by drugs. Officer Wang, her saviour, came at the most critical moment and saved her from her hopeless life. This report goes on to say that Wang later helped her to apply for community drug rehabilitation in a hospital. With the help of Wang, the local district government had aided the woman financially by helping her to apply for the minimum-subsistence allowance, and the local police station had delivered the woman daily necessities. Although at first sight this report is about a drug user, closer inspection reveals it is more about the glorification of police officers and the government. Similar with the parallel of the model drug fighters and the party-state, in this case, the caring and compassionate image of Wang is presented together with the helpful images of the local police force and the local government.

Prison director Song's dream and the party's quality

Similarly, in news about prisons for drug users, model prison officers are very often presented as 'caring parents' who want to save the inmates (X. Lu 2013). In a news report in 2012, Song Lina, the director of a drug rehabilitation centre in Yunnan is described as a benevolent mother, who treats the inmates as her children:

> The dream of Song Lina, the head of the Kai Yuan City Drug Rehabilitation Centre, is tightly linked to a special group of people. She treats them as 'children who lost their way' [*milu de haizi* 迷路的孩子]. (X. Lu 2013)

The drug addicts inside the prison are described as naive, or at most naughty 'children' who went down the wrong path. Song in this report is not the stern prison guard who punishes or controls the prison inmates. Instead, she is a caring mother, who wants to save the lost children:

> She fully employs her patience and tenderness as a woman. She has changed the relationship between the officers and the inmates from 'control' [*guanli zhe* 管理者] and 'being controlled' [*bei guanli zhe* 被管理者] to 'teachers and students' [*shisheng* 師生] alike, and to friends [*pengyou* 朋友] too. [She] respects them and takes care of them. (X. Lu 2013)

The two quotes above have demonstrated the feminine and caring qualities of Song—patience, tenderness, and an urge to save the 'children'. Audiences can almost sense the aura of care and goodness that envelops her. Again, in the news report, 'sacrifice' is one of the main themes. In the story about Song, what she had sacrificed for these 'children' is her precious 'youth' (*qingchun* 青春).

> One day in October 1995 Song Lina, a 20-year-old girl, was assigned to be an officer in the Kai Yuan City Drug Rehabilitation Centre. When other girls are enjoying their 'time of youth' (*qingchun nianhua* 青春年華), Song was trapped inside the walls of incarceration with those people [inmates] with tattoos and cruel eyes.... Inside this girl who had seen little of the world were fear and confusion. (X. Lu 2013)

This little story of Song informs the audience that she has grown from an innocent young girl who was scared by the drug addicts to a compassionate and experienced prison director. This is how the journalist described her: 'Those who know Song Lina well would evaluate her in this way: 'Every time you see her, she is always smiling warmly. It seems like she is always so energetic' (X. Lu 2013).

With her personal charm and sacrifice, she changed the prison to a better place for the good of the inmates at the cost of her precious youth. While other girls enjoy their time of youth outside in the big wonderful world, Song has devoted her youth to saving the poor and suffering drug addicts. Personal characteristics like warm, energetic, easy-going, and willing to sacrifice one's good for the drug users are all examples of the 'benevolent model officers'. In another report, the presentation of male prison officer Xiao Jianfeng again shows these exemplary personal qualities. Below are three quotes in the report about Officer Xiao:

> The first impression [of the reporter] of Xiao is that he is 'competent' [*ganlian* 幹練] and 'easy-going' [*suihe* 隨和]. He is slim and tall. He has a clean white face, a sharp nose, and a pair of small eyes. He smiles like a 'blooming sunflower' [*shengkai de xiangrikui* 盛開的向日葵]. (Beijing People's Broadcasting Corporation 2014)

Officer Xiao is presented as a charming person. In order to have a better understanding of the prison inmates, Xiao not only lived inside the prison with the inmates for twenty-four hours a day over six months; he also obeyed the regulations that the inmates needed to obey. In the interview, Xiao said:

> My family member drove a very long distance to see me. A police officer in the visitors' room called me and told me to see my family members. I didn't know how to explain it to him [the officer], but no one can understand me. A police officer lives inside [the prison] and obeys the same regulations [as the inmates]. I could not see my family members. I didn't know how to explain it to them. I saw them from the window.... They left disappointedly. When I saw them leave, I was very upset from the bottom of my heart. (Beijing People's Broadcasting Corporation 2014)

This is how the reporter comments on Xiao:

> Just like an 'ascetic monk' [*kuxingseng* 苦行僧], Xiao is strict with himself [*yange yaoqiu ziji* 嚴格要求自己].... He did all this for other people [the inmates]'s 'happiness' [*xingfu kuaile* 幸福快樂] ...
>
> He is saving lives [*wanjiu shengming* 挽救生命], and he is also saving souls [*wanjiu linghun* 挽救靈魂].... Starting from 2003, Xiao started to trace and visit different discharged drug users. All these former drug users see Officer Xiao as their family member.... Xiao always says, 'Give yourself hope, give society a miracle.' He used his loyalty and faith to perform the duty of a People's Police.' (Beijing People's Broadcasting Corporation 2014)

Similar to previous model police officers, the model prison officer in this case is clearly connected to the party as a whole. Self-sacrifice, giving hope to the people, creating a social miracle, and being loyal and faithful—all these exemplary qualities were described as belonging not only to the model officers but also the Communist Party members who are representing the party-state.

The spirit of self-sacrifice

'Sacrifice' is an essential theme in different types of social myths (Bakken 2000). In these narratives of sacrifice, three levels of forces are usually present: the heroic forces, the evil forces, and the victims. One fundamental quality of the heroic forces is their spirit of self-sacrifice. The exemplary model narratives I have cited here all share this theme. The 'heroic forces' are represented by police and prison officers.

The drug dealers represent evil, and the drug addicts and their families are clearly the victims. In the Anglo-Saxon context, drug crimes are either 'criminalized' or 'medicalized' (Conrad and Schneider 1980); in Chinese propaganda the drug issue as well as other deviant acts may be described in the same way, too, but essentially the stories are 'moralized' to a much greater extent (Bakken 2013). The theme of this propaganda is clear: the heroic police officers are fighting the evil drug dealers; the police and prison officers are benevolent saviours of the pitiful addicts and the interests of the people; and the heroic and benevolent state and party forces are fighting the evil forces to save the innocent addicts. It all boils down to an epic struggle of good against evil. Moreover, these stories are only a few in a compendium of similar moralistic tales of heroism in Communist China. The style used in the report on Shi Xiangning's sacrifice is almost identical to the widely propagated heroic deeds of other 'models' like wartime hero Dong Cunrui, who blew himself up on a bridge in order to stop the enemies from passing, and Wang Jie, who threw himself on the exploding grenade so as to save the bystanders (Bakken 2000; Wanyan 2013).

Recent observers suggest that 'model figures' propagated in Chinese education have undergone a change from the 'heroes' to 'normal persons' (*putong ren* 普通人) (Ding and Li 2010). However, although it might be true that more and more 'normal people' are replacing wartime heroes in government propaganda, as demonstrated in the news reports quoted here, the 'heroic' themes of sacrifice are still very much part of the ongoing propaganda. One good example of this is shown in a television show broadcast by Hunan Television (Hunan Weishi 湖南衛視) running every Monday and Tuesday evening at six. The show is called 'Heroic Civilians' (*Pingmin yingxiong* 平民英雄) and basically tells stories about 'fearless heroic civilians who stand out to help' in times of crisis. Sacrifice and heroic deeds are still very much the main themes of these narratives.

Exemplary Tales

The stories of the model police officers and prison officers are very similar to what Bakken calls 'cautionary tales' (Bakken 2000, 366). In *The Exemplary Society* Bakken points out a type of narrative that is told again and again in a similar format to warn against 'premature love', which is associated with the alleged 'degeneration' of young girls. The standard storyline in those cautionary tales started with the girl rebelling against family and school authority, then losing her virginity, and finally 'losing everything'. This narrative of 'danger' was told repeatedly in different stories. In a very similar fashion, stories about model police officers and model prison officers, drug dealers, and drug users follow the pattern—the heroic and wise protectors against danger, and the misfortune that befalls the evil and the mistaken drug dealers and users. In many cases, such cautionary tales may be based on true stories, but certainly come embellished with the well-known features of party propaganda. Many of the former prisoners did not doubt the validity of these stories. However, what I want to illustrate here is that this style of representation has constituted what the former prisoners called 'what they say', which is again forming the basis of the 'hypocritical world' seen through their experiences.

The creation of moral expectations

The media is used as the mouthpiece of the party in China, and information provided in the media is perceived by the public as reflecting official rhetoric. It is not clear how these reports or the propaganda have affected other audiences' perception of the police officers or the prison officers in the real world. However, it seems to be quite clear that it affects former prisoners' expectations of what 'should be' the government's attitude towards the issue, and what the government 'should do' according to these standards. What they had read was not only the surface value or messages presented in the propaganda. Instead, they kept a certain distance to this propagandistic ideology and formulated their own interpretations based on their own experiences.

In the international literature on the subject, it has long been said that popular culture sometimes give a 'CSI effect' to its audiences (Surette 2011),[1] which means that audiences' expectations about the criminal justice system might be affected and distorted by the content viewed in criminal justice–related movies or novels. In the case of former prisoners, their perceptions of the police, party, and government are clearly influenced by the party's presentation of drug-related issues in the media. The effects are quite different from what the party tends to expect. Instead of the formation of positive images of the police and the government, these media reports and propaganda somehow shape former prisoners' expectations about what the police should do to drug users and drug dealers, and what the appropriate motivation behind police officers' actions should be. In other words, from the drug users' point of view, the police officers are supposed to 'educate' and 'rescue' the drug users and 'combat' the drug dealers. They believe that the motivation for the police to act should be for the good of the drug users and the public in general. This expectation is essentially a moral expectation. The former prisoners expect, even demand, the police officers and prison officers to be morally upright and somehow willing to sacrifice their own interest to the good of the drug addicts, just like the propaganda prescribes. However, these expectations stand in sharp contrast to their actual daily life experiences. In other words, what must be an unintended consequence seen from the point of view of party propaganda, the approach backfires and creates an impression of hypocrisy and feelings of cynicism among the drug users.

In this chapter, with examples from the mass media, I have outlined how the image of the police officers and prison officers is presented in party propaganda. Different 'model' officers are presented in ways highlighting their 'exemplary

---

1. CSI refers to the US crime television show called *CSI: Crime Scene Investigation*.

qualities', like their willingness to sacrifice self for public good, and emphasizing their heroic and benevolent personal characteristics. The stories of these model figures can be conceptualized as 'political performances' (B. Xu 2012). The presentations of the stories and these models, as previous scholars like Bakken (2000), B. Xu (2012), and R. Yan (2004) have already pointed out, are carefully tailored in order to serve two basic functions—to educate the public and to enhance the moral legitimacy of the party and its government. Both functions can be seen as aiming at strengthening party control over its population. However, mirroring Scott's warning against the potential danger of 'public transcript' (1990), from what I have experienced dealing with former prisoners, it seems that the effect of such propaganda is going against such control. What the former prisoners had experienced in their own lives went almost completely against the staged cautionary tales of propaganda. This propaganda has instead planted the seeds of what they have come to see as a 'hypocritical society'. I will next take us into what kind of daily life experiences form this view among the drug users. These daily life experiences will let us understand much better and in much more detail why these notions of cynicism and 'hypocrisy' find such fertile ground among the ranks of the drug users.

3
Police and the 'Hooks'

This chapter examines former prisoners' experiences of being arrested and their views on the police officers who arrest them. With the example of the use of informants, which the former prisoners called 'hooking' (*diaogou* 釣鉤), I argue that the police officers' concern for intelligence collection and meeting arrest quotas had overridden the concern for 'saving the drug addicts'. The former prisoners were exposed to the media presentation of 'model police officers' on the front stage and the actual practices of 'hooking' on the backstage simultaneously. I argue that this had contributed to their feelings of injustice and to a structural system of hypocrisy formed by the material circumstances of the prison as well as outside bureaucratic performance criteria like the arrest quota and different types of performance measurements linked to the daily police operation.

Lawrence Sherman (1993) points out that whether offenders perceive their punishment as fair and just matters a lot in offenders' correction and rehabilitation. Every former prisoner in this study had the experience of being 'caught' by the police officers, and they generally perceived this process as unfair and unjust. This is one of the most important experiences in their lives since it is the moment that marks the beginning of their painful experiences with the criminal justice system. It is also the first out of the four aspects of 'what is done' by the authorities being completely opposite to 'what is said' in the propaganda. This important process is, however, seldom systematically addressed in previous research. The way that the police officers 'catch' or 'arrest' offenders in China is an important factor that affects the offenders' perceptions of whether the punishment they received was just or not. It also has a serious impact on the image and their perception of the police officers and the party-state. Moreover, in a broader sense, the local police practice of 'making arrest' also contributes to the systematic production of hypocrisy.

In Chinese, the word *daibu* (逮捕) refers to the process of arresting criminal suspects, submitting requests to the procuratorate, obtaining the warrant, and presenting the warrant to the suspects (National People's Congress 2013). However, here when I say 'arrest', I am adopting the more colloquial use of the term, which refers to the police's acts of placing a person under restraint or custody. In Chinese it is called *zhua* (抓), which in English literally means to 'catch', 'grab', or 'seize'.

As mentioned in the last chapter, in the party propaganda, police officers are very often depicted as selfless and wise 'heroes' who sacrifice their own good to fight the 'evil' drug dealers. The government continually glorified police officers who 'fight drug crime' (*yanda dupin fanzui* 嚴打毒品犯罪) (Office of China National Narcotics Control Commission 2010; 2011; 2013). However, instead of regarding them as 'selfless', 'brave', or 'wise', the former prisoners felt that most of the police officers are immoral, cunning, and self-interested. Although some former drug users said that they had met one or two 'good officers', they usually depict them as 'exceptions' to the rule. The saying that 'police and criminals come from the same family' (*jingfei yijia* 警匪一家) reflects an extreme form of former drug users' attitudes towards the police officers in general.

In this chapter, I will specifically address one of the police practices that has contributed to the shaping of the former prisoners' perception of the police—the use of 'hooks' (*diaogou* 釣鉤). A hook is similar to an informer, snitch, or what the English literature has recently called the 'covert human intelligence sources' (Billingsley 2009; Greer 1995; Innes 2010; Rosenfeld, Jacobs, and Wright 2003). 'Hook' is a term that the former prisoners use to refer to drug dealers or drug users who give information to the police officers for material rewards or freedom. In government propaganda, the police officers outwit the drug dealers for public good. However, from former detainees' view, hooking is an immoral strategy used for police officers' self-interest and completely contradicts the party propaganda's depiction of police officers.

I begin this chapter by placing 'hooking' in the context of the use of informants in China for intelligence collection in general. I then examine former prisoners' account of different types of hooks. I further argue that the use of hooks has reshaped not only the former prisoners' perceptions of the police officers in particular but also their interpretations of their social surroundings more broadly. I will also demonstrate how hooking has contributed to the formation of the 'system of hypocrisy'.

'Hooking'

In China taking drugs is not an offence according to the 'criminal law' (*xingfa* 刑法). It is, however, an offence according to several 'administrative regulations' including the Law on Penalties for Administration of Public Security and the Antidrug Law (*Jindufa* 禁毒法) (National People's Congress 2006, 2008). In other words, none of the arrested drug users went through any legal trial in the court before they were detained. Police officers acting on their own initiative can put drug users into custody for up to three years in the name of drug rehabilitation. Based on related regulations, the formal procedures of arresting drug users in general consist of three steps: First, the police officers identify persons suspected of using narcotic drugs. Then they conduct drug addiction verification tests for the suspect. Once a person is verified to be a drug addict, he or she can be subjected to ten to fifteen days of detention (*juliu* 拘留), and two to three years of incarceration in compulsory isolation for drug rehabilitation centres (*qiangzhi geli jiedusuo* 強制隔離戒毒所). Among these three steps, the strategies that police officers use to identify drug users most particularly create the contradiction between people's experiences and the official presentation of the issues concerned. The process is commonly known as 'hooking'.

'Hooking', according to the former drug users, is a strategy that involves the collusion of the police and the 'current users'. Put simply, the police use some 'current users' or 'current dealers' as their informants. In return for not being detained, these 'current users and dealers' are required to occasionally or regularly provide information about other current users to the police. They are sometimes required to entrap other drug users to use or buy drugs at a particular point of time or in a particular place so that the police can come and arrest them conveniently. This strategy is related to two policing strategies that have been widely used in Chinese criminal investigation (Cai 2013; Wu and Sun 2001; D. Yang 2010; K. Zhang 2012). They are the use of 'enticement detection' (*youhuo zhencha* 誘惑偵查) and the use of 'informants' (*xianren* 線人).

The use of informants in China

Chinese scholars trace the use of informants to the tactic of 'using spies' (*yongjian* 用間) described in the ancient Chinese military treatise, *The Art of War*, written by Sun Tzu in approximately 500 BC (B. Xu 2011; D. Yang 2010). According to Dutton (2005b), since 1938 the Chinese Communist Party has used informants for political and military purposes. These informants, who were then called 'liaison personnel' (*lianluo yuan* 聯絡員), were responsible for providing information to the Communist Party about their neighbours' political reliability. The system of informants was formalized after the establishment of the People's Republic of China in 1949. Before the Cultural Revolution, informants were mainly used to collect information about political enemies of the Communist Party. It was not until after the Cultural Revolution that different informants were recruited for the surveillance of criminals (Dutton 2005b). In China nowadays, the use of informants for criminal investigation has become institutionalized. Broadly speaking, there are two types of informants. The first type of informants is law-abiding people, including former criminals. The second, more common, type of informants is active criminals.

The first type of informants is called 'security eyes and ears' (*zhi'an ermu* 治安耳目). They are under the direct supervision of a subunit of the 'local police station' (*paichu suo* 派出所) called the 'district police' (*zerenqu minjing* 責任區民警) (Pan and Lü 1999). One of the main duties of the 'district police' is to collect different intelligence information that can be used to maintain 'political stability' (*zhengzhi wending* 政治穩定) and 'social stability' (*zhi'an wending* 治安穩定) (Ministry of Public Security 2002). According to a regulation issued by the Public Security

Bureau in 2002, the district police who has successfully collected valuable information provided by the 'eyes and ears' would receive different awards including better promotion opportunities.

In practice, district police officers recruit different people, including former criminals, to be their 'eyes and ears'. 'Eyes and ears' who provide important intelligence to the district police would also be rewarded with cash sums ranging from ¥200 to ¥500 (Tong 2011). There are no official criteria in the selection of 'eyes and ears'. One local police station discloses information about the three types of 'eyes and ears' they need on their official website (Lan Yi District Police Office 2012). The first type is 'red eyes and ears' (*hongse ermu* 紅色耳目). They are the 'civilians who are enthusiastic in maintaining social security' (*rexin zhian gongzuo de qunzhong* 熱心治安工作的群眾). The second type is the 'green eyes and ears' (*lüse ermu* 綠色耳目). They are people who have benefited from social welfare and are willing to assist in maintaining social stability. The final type is the 'grey eyes and ears' (*huise ermu* 灰色耳目). They are former criminals or offenders who are now 'rehabilitated' (*gaixie guizheng* 改邪歸正). According to Dutton's estimation, in some Chinese cities, 60 to 70 per cent of all eyes and ears are former criminals (Dutton 2005b). All types of eyes and ears are supposed to be currently clean and law-abiding. The recruitment and the use of 'eyes and ears' is no secret in China. The term 'eyes and ears' is often mentioned in the media, and the stories of 'eyes and ears' are sometimes covered in news reports (J. Fu 2007; Luo 2006; Tong 2011; Chinese Police Network 2014; Zhu 2005). It seems that the use of 'law-abiding informants' is quite overt in China. However, the recruitment and the use of current criminals in intelligence collection is more covert.

Lines

There are different names for the second type of informants in China: the 'investigative line' (*zhencha xianren* 偵查線人), 'line' (*xianren* 線人), or 'special agent' (*teqing* 特情). Unlike the eyes and ears, lines and special agents are very often current criminals. There is currently no law in China that regulates the use of lines, except some secret internal guidelines (Zhu 2005). Some reported that they are selected and verbally appointed by individual police officers without going through any formal procedures (Zhu 2005). Others have reported that police officers need to seek the approval from higher-level police stations if they want to appoint 'lines' (L. Chen 2011). Generally speaking, lines are expected to win the trust of their fellow criminals by concealing their identities, telling lies, and spying so as to obtain related intelligence (D. Yang 2010). Similar to eyes and ears, lines are widely used in China. In some local districts, the lines have even outnumbered the police officers. The lines provide information to the police officers about different criminal cases like organized crimes or drug crimes. In return, lines receive monetary rewards from the police (K. Zhang 2012).

It is said that police officers need lines to enhance the crime-cracking rate (*po'an lü* 破案率) (Zhi 2013). A very similar argument can be found in the United Kingdom. The UK Audit Commission declared that informants are 'the lifeblood of CID [Criminal Investigation Department]' (Innes 2010). In China, according to a report in 2009, police officers and local police offices are evaluated according to the 'number of cases handled' (*ban'an shuliang* 辦案數量), crime-cracking rate, and 'big crime–cracking rate' (*po da'an lü* 破大案率). Different quotas are also set for each of these 'numbers' and 'rates'. Whether police officers fulfil the quota can directly affect their chances of promotion (Han 2009). In the United States, police detectives either pay their informants with their own money or through a departmental 'confidential informant fund' or departmental 'financial bonus program' (Manning and Redlinger 1977, 296; Tucker 2014). In the United Kingdom, it was reported that Scotland Yard had paid more than £9 million to 'snitches' since 2008 (Robinson 2013). In Hong Kong the police force spends around HK$80 million annually on secret actions, including paying lines, which is officially called 'expenditure of reward and special services' (Hong Kong Police Force 2014; Lai 2010).

In mainland China it is not clear whether such payment is out of the police officers' own pockets, or whether there is a fund provided by the local government. According to a line who claimed to have worked for the Guangzhou government for ten years, he was paid ¥1,000 to ¥10,000 per month for his work (J. Fu 2004). According to another report, in Guangzhou city there are about a hundred of these kinds of 'lines'. They were paid from a few hundred up to ¥1,000 for each operation (J. Fu 2007). In a Yunnan city, Mengzi, it was reported that the police paid up to ¥300,000 a year to police 'lines' (*Chinese News Weekly* 2012).

By looking into the former prisoners' stories, all the hooks were kinds of lines instead of eyes and ears. These hooks were all current drug users and drug dealers. What we can see from the above is that the police officers, the eyes and ears, and the lines are motivated and sometimes under pressure to not only collect intelligence but also to successfully catch drug users. To achieve this purpose, one controversial tactic is sometimes used in the process of investigation and arrest of drug users: the 'enticement detection'.

Enticement detection

Local research and reports show that informants are widely used in dealing with felony cases like drug dealings, counterfeit money production, and forced prostitution (Cai 2013; D. Yang 2010). Sometimes enticement detection is used during the process of arrest. Chinese scholars define 'enticement detection' as a strategy that the law enforcement agency uses to intentionally provide the person the conditions for an illegal act, or they create a certain environment to attract a person to commit an illegal act and then arrest the person after he or she commits the illegal act (Ma 2000; J. Xu 2011; Z. Yang 2008). There are two types of 'enticement detection'. The first type refers to the law enforcers' act to attract people who have criminal intentions to commit crime. It is called the 'providing-opportunity type' (*jihui tigong xing* 機會提供型). It is similar to the 'law enforcement encouragement' found in the United States (Potenberg 1963). The second category refers to law enforcers' act to provoke innocent people's criminal intention and provide them with opportunities for criminal acts. This is called 'provoking-criminal-intention type' (*fanyi youfa xing* 犯意誘發型). This practice is similar to 'entrapment' in the American context, which is defined as 'the conception and planning of an offense by an officer, and his procurement of its commission by one who would not have perpetrated it except for the trickery, persuasion, or fraud of the officer' (Colquitt 2004, 8).

Strictly speaking, enticement detection is not allowed in China. The 1979, 1996, and 2013 versions of Chinese Criminal Procedure Law state that enticement and deception are prohibited in extorting confessions (National People's Congress 2013; J. Xu 2011). It is, however, still widely used in practice (Wu and Sun 2001). Chinese commentators generally suggest that the providing-opportunity type of enticement detection is acceptable, while the 'provoking-criminal-intention type' is not acceptable (Wu and Sun 2001; J. Xu 2011; Yao and Wang 2012). But by looking into former drug users' narratives, signs of both types of enticement detections can be found in the policing of drug users.

Moreover, current literature and media reports allege that enticement detection and informants are used only in criminal investigations. That said, if what former drug users say about hooking is true, enticement detection and informants are used also in the investigation of administrative cases like drug taking. Almost every former prisoner told me something about 'hooking' when talking about how they were 'arrested'.

Three Types of 'Hooks'

When talking about their experiences of being arrested, most former drug users said that the police were able to identify them only because they colluded either with other drug users or drug dealers. In my survey, twenty-two of the twenty-eight former prisoners believe that it is common for the police officers to use a hook when they want to catch drug users.

Some of the information that former drug users gave me about hooks is based on their personal experiences of being recruited as hooks. Others' narratives either came from stories that they heard from police officers or from other drug users. Before looking at how these information and stories spreads and how these stories influence former drug users' world view, I will first describe three types of hooks that I identified according to their recounts. For the sake of analysis, I call these three types of hooks the 'one-off hooks', 'drug user hooks', and 'drug dealer hooks'.

One-off hooks

A 'one-off hook' is a drug user or a former drug user who has already been identified and arrested but not yet incarcerated. Usually during the time of interrogation the police would require arrested drug users to give names and information of several other current drug users. Many former drug users told me that police officers sometimes ask drug users to betray their friends in exchange for their own freedom. Ling, a 40-year-old woman, gave me an example:

> Ling: Several police officers came to me after I bought the things. I felt like, it's over. I will spend my next two years in prison again. They brought me to the police station [*paichu suo* 派出所]. One of them said if I gave them three names they will let me go.
> Author: Did you?
> Ling: I couldn't think of other methods. I gave them three names. [*Her voice trembles*]
> Author: Did they let you go?
> Ling: Yes. (Ling, non-audio-recorded conversations in a cafe, 2012)

The police kept Ling in the interrogation room until they arrested all three drug users whom she had mentioned. Ling was under great pressure at the time when she was kept in the police station. She had been incarcerated for two years because of drug use. She still remembered the pain of incarceration and did not want to go back there again. She had to make the choice between temporary freedom and betrayal. To her, the police officers were tempting her, if not forcing her, to betray her friends. This temptation, to Ling, is evil by nature. Qiang, a 40-year-old former drug user, told me about another 'evil' method that the police used to tempt the arrested drug users to leak information about other drug users in the early 1990s:

> We are all 'drug friends', so-called drug friends, but you cannot blame them. Once arrested, after the police torture, once he is psychologically collapsed, he will tell anything he knows. . . . They kept you in the interrogation room and waited until you start craving drugs. They put some drugs in front of you and tell you that if you give names, you can take those drugs. This is just a 'soft' way. There are other 'hard' ways, but I do not want to talk about that. (Qiang, interview, 2012)

Qiang refused to talk about what he meant by 'torture' and 'hard ways'. He was also the only person who told me about how 'drugs' were used by the police to tempt drug users to give information about other drug users. To Qiang, the police officers were supposed to help the drug users to quit drugs, not use drugs as a temptation for the drug users to betray their friends. Qiang's might be an extreme case. However, one similarity between Qiang's and Ling's cases is that, from their point of view, the police officers used filthy tricks to tempt them during their most vulnerable time, when they deeply feared being incarcerated and were suffering from the unbearable pain of craving.

The one-off hooks cooperate with the police officers on a short-term basis. They were caught, but refused to betray their friends, and put in jail, or caught and released after they gave the police officers information about other drug users. However, according to the former prisoners, there were two other types of hooks who cooperated with police officers on a more regular and long-term basis. We may call them the 'drug user hooks' and the 'drug dealer hooks'.

Drug user hooks

The second type of hooks was the individual drug users who were recruited by police officers to be their informants—the drug user hooks. They are usually active members among one or several groups of drug users. With these social connections, they could give names of different drug users to the police officers when asked by the police officers to do so. Some of the drug user hooks were known to other drug users, while others were more anonymous. Former prisoners hate this type of drug users and the police officers who recruited them not only because they abuse the trust among drug users but also because of their use of 'enticement detection'. These drug user hooks were used because they could 'seduce' some drug users into using drugs at a particular moment, so that the police can come and arrest these drug users. Lili, a female former inmate who had used heroin for five years, told me how police arrested her through the help of a hook:

> It was a morning in August. I was running out of heroin. The drug dealer whom I used to go to in order to buy heroin was just arrested. I went to Huzi's house to see if there was some heroin left. Huzi's house was a 'drug den' [*yaokou* 窯口] where some other drug users came to use drugs. In return for providing the venue, Huzi and his wife could share some of the drugs that the visitors brought. There were some rumours saying Huzi was a hook, but I could not stand the craving and went straight to Huzi's house. Huzi and his wife were both craving as well when I rang their doorbell. I gave him ¥200 and told him to buy some heroin. Huzi soon came back with heroin. I lay on a sling chair after injecting the heroin. I saw a mobile phone in Huzi's room when I was smoking. I suddenly remembered the 'hooking' things. I stood up and told Huzi that I was leaving. Huzi said, 'You are leaving now? Stay longer.' I insisted and left his house. When I was crossing the road, I saw a uniformed police walking towards me. My brain went blank. The police caught me and handcuffed me.

It was obvious to Lili that Huzi was a police informant. If what Lili said were true, what the police had done in Huzi's case can be seen as an 'opportunity-provision type' of enticement detection. By ambushing the user outside Huzi's house, the police could arrest drug users whenever they wanted. Another former drug user mentioned a similar experience. The only difference is that he did not plan to take drugs at that time. Laoda, a former inmate in his fifties, told me how he was 'seduced' by his neighbour to use heroin and then was arrested by the police:

> My neighbour suddenly came to my place that day. He said he wanted some 'thing'. . . . We sometimes play [use drugs] together. . . . I went out to buy those 'things'. . . . After I smoked the first puff, they [the police] knocked at my door. . . . After a while, I realized he was a hook.

If what Laoda said is true, then a drug user hook is not only an informant who provides police officers with information about other drug users; they also carry out the 'provoking-criminal-intention type' of enticement detection. From Laoda's point of view, under the police officers' instruction, his neighbour deliberately provoked him to use drugs.

Drug dealer hooks

The third type of hook is the 'drug dealer hook'. They are drug dealers who work for police officers. According to former drug users, they sell out some of their customers for their own freedom. Dong, a 35-year-old woman who had used heroin for several years in the 1990s, told me how it works:

> The buyers usually call the dealers before they come to [the dealers' apartment to] buy 'things'. The dealers will then call the police. The police officers would ambush the buyer outside the dealer's apartment. When the buyers left the dealer's place after they bought 'things', the police would come to arrest him.

Among the forty-one former drug users that I met, Dong was the only one who had this kind of experience. However, most of them believe that such phenomena are not rare. Many of them had asked this question: 'Why do the police not arrest the drug dealers but instead arrest the drug users?' Their answer to it is usually, 'So that they can arrest more drug users!' The narrative of dealer-police collusion is intensified further by other personal experiences and stories heard from other drug users. Sun had worked for a drug dealer for a few months in the mid-1990s. According to him, the drug dealer that he had worked for had a good relationship with a police officer. In his words, they are like 'brothers'. He told me how the police officer helped the drug dealer by arresting several people who came to take revenge on him:

> They came with weapons. He [the drug dealer] just gave a call to that policeman. A team of police officers came within three minutes. . . . They [the police] soon defeated them [the robbers]. Then—here comes the exciting part—the police put a pill and hundred-dollar notes into his [one robber's] hand and took a picture of him, putting a pipe in his hand. This is the evidence. . . . They later sentenced him to life imprisonment.

The Circulation of Information about 'Hooking'

Whereas I had assumed that the use of enticement detection and informants was a secret known only to a few drug users, in fact I found that every single former drug user 'knows' something about it. This knowledge of hooks is widely spread among both drug users and former drug users. It raises the question of how the word about hooks is spread. Compiling former drug users' accounts, there are two main sources of these narratives. The first narrative is that of former drug users and current drug users who have been recruited as hooks. The second one is former users and current drug users who believed that they had experienced hooking.

Hooks

All three types of hooks can be a source of knowledge about hooking. In my survey with the twenty-eight former prisoners, twenty-two of them had been approached by at least one police officer to recruit them as a hook. Among all the former drug users in this study, only two of them admitted that they have been recruited as hooks. Both of them were recruited as one-off hooks. As mentioned above, Ling explained her experience of becoming a hook to other drug users and former drug users as 'my friend has become a hook'. Unlike Ling, Laoda is another former drug user who told me about his experiences of being recruited as a hook. Laoda said on the contrary that he refused to betray his friends:

> I was clean at that time. I didn't use drugs before they arrested me. They had no way of threatening me. I refused to do that when I was taking drugs, not to mention now when I am clean.

Regardless of the authenticity of Laoda's story, he did raise a scenario that one-off hooks would be more willing to tell other about their experiences of being recruited as a hook—that is, when they had not taken drugs, or at least had not taken drugs for long enough to test negative.

As was the case with the one-off hook, the drug user hook and drug dealer hook sometimes spread information about hooking. Although they are police hooks, they sometimes also act as informants for the drug users. From a former drug users' narrative, these hooks are by no means loyal to the police officers. On the one hand, drug user hooks and drug dealer hooks give information about drug users to police officers, but they also sometimes provide drug users with information about the police—information that could help drug users to be more aware of police arrest. In other words, some of the hooks are 'double agents'. As Ling said, 'They [the police] have people among us, but we also have people among them.' This type of drug user–hook relationship is usually based on some kind of 'commonality' (*tong* 同). In China 'commonness' forms connections that link different people of common birthplace, family, and workplace together (Bakken 2000). This is also the case in the drug user–hook relationship. They are usually either living in the same community—or, in their words, they 'grow up together'—or they have studied in the same school or belong to the same kinship. Because of the commonness, hooks sometimes told their drug user buddies to be aware of other hooks and police, especially during specific police campaigns against drug users. That might also explain why, although some drug users and drug dealers are known to be hooks, they still are able to remain in the community. While their existence may threaten some drug users, they sometimes can also help other drug users to avoid police arrest.

'Being hooked'

Drug users who believe that they have been hooked are another major source of information about hooking. Twenty-four out of twenty-eight of the former prisoners in my survey reported that they had been hooked. Although some former drug users know drug user hooks and drug dealer hooks in person, none of them have become these two kinds of hooks.

Neither Laoda nor Lili had solid evidence to prove that Huzi and Laoda's neighbour were hooks. Their judgements originated either from personal knowledge of hooking or from stories that they heard from other drug users. During my fieldwork, whenever there were rumours about some drug users being arrested, former drug users almost always said 'He or she is hooked.' However, in some cases drug users might be mistaken as hooks. Juan was arrested and put in a detention centre because of using heroin. According to current regulations (Ministry of Public Security 1991; State Council 1990), the detention officers collected all her personal belongings, including her mobile phone. One of her drug friends, Xi, called her mobile phone after she was incarcerated. Xi's telephone number was shown on Juan's mobile, and it was exposed to the detention officers. Xi was arrested and put into the detention centre soon after that:

> She insisted that I was a hook. She didn't believe me no matter how I explained. We fought in the detention centre because of that. She insisted, but I had nothing to do with it. (Juan, interview 72, 2012)

If what Juan said is true, it might be possible that some drug users had occasionally mistakenly attributed their arrests to hooking. Reviewing my data, I cannot tell how widespread hooking is in practice. Apart from those cases in which former drug users are directly recruited as hooks, all other cases are merely speculative. However, from the former drug users' point of view, it becomes 'real' that almost all these cases are caused by hooking.[1]

So far I have described former drug users' accounts of their experiences of hooking. I have also talked about how former drug users interpreted their

---

1. There are two exceptions: two drug users had been reported to the police by their parents. Their parents reported them because they believed that it could help the drug users to get rid of their habit.

experiences of being arrested according to 'hooking' narratives. In the following, I am going to examine how these hooking narratives are affecting former drug users' interpretations of the police and the state. These interpretations go completely against their expectations and what the state would like to portray in the media. As I would argue, these contradictions have contributed to the destruction of former drug users' trust in other drug users, the state, and the police; they have also created a clear atmosphere of 'others' and 'us' in the social world of the former drug users.

Reinterpretation of the Propaganda

The cunning police

Former drug users' experiences of arrest and their interpretation of the police have destroyed the image of the 'brave and benevolent police'. To them, the police that they meet are by no means 'brave' or 'benevolent'. None of the police arrest them by 'risking their lives' or by any of the 'outstanding' investigative tactics portrayed in the media. Instead, they are using hooks, a stratagem perceived by the former drug users as 'cunning' and 'dirty'. When I asked former drug users what kind of investigation tactics are 'appropriate', few of them could give a very systematic description. For Sun, the appropriate methods for police to detect or identify drug users should be their 'professional knowledge'. This kind of professional knowledge includes detecting the unusual facial expressions, pale faces, unfocused eyes, and arms with needle tracks. Although Sun has never been professionally trained in criminal investigation, he had formed a set of perceptions about what constitutes professional police officers. In the words of many former drug users, 'It's natural for cats to catch rats.' However, they care a lot about the ways that the police go about catching drug users. As Sun put it,

> If the police identify us by carefully examine our appearances, this can at least show their 'professional quality' [*zhuanye sushi* 專業素質]. . . . Hooks are people whom we originally trust. If we do not trust them, it would not be possible for them to hook us. They are for sure people that you would never expect to betray you. It's the feeling of being cheated that hurts me. (Sun, conversation in a cafe, 2013)

To former drug users like Sun, the police's use of hooks is certainly inappropriate. It is inappropriate in the sense that they believe that 'cheating' and 'betrayal' are by nature 'dirty'. Through hooking the police are not only 'cheating' the drug users but are also provoking 'betrayal' among drug users. Former drug users perceived police officers to be abusing the trust between drug users and sowing discord among them. From their point of view, this is 'evil'. When I talked with Ling about her experiences of becoming a one-off hook, she felt that she was forced by the police to betray her friends. She was forced by the police to do things that she is ashamed of. When I asked Sun to compare the hooks and the police officers, he maintained that the police are much worse than the hooks:

> Hooks are bad, but understandable. No one wants to go to jail. Although they betray their friends, they do it only to avoid pain. The police are different. They do it for their own petty benefits. (Sun, conversations in a cafe, 2012)

Police–drug dealer collusion

As described in the last chapter, in government propaganda drug dealers are described as the force of evil which is 'extremely fierce and vicious', 'mad', 'tricky', and 'shrewd and crafty'. The mission of the police is to fight them bravely, wisely, and selflessly. Former prisoners did expect the police officers to fight the 'evil' drug dealers. However, their experiences taught them that it is completely the opposite. Although former drug users do not have much evidence to prove that the police collude with drug dealers when they arrest drug users, they do believe that it happens. Former drug users arrested shortly after buying drugs from drug dealers are justifiably suspicious. In the social world of former drug users, when compared with drug dealers, they are good people who never hurt anyone because of their drug use, while the 'bad guys' are those 'bad drug dealers' who sell them drugs. Ying once commented on this:

> I thought they are supposed to bust the drug dealers? Now it's completely the reverse. They do not arrest the drug dealers but arrest the drug users. They 'feed' [*yangzhe* 養著] the drug dealers, so that the drug dealers can help them to meet the arrest quota! (Ying, interview 7, 2012)

Rumours freely circulate among former drug users about the 'bad drug dealers'. One recurring rumour is that the bad drug dealers dilute heroin with harmful substances like chalk, lime, and rat poison. This, according to the former inmates, is the trick that the drug dealers use to lower the cost but maintain the dizzying effect of the heroin. Similar speculations can be found among drug dealers and users in other countries (Coomber 1996, 1997). Another rumour is that drug dealers lure 'innocent' people into taking drugs by giving them free drugs. None of the forty-one former inmates have any first-hand evidence to prove any of these two rumours. However, all of them believe either one or both of these rumours. In their words, 'Although I have never seen it, I am sure it is true.' This kind of 'bad guy' image of drug dealers is further reinforced by the state propaganda mentioned above. There are many drug-related television dramas, infotainment programmes, and news reports in China. The media hype on drug issues peaks every year during the UN Office on Drugs and Crime's 26 June campaign. One of the main themes of these reports and television programmes is that the wise, brave cops catch the bad, cunning drug dealers. Law and the police, according to this view, should target the bad drug dealers instead of the drug users. However, former drug users' belief in the existence of drug dealer hooks further debunks the image of the 'bravery and righteousness' of police officers. To them, police officers are colluding with drug dealers. To them, the real reason behind such collusion is that the police want to meet their arrest quota and get monetary bonuses. This allegation points to another contradiction between former drug users' perceptions of the police and the official portrayal of the police—they accuse the police of acting out of self-interest.

The self-interested police

To be 'selfless' is an important personal characteristic that official propaganda frequently uses to describe police officers. However, former drug users' experiences with hooking had informed them that police officers are certainly not selfless. It is often claimed in official propaganda that the police's goal is to 'educate' and 'rescue' drug users, claims which former drug users refute.

Cash bonuses

Dutton (2005b) has convincingly demonstrated that monetary incentives have increasingly been used to motivate police campaigns in post-Mao China. Prostitution has become one area where the police force used to get monetary gain through fines. In the words of Dutton (2005b, 205), prostitution became 'a milk cow that would pay, through fines'. However, through looking into other existing literature, there are no records about cash bonuses that the police can get through arresting drug users. I had consulted a professor who was teaching in a local police academy and he denied that the police get any monetary bonuses by arresting drug users. Yet every former drug user with whom I have spoken believed that monetary gain is one of the most important motivations behind police arrest. One possible reason underlying such speculations is that informants who provide information to the police do receive monetary rewards (Cai 2013; J. Fu 2004, 2007; K. Zhang 2012). Some former drug users have personally witnessed these payments. Shan told me about one such experience in 2009, right before the sixtieth anniversary of the People's Republic of China. He was caught by several hooks after taking heroin. Some police officers came and paid them ¥800 right in front of his eyes. The logic behind the former drug users' speculation is that, if the police are willing to pay informants ¥800 out of their own pockets, they must be able to get even more cash bonuses themselves by arresting drug users.

Pressure for making arrest

The second reason motivating police officers to arrest drug users, according to former drug users, is that the police need to meet their arrest quota. Lily told me about a conversation between her and a police officer. She was arrested through hooking in the early 2000s. She felt very unfairly treated and questioned the police officer: 'Why do you arrest me, but let her [the hook] go?' According to Lily, the police answered, 'Because I have met my quota.' Many former prisoners personally knew one or two police officers in their local districts. Many of these police officers had told them things about arrest quotas.

The practices of arrest quota performance are not a secret in China. It has been reported and debated openly in local newspapers (*Chinese News Weekly* 2012; L. Wang 2006; G. Wu 2009). A case in 2009 brought media attention to the police arrest quota. A 1.7-metre-tall guy was mistaken by police officers for being a drug user because he looked 'thin and weak'. He was arrested by police officers responsible for another administrative region instead of police officers in his own region. The reason behind this 'cross-region arrest', according to a deputy police chief, is that there was a rise of 50 per cent in the 'security quota' during that year (G. Wu 2009). It is reasonable to believe that the officers are under pressure to make arrests. A recent news report about a local police station in Guangdong Province shows how local police officers respond to such pressure:

> In mid-October, Xiayang District Police Station was among those in the lowest ranks in term of 'cracking drug crime' [*po du'an* 破毒案] and 'catching and rehabilitating drug users' [*shoujie xidu renyuan* 收戒吸毒人員]. This had also dragged down the ranking of the security bureau [*gongan ju* 公安局].[2] On 17 October Xiayang District Police Station was named and criticized [*dianming piping* 點名批評] in the public security bureau anti-narcotic evaluation meeting. The head of the police station called a meeting immediately after the evaluation meeting. The meeting concluded that the source of their failure was the inefficient intelligence source.
>
> On 18 October, with the intelligence from the public, the police officers arrested three drug users on a farm. On 21 October a drug den was busted and six drug users were arrested. On 24 October five drug users were arrested. On 30 October and 4 November two drug users were arrested. On 5 November there was a crackdown on another drug den; six drug users and one drug dealer were arrested. (Z. Chen 2013)

This news report reveals that the individual officers were under pressure to arrest drug users. Police officers who fail to meet their arrest quota are shamed and criticized along with their police stations; even the county security bureau might be criticized. This collective responsibility system had imposed immense pressure on police officers to make arrests. Although there is no clear evidence to prove that former drug users in my study were arrested because of an arrest quota, it would be reasonable to believe that these police officers were under very similar pressure. Moreover, from the former drug users' point of view, it is one of the main reasons

---

2. The local police station (*paichu suo* 派出所) is under the county security bureau (*xian gongan ju* 縣公安局).

that explain why the police use hooks. To them, hooking is similar to a 'pyramid scheme'. By arresting one drug user, the police officers can conveniently find three more drug users. Through these three drug users, the police officer can find nine more drug users. It is simply mathematics.

From the former drug users' narratives, we can see that they perceived the police as motivated simply by selfish interests. All the police officers' actions, including hooking, are interpreted by former drug users as something that is done out of police self-interest to meet their arrest quota and to get monetary bonuses. By debunking the 'selfless' image of the police, the former drug users also cast judgement on the government as hypocritical.

The hypocritical government

In China the official name of many state organizations and agencies starts with the term 'People's' (*renmin* 人民)—for instance, People's Republic of China, the People's Hospital, the People's Liberation Army, and the People's Police. However, former drug users seldom use the term 'People's Police' when they talked about police officers. Examples of terms that they often use when referring to the police are *jingcha* (警察, which literally means 'police'), and *gongan* (公安, meaning 'public security'). However, I found one term that they often used surprising in the very beginning: *zhenfu* (政府, meaning 'government')—or sometimes the *gongchan dang* (共產黨, meaning 'Communist Party'). In their conversations, the term 'government' occurred together with and sometimes interchangeably with 'the police'. When I asked them, 'Are you talking about the police or the government?' they answered me in a tone that made me feel like I was an idiot. 'It's the same!' they said. In the official propaganda that I have mentioned above, police officers are glorified, and at the same time such glorification was also applied to the government as a whole. In these propaganda narratives, the police and the government are treated as if they were the same thing. Former drug users, in accordance with the state propaganda, sometimes simply called police officers 'government people' (*zhengfu de ren* 政府的人). This explains why many former drug users said that *the government* is hypocritical. To former drug users, the government is hypocritical not only because the government 'talks the talk but doesn't walk the walk', but also because they thought that the government had bragged too much in the propaganda while the reality was that what they had perceived was totally opposite to what was claimed in the propaganda. News and reports about 'exemplary police officers' can be seen so widely all over the different types of media in China. The more they heard about the 'brave, wise, selfless, and benevolent' police officers in the media—the more they compared them with the 'cunning' and 'self-interested' police officers from their experiences who 'colluded with evil drug dealers'—the more they felt that the government was hypocritical. When describing the government's hypocrisy, former drug users are not only referring to the fact that the 'behaviour of the government' is different from the 'claim of the government' but also to their perceptions that the 'behaviour of the government' is completely opposite to the 'claim of the government'.

In this chapter, I have examined the former prisoners' accounts of their experiences with the police officers when they were arrested. The feeling of unfairness and injustice has been shown in former criminological literature to be counterproductive to offender rehabilitation (Sherman 1993). Former prisoners in this study perceived that the methods that police officers used to arrest them, especially the use of hooks and enticement detection, had made their arrests unfair and unjust. From the former prisoners' perspective, making arrests was supposed to be for the purpose of fighting the force of evil as explained in official propaganda. But they insisted that the police officers' 'collusion' with other drug users and especially their collusion with the 'evil' drug dealers, as well as the use of enticement detections, both the providing-opportunity type and the provoking-criminal-intention type, were definitely not appropriate methods to make arrest. Former prisoners expected the police officers to use their 'professional skills' or their wisdom to make arrests in precisely the way represented in the party propaganda. The narrative of the brave, wise, and selfless police officer had turned out to be a complete fiction in the eyes of the former inmates. A careful examination of the former prisoners' accounts, different Chinese reports, and local studies (Z. Chen 2013; G. Wu 2009; Zhi 2013) grounds the belief that local police officers were under strong pressure to collect intelligence and make arrests according to plan. Not only the individual police officers but the whole police station might be criticized if the police officers could not meet the arrest quota—hence the alleged normalization of informants and enticement detection. One unintended consequence is that the 'impression management' (Goffman 1958) in the front stage of propaganda is presented to the former prisoners alongside the 'backstage' performance of the 'real' police officers.

This chapter has unearthed the first fragment of a system perceived as structurally hypocritical. Former prisoners saw the contradictions between the model police officers in the party propaganda and the police officers they met in real life. The experiences of being arrested can be seen as an orientation to the wider 'managerialist'—and as a consequence hypocritical—criminal justice system where propaganda and real-life managerial criteria clash in open view of the arrested drug users. What they experienced later in the *laojiao* ('re-education through labour') forced them not only to witness more and more hypocrisy as clashes between ideals and reality escalated but also to learn to *be* hypocritical themselves in order to survive the reality of incarceration.

4
Initiation Ceremony in Drug Detention

In this chapter I will further examine former prisoners' experiences in the early phase of their imprisonment.[1] With the example of the prison culture of 'initiation ceremonies', I argue that prison officers' concern of maintaining control and order in the prison goes beyond producing the form of structural hypocrisy discussed in the previous chapter and actually forces former prisoners to act in hypocritical ways themselves. What should have been a process of learning and rehabilitation through education turns instead into a veritable culture of hypocrisy.

In 2009 over 173,000 drug users were incarcerated in China for the purpose of drug rehabilitation. The number has practically doubled to 340,000 in 2015 (Office of China National Narcotics Control Commission 2010; 2016, 35, 61). Incarceration has been used as one of the major means of drug rehabilitation in China. All former drug detainees in this study regarded their incarceration as a very painful experience. One of their most painful memories of imprisonment which still comes back to haunt them originates in what I call the 'initiation ceremonies'. By 'initiation ceremony', I am referring to a short but intensive period of ceremonial initiation rituals organized by both the prison authority and the 'inmate authority'—that is, the power authority within the inmates' community—upon the new inmates' arrival to the prison. The purpose of these ceremonies is to socialize the new inmates into obedient subjects of the prison regime. From the former prisoners' points of view, during this process, instead of 'educating' and 'saving' the new inmates, both the prison officers and the experienced inmates constantly and intentionally inflicted physical and mental pain on them for the purpose of control. It was also in this period that some of the former prisoners were forced to participate in a system of hypocrisy in which they had to tell lies in order to survive.

On the conceptual level, this process is related to the 'prison culture' literature (Clemmer 1966; Mathiesen 1990; Sykes and Messinger 1960). The experiences of being imprisoned are essentially painful and many of the 'pains of imprisonment' (Sykes 1958) are assumed to be the intrinsic and universal characteristics of imprisonment. However, in this chapter I propose that many of the particular Chinese

---

1. A slightly different version of this chapter is published as a book chapter in Børge Bakken, *Crime and the Chinese Dream* (Hong Kong: Hong Kong University Press, 2018).

pains of imprisonment are rooted in Chinese educational, penal, and social control philosophy. In Chinese prisons both the prison authority and the inmate authority consciously attempt to 'prisonize' the new inmates. Many of the techniques that they used to prisonize new inmates are not simply casual by-products of an informal prison culture. This system also originates from a characteristic Chinese control philosophy. This combination of the informal and the formal represents the double-edged sword of pain that may not be exclusive to the Chinese system but has its own specific rationality in a Chinese philosophy of pain and control. While criminologists suggest that 'pain' is very often counterproductive to offender rehabilitation (Christie 1981), the Chinese prison and inmate authority had actively used 'pain' to train the new inmates for the purpose of control. This also resonates with Chen's discussion of the use of 'disintegrative' shaming to 'deter' offenders, or to 'teach the offenders a lesson' through pain (2002).

Prison Culture

Individuals in prisons can generally be divided into two categories: 'informal group', which means the prison inmates, and the 'formal group', which refers to the prison authority (Caldwell 1956; McCorkle and Korn 1954). Prison inmates form their own culture and related code of behaviours, which is also called the 'prison culture' and the 'inmates' code'. The process through which the inmates adopt the prison culture and the inmates' code of conduct is generally called 'prisonization' (Clemmer 1966; Mathiesen 1990; Sykes and Messinger 1960; Thomas 1977). Prisonization describes a process whereby the prison inmates take on 'in greater or lesser degree of the folkways, mores, customs, and general culture of the penitentiary' (Clemmer 1966, 299). The content of prisonization basically stems from two sources: the norms of conduct that prison authorities impose on the inmate, and the norms of conduct originating from the prison community itself (Wellford 1967). Some studies have focused on how prison authorities attempt to change the behaviours and thoughts of the prison inmates (Foucault 1977; Goffman 1968a), but most other studies on prison culture concentrate on the norms of the prison community itself (e.g., McCorkle and Korn 1954; Mears, Stewart, Siennick, and Simons 2013; Tasca, Griffin, and Rodriguez 2010). There are two main approaches in the explanation of the content and the formation of inmate codes: the 'deprivation model' and the 'importation model'.

The deprivation model argues that prison culture is created by prison inmates so as to adapt to different kinds of pains and deprivations in the prisons. These deprivations include the loss of freedom, right to food and sex, and the psychological harm caused by incarceration (McCorkle and Korn 1954; Sykes and Messinger 1960; Thomas 1977). The deprivation model sees prison culture as something produced within the prison. The importation model suggests that prison culture is an imported product. From this perspective, criminals bring lower-class culture and criminal culture into the prison and use them to deal with the hardships that they encounter in the prison environment (Cao, Zhao, and Van Dine 1997; Irwin and Cressey 1962; Mears et al. 2013; Olin 1956; Tasca, Griffin, and Rodriguez 2010). Prisonization is basically the process of internalizing specific prison norms and prison conduct, and may be seen partly as the effect of a strategy intentionally enforced by prison authorities to 'reform' the inmates by indoctrination or punishment. The effects of this process seen from the vantage of the authorities may be intended or unintended, effective or ineffective depending on the anticipated outcome.

Prisonization may also be seen as a specific 'prison culture' or behavioural strategy among inmates in order to 'survive' or cope with the 'pains of imprisonment'. The inmates may be more or less dependent on such coping strategies, and there are studies on how deeply ingrained in the prisonization process inmates become during the process of incarceration (Clemmer 1951, 1966; Mathiesen 1990). To understand prisonization in the Chinese prison/*laojiao*/*qiangge* system, it is important to recognize the discrepancy between the promised official narratives of 'reform' and inmates' experiences of 'pain' in the daily experiences of prison life. In my interview data the clash between the promises of 'reform' and the experiences of utterly *useless* pain develops a strong feeling of 'being conned' or manipulated. This in turn creates strong resistance against what is perceived as official 'hypocrisy' among the inmates: 'They promised to help us; they actually harm us.' One may even say that the specific culture of prisonization itself develops this unintended effect among the inmates. The authorities no longer seem to control the outcome of prisonization, and the intended 'steered' process of 'reform' produces results seemingly dysfunctional for the prison authorities. Prisonization may therefore be seen as partly a culture of intended oppression, partly a culture of unintended resistance.

Prisons and Drug Rehabilitation in China

Before I describe the daily life of the prisoners, more has to be said about the system of 'jails' or 'prisons' here. The English language distinction between 'jail' and 'prison' may not apply directly to the Chinese institutional system that makes a difference between *laojiao* and *jianyu*. Because of such differences, I found it necessary to repeat myself on my use of the term 'prison'. As I mentioned in the introduction, what I am talking about here is not the formal prison system but other administrative systems of incarcerations, including 're-education through labour' (*laodong jiaoyang*), 'compulsory isolation for drug rehabilitation centres' (*qiangzhi geli jiedu suo*), 'compulsory drug rehabilitation centres' (*qiangzhi jiedu suo*), and 'detention centres' (*kanshou suo*). I still talk of 'prisons' and 'prisoners' in this respect.

Scholars in different disciplines have conducted a variety of studies on Chinese prisons. These include studies on Chinese prisons' historical roots and developments (Dikötter 2002; Dutton 1992; Seymour and Anderson 1998; V. Shaw 1998;

Williams and Wu 2004), the economic dimension of Chinese prison labour (Dutton 2005a; Liu and Chui 2016; Seymour and Anderson 1998; Seymour 2005; 2006; V. Shaw 1998; H. Wu 1992), discipline and control over inmates (Bakken 2000; Cheng 2009; 2010; Dutton 1992; Williams and Wu 2004; H. Wu 1992), and inmates' lives and resistance (Bakken 2000; Cheng 2009; 2010; Tanner 1994; Williams and Wu 2004). When former drug users recalled their memories of incarceration, one typical remark was that 'they do not treat you as a human being' (*bu ba ni dang ren* 不把你當人). Many stories about how prisoners were physically and mentally tortured during their incarceration have been reported in previous studies and memoirs (Liao 2013; Saunders 1996; Williams and Wu 2004; H. Wu 1992; 1993). However, most of these books have been about 'political prisoners' who were regarded in the political language of 'friends and enemies'. Literally, such relations are seen as 'enemy-and-me' (*diwo maodun* 敵我矛盾) relationships by the party-state. The former prisoners in this chapter were incarcerated in administrative detention institutions. They were defined in the old Maoist language of politics as being 'conflicts among the people' (*renmin neibu maodun* 人民內部矛盾). There is a lack of comprehensive studies on prison inmates who had been put under administrative detention, and even fewer have specifically examined the use of imprisonment in drug rehabilitation. The important point here is that the *laojiao* is an *administrative* system. That means that the police have full discretion in terms of arrest and incarceration of drug addicts, and that the system is effectively not 'judicial' since it does not involve a court system. The use of drugs is not in itself a 'criminal' act in the legal sense; it is basically a 'mistake' that has to be corrected. The 'reform-through-education' system is basically a political-administrative system set up in order to 'correct' erring individuals. From this follows the focus on 'reform' and 'education'. Drug addicts are thus seen, not as 'enemies of the people', but as 'erring members of that same 'people'. The narrative of 'improvement and reform' follows directly from this logic. Still, of course, we talk very much of a prison-like system here, and in this book I use the expressions 'inmate' and 'prisoner' synonymously.

The use of confinement for drug rehabilitation was introduced to China around 1860 by foreign missionaries during the late Qing dynasty (Dikötter, Laamann, and Zhou 2004). After 1911, although some of the missionary-run drug treatment centres were still functioning, drug rehabilitation was mainly carried out in detention centres, health clinics, and prisons. During the Republican period, in 1934, a system to convert 'addicts' into productive labour was proposed and implemented in Beijing. Drug users were forced to work in agriculture, construction, or factories. In those factories 'moral instruction' was provided in the form of lectures, formal education, and leisure activities to save the inmates from the 'evil of smoking' (Dikötter, Laamann, and Zhou 2004, 130–34).

The formal legislation about the establishment of 'compulsory drug rehabilitation centres' in Communist China was not implemented until 1995 (State Council 1995). Most of the former drug users I met were incarcerated after 1995 and before

2008. In that period, most of the arrested drug users went through very standardized penal procedures. Many drug users were first incarcerated in a 'detention centre' for about a week. They would then be sent to a 'compulsory drug rehabilitation centre' (hereafter referred to as *qiangjie*) for three to six months. Some former prisoners reported that they were sent directly to the *qiangjie* without staying in the detention centre. The first-timer would be discharged after staying in the *qiangjie*. Recidivists would be incarcerated for about a month in the 'compulsory drug rehabilitation centre' and would then be sent to a 're-education through labour' (hereafter referred to as *laojiao*) for one to three years. Officially, after the implementation of the new Anti-drug Law in 2008 'compulsory isolation for drug rehabilitation centres' (hereafter referred to as *qiangge*) were set up to replace *laojiao* as the institution for drug rehabilitation (National People's Congress 2008). According to the new regulation, all arrested drug addicts would be incarcerated for one to three years in the 'new' *qiangge*.

According to the current laws and regulations (National People's Congress 2008; State Council 2011), every arrested drug user in China nowadays is supposed to have an opportunity to participate in 'community-based drug treatment' (*shequ jiedu* 社區戒毒). The law states that every drug addict has an opportunity to have their drug rehabilitation carried out in the community instead of in prison. According to the regulations, the local government is required to formulate and implement treatment programmes for drug addicts who are participating in the community-based drug treatment programme. However, the main ways of conducting drug rehabilitation in China today is still by incarceration alone (Zhu, Dong, and Hesketh 2009). The next section will briefly outline each of these prisons.

Detention centres

At least twenty of the former prisoners in this study had been incarcerated in the detention centre, while other were sent directly to the *qiangjie* or *qiangge*. Detention centres are used to incarcerate various types of inmates in addition to drug users. Inmates include detained and remanded suspects, criminally detained offenders, administratively detained offenders, and criminals who are sentenced for less than one year (National People's Congress 2008, 2013; State Council 1990). One characteristic of detention centres that makes them different from other places of incarceration is that suspects and offenders who are accused of different types of crimes and offences are usually put in the same cell. Drug users in detention centres are categorized as offenders who are 'administratively detained'(*xingzheng juliu* 行政拘留). They are usually detained in the detention centre for about fifteen days. Besides incarcerating inmates, the detention centre is also a place where police officers interrogate suspects in order to obtain confessions (Williams and Wu 2004). Sometimes these interrogations, according to the former drug users, are conducted right in front of other inmates.

Compulsory drug rehabilitation centres

Forty-four former prisoners in this study had been incarcerated in *qiangjie*. *Qiangjie* was used solely for the purposes of drug rehabilitations before the enactment of the 2008 Anti-drug Law. There are usually two types of inmates in *qiangjie*. The first type is drug users who were arrested by the police. The second type is drug users who voluntarily request to stay in *qiangjie* for drug rehabilitation. Both arrested and voluntary inmates are required to spend three to six month in *qiangjie*. Practices in drug rehabilitation in different *qiangjie* are different. Some provide pills free of charge to the inmates to help them to go through the period of withdrawal, and some charge a certain amount of money. Some *qiangjie* employ what is called the 'cold turkey method', sometimes called 'natural therapy' (*ziran liaofa* 自然療法), for drug rehabilitation. This means that inmates are not provided with any medical assistance during their drug abstention and withdrawal period. After 2008 *qiangjie* has become a place for physical detoxification before the inmates are sent to *qiangge*.

Re-education through labour and compulsory isolation in drug rehabilitation centres

Thirty-seven former prisoners in this study had been incarcerated in *laojiao* or *qiangge*; thirty-one had been incarcerated in *laojiao*, and eight had been incarcerated in *qiangge*. Before 2008 *laojiao* was widely used for drug rehabilitation. According to official rhetoric, forced physical labour at *laojiao* is a means to reform the inmates. Similar to detention centres, *laojiao* incarcerates people who are accused of various kinds of offences, though they are usually incarcerated in different cells. Inmates in *laojiao* are divided into two main categories. The first type is made up of those who are put under 'drug reform' (*yanjiao* 煙教). They are people who are accused of drug abuse. The second type of inmate is under what is called 'social reform' (*shejiao* 社教). It generally refers to inmates who are incarcerated for any reason other than drug abuse and prostitution. After the enactment of the 2008 Anti-drug Law, *laojiao* is officially no longer used as a place for drug rehabilitation.[2] Such functions are now replaced by the new institution called *qiangge*. Officially, *qiangge* has changed from an 'administrative detention penalty' (*xingzheng chufa cuoshi* 行政處罰措施) to a 'compulsory education and treatment measure' (*qiangzhi xing jiaoyu yiliao cuoshi* 強制性教育醫療措施) (Jia 2010; National People's Congress 2008).

In 2012 I had the opportunity to spend an afternoon visiting a *qiangge* in China. While I was waiting for the officer who was coming to fetch me, I saw about thirty people standing in front of the big gate of the rehabilitation centre. I discovered through talking with some of them that, to my surprise, quite a number of the inmates were incarcerated because of minor offences like gambling and theft

---

2. In 2013 the Standing Committee of the National People's Congress officially announced the abolishment of *laojiao*.

instead of drug use. Then I saw that there were signboards on both the right and left side of the gate outside the rehabilitation centre. The one on the right read '[Name of that city] compulsory isolation for drug rehabilitation centre' and the one on the left said '[Name of that city] centre for re-education through labour'. In accordance with the experience of former drug users, instead of building new institutions for 'drug rehabilitation', *qiangge* is usually established by either changing the name of the 're-education through labour' to 'compulsory isolation for drug rehabilitation centre', or by putting the sign 'compulsory isolation for drug rehabilitation centres' side by side with the sign of 're-education through labour'. The same prison officers were working in the same facility (S. Li 2009; D. Yan 2009).

There are two possible interpretations of the change. The first is that the so-called *qiangjie* is just a 'new bottle with old wine'. Instead of establishing a new type of institution with new rehabilitation philosophies for drug rehabilitation, *qiangjie* is merely an additional name given to the existing *laojiao*. The other interpretation is that the *qiangjie* system has become a sub-branch within the *laojiao* system. That is to say that although *qiangjie* might have its new penal/rehabilitation philosophy, it is still operating under the *laojiao* framework.

Officially, inmates in *qiangge* are those who are defined by the public security organs as 'drug addicts', including those who refuse to participate in community-based treatment, those who relapse during community-based treatment, those who break community rehabilitation regulations, those who relapse after they are discharged from either community rehabilitation or *qiangjie*, those drug addicts whose addiction is too serious to be cured by community rehabilitation, and those who hand themselves in to the police voluntarily for compulsory rehabilitation (National People's Congress 2008; Song and Xu 2011). Males and females are put in separate facilities, and all inmates would be incarcerated from two to three years.

New Inmates' Initiation Ceremony

Now let us turn to the daily life of the people incarcerated in these institutions. One common experience of the former drug users during the early stage of their incarceration is a feeling of pain, fear, and shame. Jones and Schmid (2000) describe a process called 'prison orientation', signifying a process wherein prison inmates acquire knowledge about the 'real' experience within the prison world. A new prisoner who is experiencing prison orientation is identical to what Turner (1987) called the 'liminal *persona*', whose identity is betwixt and between that of a 'normal citizen' and a 'prisoner'. According to Turner, liminal personas are often supervised by 'instructors' or 'elders' who carry out initiation rituals that introduce the liminals to their proper new roles. During this period, the instructors or the elders have complete authority over the liminal persona. What Turner describes is quite similar to the situation of the new prison inmates in China. However, one special characteristic of the prison inmates in China is that they were 'initiated' by both 'prison officers' and 'powerful inmates'. During this liminal period, new inmates were not free citizens and did not qualify as 'proper' prisoners', nor were they 'proper cellmates'. They were required to go through two processes that would 'initiate' them into the roles of proper prisoners and proper cellmates. This process, as I will conceptualize, is the active 'prisonization' carried out by both the prison officers and the existing powerful inmates, who act as 'instructors' during this period.

Goffman documented a standard process of such initiation ceremonies in his study of total institutions (Goffman 1968a). He called this process the 'admission procedure' (Goffman 1968a, 24), which is a process of 'deculturation' in which new inmates bit by bit leave their old culture behind and adopt a new one. During this process, new inmates' original possessions are taken away by the authorities and substituted with uniformed items. The admission procedure does not only take physical possessions away from the new inmates; it also strips their previous identities and dignity. The main purpose of this admission procedure is to force the inmates to dispose of their past and take up the role of obedient subordinates in a total institution. In accordance with Goffman's description, new prison inmates in China experience similar types of admission procedures. In this study I refer to these admission procedures as the 'initiation ceremony'. The main reason that I chose the term 'initiation ceremony' instead of 'admission procedure' is that I would like to stress the individual agency of the new inmates. By envisioning this process as an administrative 'procedure', Goffman has focused on the authority's intentions, rationale, and practices in the total institutions only. By envisioning this process as a 'ceremony', I would also like to examine the ways in which the former prisoners—the participants of the 'ceremony'—understand and interpret the ceremony. In other words, we have to look beyond the administrative side of the ceremony.

Officers' initiation ceremony/prisonization

The initiation ceremonies held by the prison officers are well organized and institutionalized. There are two main elements in the ceremony: stripping and admission training. Stripping is the ceremony that exemplified the practice of 'deculturation' (Goffman 1968a) in which new inmates' personal belongings as well as their individual identities are systematically confiscated. The admission training is the process in which new inmates undergo a whole set of disciplinary training and education programmes. Both ceremonies aim at transforming the new inmates into 'appropriate' inmates from the perspective of the prison officers. However, this process, especially the 'education training', had also 'initiated' the new inmates into a hypocritical system. In the following, I will discuss the content and practices of strip-search and admission training in more detail.

Stripping: Obedience test and the 'mortification of self'

Mortification of self is a process through which individuals' dignity and identity are deprived (Goffman 1968a). Strip-search is one important component of self-mortification in total institutions. Previous studies have documented different kinds of strip-searches that new inmates have experienced in prisons (Goffman 1968a; Hassine 1996; Jones and Schmid 2000). Similar to these practices, in China, immediately after the new inmates' arrival to the detention centre, they are usually taken to an office where they are strip-searched. Inmates are also required to hand over all their personal belongings, including items like lighters, watches, necklaces, rings, and glasses with metal frames. They are required to take off all their clothes. After a simple body check, they are then required to stand, squat, or sit in humiliating postures. Sun recalled his memory in detention centre in this way:

> Sun: They stripped you of your clothes. They body-checked you, and then it's the show time [*jiemu shijian* 節目時間].
> Author: What do you mean by 'show time'?
> Sun: They forced you to squat, to jump, to do handstands and push ups. (Sun, conversations in a cafe, 2013)

Sun's experience is very similar to Goffman's descriptions to the 'mortification of self' in total institutions. One core element in the 'mortification of self' process is the 'obedience test' (Goffman 1968a, 27). In this 'test', the total institution authority intentionally humiliates the new inmates verbally and physically—for example, by addressing them with humiliating nicknames like 'fish' or 'swab', or they might require the new inmates to perform humiliating gestures. Any new inmate who fails to follow the officers' instructions is immediately punished. According to Goffman, the main purpose of this obedience test is the creation of obedient subordinates. The stripping in Chinese detention centres can also be seen in a similar vein.

After the stripping, according to the experience of the former prisoners, in the detention centre new inmates are usually allowed to wear their own clothes. In some detention centres inmates are required to wear a uniform vest on top of their own clothes. According to the regulations in the detention centre, all items that are made of metal on new inmates' clothes and shoes will be taken off. This is done in the name of protecting the inmates from using them as weapons to harm themselves and others. Such destruction of clothes right in front of the new inmates, however, can be a shameful and painful experience. Bang, a 40-year-old man who had been incarcerated in a detention centre, recalled his experience:

> The Dunhill jacket (¥2,400), the belt (¥2,600), the Clarks shoes (¥1,500) . . . They cut the zippers on my jacket off with scissors. They took my belt, my lighter, and my wallet. Then they cut off my shoes' uppers, because there is a copper plate on them. I tried to stop them. They said, 'You are here. What do you expect?' It was awful, but I dared not resist. (Bang, interview 6, 2012)

It is said that 'through clothing people communicate some things about their persons' (F. Davis 1994, 4). Your clothes are about more than what you wear; they also reflect who you are, and maybe, more important, who you want other people to think you are. Personal belongings like lighters and watches also serve the same function as the clothes. To Bang, those metal plates on his clothes and shoes do not only symbolize their brand and the monetary value but also who he is. He tried to convince me of the importance of wearing 'proper' clothes: 'I wore luxury brands. . . . These clothes might not be particularly comfortable, but when people see these brands on you, they look up to you, they think you are superior' (Bang, interview 6, 2012).

Not every former inmate shared Bang's view on luxury brands, but as we are informed by the sociology of fashion, people actively use taste and fashion as a 'body technique' to give themselves a sense of uniqueness and a sense of self-identity (Bourdieu 1984; Craik 1994; Ritzer 2008). This sense of uniqueness, however, is seen as harmful in the prison environment. Cutting metal plates from new inmates' clothes and asking them to wear uniforms can be seen as a process of depersonalization that aims at eliminating the uniqueness of the new inmate. While detention centres usually allow their inmates to keep their own clothes, in *laojiao* and *qiangge* inmates are required to wear prison uniforms.

After seven to fifteen days of detention, a group of detention inmates are usually sent to *laojiao* or *qiangge* on a particular date every month. Shortly after new inmates set foot inside the *laojiao* or *qiangge* they are taken to a public area. They are then required to stand or squat in a uniformed manner. In front of them are usually some prison officers and some current inmates. There would usually be a talk given by a prison staff officer. Inmates are required to stand or squat while listening. They would be surrounded both by the officers and some of the current inmates. Hui told me about his first day in *laojiao*:

> There were about eighty newcomers. We were placed in a big playground. It was my first time. It was a hot summer's day, around July or August. . . . There were about twenty officers standing at the four corners of the playground. Each of them had two electric batons in their hands. We had to squat and put our hands on our heads. The floor was at least fifty to sixty degrees [Celsius] hot. We were not allowed to move. Whoever moved would be beaten by the police and forced to do push-ups. (Hui, interview 59, 2012).

Then the current inmates would hand over to the newcomers some daily necessities like washbasins, soaps, towels, toothbrushes, some clothes hangers, and sanitary pads for female inmates. The new inmates were then required to stand in a line, take off their clothes, and change into prison uniforms, sometimes in front of the officers and other current inmates who assisted the officers.[3] Prison uniforms are,

---

3. Prison officers in China usually assign some prison inmates to be their assistants in daily administrations. I will talk more about that in a later section.

however, not that 'uniform'. According to former prisoners' experiences, not all of these prison uniforms were new. The new inmates do not have the right to choose which prison clothes they would like to wear. They are required to wear whatever uniform they were assigned to wear. Juan said:

> They give you the uniform. . . . There was a yellow T-shirt, a pair of cotton trousers, two washbasins, one for face washing, one for foot washing, a soap, a towel, a toothbrush, and some hangers. What else? Sanitary pads . . . I paid ¥500 for all these things. . . . You can't argue with them. Those things are terrible. There are two big holes on the trousers that they gave me [she pointed at the side of her thigh]. I asked her [the inmate assistant] how I can wear these trousers now. She refused to give me a new pair. (Juan, interview 73, 2012)

Besides wearing uniforms, like in prisons in other contexts, new inmates were required to change their hairstyle. All male inmates' hair would be shaved to about a length of one inch. All female inmates' hair would be cut to shoulder length.

The prison authorities use the concern for tidiness and safety to justify what they do to the new inmates (He and Zheng 2002). However, from the perspective of the inmates, it was neither the filthy ragged prison clothes nor the zipper-removed jacket that gave them the deepest pain. It was the process of being coerced to obey that gave them the most pain and shame. Clothes being cut into pieces and taken away by the prison officers, squatting on the floor with both hands on their head, being beaten up or being forced to do push-ups in front of other officers and inmates, being forced to get naked in public, all these experiences were clearly seen by the inmates as public humiliation in violation of their dignity. As Sun comments:

> To me this is simply an insult to basic human dignity [*dui renge de wuru* 對人格的侮辱]. Yes, I had made a mistake. I was already taking my punishment there. Why would you [the officers] still humiliate me? (Sun, interview 56, 2012)

To the former prisoners, this public shaming could by no means be connected to education or rehabilitation. To them, the prison officers simply want to shame them. The stripping was only the start of the painful experience of the official initiation ceremony. The core part of the officers' initiation ceremony is the 'admission training'.

Official admission training

In China prison officers organized an intensive training for every new prison inmate. There are different names for these procedures—for instance, 'admission training' (*xinshou jixun* 新收集訓), 'transitional education' (*guodu jiaoyu* 過渡教育), and 'strict-control period' (*yanguan qi* 嚴管期). By looking into the former prisoners' experiences, 'admission training' is usually carried out in a segregated area within the prison—'the newcomers' district' (*xinshou qu* 新手區). 'Admission training' generally consists of the 'correction of acts' (*xingwei jiaozhi* 行為矯治) and the 'correction of thoughts' (*sixiang jiaozhi* 思想矯治) (Zhang and Yao 2005). The 'correction of acts' would be mirroring the disciplining of the body as discussed by Foucault (1977). It requires that new inmates learn to move in 'correct' postures. It is similar to the 'five regularities' (*wu gu ding* 五固定) in the Chinese prison which regulate inmates' 'sleeping berths, study places, eating positions, workstations and one's place in queues' (Bakken 2000; Dutton 1992). The 'correction of thought' on the other hand is connected to the traditional Chinese belief in repetition, memorization, and recitation in education as well as in changing individual habits (Bakken 2000, 99, 141; Dahlin and Watkins 2000). Both the 'correction of acts' and the 'correction of thoughts' involve certain physical and mental pain. 'Pain' plays an essential role in Chinese education and penal philosophy. It was believed that through pain one could be educated and rehabilitated (X. Chen 2002). As I have discussed in Chapter 2, the ancient character of 'to educate' (*jiao* 教) is composed of a child holding teaching materials and a person holding a whip in his hand (Bakken 2000). The whip stands for 'discipline' and also stands for 'pain'. The idea is that through pain one can learn. Discipline and the training of body in Chinese prison were essentially painful. However, to the former prisoners, these pains had nothing to do with 'education'. Indeed, as I would also argue, the process is more about 'control' rather than education. 'Pain' is thus an important component of 'reform', and 'reform' can in itself again be seen as a kind of 'educative pain'.

The 'correction of behaviour': Paramilitary training

One major means that the prison officers use to 'correct' new inmates' behaviour is paramilitary training. Zhang and Yao (2005), two *laojiao* officers, pointed out the importance of paramilitary training in drug rehabilitation. They assumed that drug users 'have extremely abnormal behaviours and habits' (*xingwei xiguan ji bu zhengchang* 行為習慣極不正常), 'pay no attention to hygiene' (*bujiang weisheng* 不講衛生), 'are impolite' (*meiyou limao* 沒有禮貌), 'are lazy and idle' (*landuo sanman* 懶惰散漫), and 'sleep lazily during daytime and are active at night' (Zhang and Yao 2005, 237). Through paramilitary training, according to the prison authorities, the inmates can 'get rid of their bad habits' and learn to 'regulate what they say and how they behave' (*guifan yanxing* 規範言行). Different kinds of training might exist in different *laojiao*. Most former prisoners mentioned three types of paramilitary training: the 'marching drill' (*bucao* 步操), the folding of '*tofu* blankets' (*doufu bei* 豆腐被) and daily paramilitary etiquette.

Marching drill included different standard military steps and radio callisthenics (*guangbo cao* 廣播操). Some of the marching drills were held inside the prison cell, others in the outdoor playground. It was usually performed early in the morning, before or after the breakfast. Inmates were required to stand in rows and march according to official instructions. This was a painful experience, especially in the hot summer. Marching drill is only one of the many nitty-gritty paramilitary elements in the admission training. The paramilitary training included a whole set of etiquette that the new inmates needed to follow in their everyday lives in front of the prison officers. Sun told me how inmates should act in front of the prison officers:

> When you saw the officers, you bowed. The centre of the corridor was not for you. You were not allowed to walk in the middle of the corridor. When you saw the officer, you first stood idly at the side of the wall and bowed. Then you greeted the officer by saying *guanjiao hao* [管教好] three times. Then you squatted and put your hands on your head. You could only stand up after the officer had left. (Sun, interview 56, 2014).

Guanjiao hao is a deferential way of saying 'hello, officer'. When inmates were walking with the prison officers, they were required to walk with their face down, and all inmates needed to walk in front of the officers. The reason why officers walked at the back, according to former prisoners, was to make sure that the officers could see all the prisoners clearly. The practice could also prevent prisoners from attacking officers from behind. Moreover, all inmates needed to walk on the side of the corridor close to the wall when there were prison officers present. Hua, a former prisoner once joked, 'In Chinese mythology, all ghosts stick to the wall when they walk. We were just like ghosts' (Hua, conversations in a restaurant, 2013). One commonality of the above paramilitary training is that the new inmates needed to behave in particular ways when they were under the gaze of the prison officers or the experienced inmates. Their particular 'performance' (*biaoxian* 表現) were monitored so as to avoid punishment. The example of folding *tofu* blankets can further demonstrate such performance.

Inmates are required to fold their blankets into a so-called *tofu* blanket, which is a blanket that is folded into a perfect rectangular cube with twelve sharp angles. Officers would come to check their blankets every morning. Those who failed to fold it would be subjected to punishment. Compared with other training, this was seen as the most difficult task for new inmates. Some of the former prisoners said that they still had not mastered the technique of folding *tofu* blankets. Those new inmates who could not do it usually asked other inmates who were better at doing it to fold the blankets for them once. They would keep this blanket for officers' inspections and use another blanket when they slept at night.

The 'correction of behaviour': Quiet-sitting

One of the earliest pains that the new inmates faced in the admission training is the 'quiet-sitting and self-reflection' (*jingzuo fansi* 靜坐反思). Chinese Confucian, Buddhist, and Daoist practices included quiet-sitting for personal moral cultivation (R. Liu 2005). 'Quiet' (*jing* 靜) is connected to 'stability' (*an* 安), 'self-cultivation' (*xiushen* 修身), and the achievement of 'truth' (*dao* 道) and 'ultimate good' (*zhishan* 至善) (Duan and Wen 1960; Z. Lin 1991; Y. Wang 2007). In practice, according to the experience of the former prisoners, in the first few days after they arrived at the *qiangge* they were required to practice quiet-sitting for a prolonged period. Sansan told me her experience of quiet-sitting in a *qiangge*:

> I will never ever forget that. It lasted for ten days, fourteen hours a day. We sat on stools. [We needed to keep] our backs and legs at a right angle, and to keep our legs and feet at a right angle from six in the morning until eight at night. (Sansan, interview 18, 2012)

Another former prisoner, Ping, related a similar experience:

Ping: You have to sit like this [*sitting with a straight back*], put your hand here [*her right hand on her right knee and left hand on her left knee*], and keep your waist straight. You are not allowed to move, not even a little bit. You need to look straight into the back of the head of the person in front of you. . . . [It lasted for] ten days.
Author: From what time to what time?
Ping: [We] started sitting after breakfast until dinner. Then we sat until eight.
Author: Did they ask you to do anything?
Ping: [No] I would rather do something, OK? Do you want to try it? On the stool there were some holes, just like in a bee's nest. It was very hot. You sit there and you can't move. Your whole body was like paralysed, and it was very painful [for our butts]. There are some small holes on the stools. Many people's butts were cut [by those holes]. [I] needed to put iodine on [the wounds].
Author: Because of the beehive-like things on the stool?
Ping: Yes. Sitting like this with your back straight is still very tiring even without [the beehive-like holes]. (Ping, interview 23, 2012)

The new inmates were normally supervised by the more experienced inmates when they were doing the quiet-sitting. These inmates, according to former prisoners, were much worse than the officers. Lily told me,

> It was really 'cruel and inhuman' [*canwu rendao* 慘無人道]. You know we are women. When we had our periods, we urgently needed to go to the WC. [The current inmate said] no! It's really totally inhumane [*mei renxing* 沒人性]. (Lily, interview 3, 2012)

Quiet-sitting was a painful experience. New inmates were required to maintain a difficult posture for a very long time of the day (see Figure 4.1). What made it even worse was that they had no access to a clock or a watch. During quiet-sitting they did not know how long they had been sitting and how much longer they needed to sit. The worst part of it was that they were under the surveillance of officers and experienced inmates. They would immediately be punished if they deviated from the required sitting postures. They were apparently told that they were required to do so because it could help them reflect on what they had done wrong. While a couple of them said that they did use this period to reflect on their previous experiences, most others said that during the process they were simply overwhelmed by pain which prevented them from thinking about their past. In order to relieve the pain, many former prisoners said that they looked for chances when the prison officers and the experienced inmates were not looking directly at them so that they could move their limbs and backs a bit.

Both the quiet-sitting and the 'correction of behaviour' are the training of new inmates' bodies. However, they are also connected to the training of 'thoughts'. It was believed that through training one's behaviour one's thought could also be reformed. By forcing the new inmates to sit, walk, and behave in particular ways, it was believed that new inmates could change their 'minds' (J. Yang 2006; Zhang and Yao 2005). In practice, although the new inmates were required to act and behave in certain particular ways under the gaze of the officers and other inmates, these 'acts' are very often 'performance' (*biaoxian* 表現), or could even be seen as 'acting' (*biaoyan* 表演) in front of the authorities. Bakken (2000) sees this type of outward acting resulting from the overemphasis on performance as 'ways of lying'. Compared to the 'correction of behaviour', the 'correction of thoughts' forced the prison inmates to 'lie' even more explicitly. It also formed the core part of the 'participation in hypocrisy' I discuss in this chapter.

The 'correction of thoughts': 'Autobiography writing'

The 'correction of thoughts' during the admission training includes two elements: the writing of an 'autobiography' (*zizhuan* 自傳), and studying different textbooks. In the experience of the former prisoners, all new inmates were required to write an 'autobiography'. The main purpose of writing this autobiography, according to the officers, was again to 'reflect on their wrongdoings'. That might explain why some of the former prisoners referred to it as a 'remorse letter' (*huiguo shu* 悔過書). Similar to quiet-sitting, the writing of an 'autobiography' is about one's 'self'-reflection (*zixing* 自省). The Chinese word 'reflection' is *xing* (省). The ancient character of *xing* ( ) is composed of a 'shade' ( ) and an 'eye' ( ). The original meaning of *xing* is about seeing carefully through the shades. Used together with the character *zi* (自), which means 'self', it is later used to connote the meaning of seeing carefully through one's own 'self' (Gu 2003, 448–49). Confucians advocate that individuals should constantly reflect on themselves. In Confucius's classic *The Analects* (*Lunyu* 論語), it was said that people should reflect on themselves every day (*ri san xing wu shen* 日三省吾身). They should learn from virtuous people, and reflect on themselves when encountering unvirtuous people to see if they had made the same mistakes as the unvirtuous people (*jian xian siqi yan, jian buxian er nei zixing ye* 見賢思齊焉，見不賢而內自省也) (W. Hu 2002). The writing of autobiographies asks the new inmates to put their self-reflection down on paper for the officers' inspection.

The writing process usually lasted for two to three days. When I asked what they were required to write, Ling told me, 'We sat on a little chair. It was so painful for our butts. They gave us three questions. Who are you? What have you done? Why did you come here?' (Ling, interview 11, 2012).

Generally speaking, former prisoners told me that they were required to write about their own experiences with drugs, the reason behind their drug use, and the 'harmful consequences' of their drug use. After the writing was over, the 'autobiography' would be examined by the *qiangge* officers. New inmates needed to meet certain criteria in order to have their 'biographies' passed by the officers. Writing personal biographies can be seen as another form of writing a 'self-criticism'. Bakken (2000, 248) pointed out that self-evaluation and self-criticism in China 'take the form of direct criticism of self'. They are very much linked to the standards that *qiangge* officers used to judge the quality of the new inmates' 'autobiographies'.

The most important quality of a 'good' personal biography is that the new inmates admit that taking drugs is a wrongful act. Second, new inmates were asked to write about the 'reasons' behind their drug use. Instead of writing about how the circumstances of their social lives had affected their experiences with drugs, they were required to write about 'individual reasons'. In other words, they should blame themselves morally for their 'wrong deeds'. Third, they had to describe in detail the harmful effect of their act of taking drugs. In this part of their descriptions, instead of just talking about how taking drugs had harmed their bodies, they should talk about how their act of taking drugs had caused harmful effects to their friends, families, and society as a whole. A song sung by inmates in a *qiangjie* exemplified these qualities:

> Look, beyond the hill under the tree,
> Stand my pitiful parents.
> In many a cold night, my mum is in tears, dreaming
> Of her son, but sees no one,
> When waking up, only tears are falling.
> . . .
> Dear Dad, dear Mum,
> I feel ashamed when seeing you.
> . . .
> Oh, Friends, my fellow drug addicts,
> You ruined my life,
> Pulling me down to the trap, and
> Pushing me to the fire pot. (McCoy et al. 1997, 81)

Writing an 'autobiography' might be a difficult task for first-time inmates who do not know the criteria mentioned above. However, for experienced recidivists, it actually becomes very easy. As Mei said,

> We needed to write [our stories] in detail. There were many illiterate people. I was asked to help them to write [as they told me about their stories]. I said, 'You do not

need to tell me.' [I am] so tired of these... basically, those things. I just helped them to write. (Mei, interview 10, 2012)

One might expect that what the new inmates ultimately wrote could be very different from what they have actually 'reflected' upon during the quiet-sitting session. In this process, the new inmates start to realize that in order to survive in the prison one has to learn to be two-faced; they needed to learn a set of languages and performances that could satisfy the officers and let them survive during their daily interactions. The writing of 'autobiographies' and 'self-reflection', which is supposed to be about one seeing carefully through one's own self, becomes a performance that is more about seeing carefully through what the prison officers want. In the previous chapter I pointed out that former drug users had seen the hypocrisy in the behaviour of the police and prison officers. During the process of writing autobiographies inmates realized that they had to participate in this 'hypocritical drama' if they wanted to survive in the prison. More important, the more time drug users are incarcerated, the more they master the skill of 'acting'.

The 'correction of thoughts': 'Studying'

Another means that the prison officers used to 'correct' new inmates' 'thoughts' was to study different textbooks. In China, repetition, memorization, and recitation are used as a key educational method particularly geared to changing individual habits (Bakken 2000, 99, 141). The same principle is also applied in the study sessions in prison admission training. Moreover, similar to the quiet-sitting, new inmates were required to study while sitting in a standard posture. The posture, according to the ex-inmates, was like this: They had to sit upright with a straight back and hold the copied material with both arms straight in front of themselves. Both arms should form a right angle with their back. Their thigh should form an appropriate angle with their shanks so that their shanks could form a right angle with their waist (see Figure 4.2).

Some examples of the materials that inmates are required to copy, read, and recite include Chinese classics like *Standards for Being a Good Pupil and Child* (*Dizi gui* 弟子规), official doctrines like the Eight Honours and Eight Disgraces (*Ba rong*

Figure 4.1: Standard sitting posture during quiet-sitting in the admission training in *laojiao/qiangge*

Figure 4.2: Standard reading posture during reciting sessions in the admission training in *laojiao/qiangge*

ba chi 八榮八恥), the *Drug-Rehab Three-Character Classic* (*Jiedu sanzi jing* 戒毒三字經), legal documents like the Anti-drug Law (*Jindu fa* 禁毒法), and the 'inmates' code of conduct' (*xueyuan xingwei guifan* 學員行為規範). Other materials also include texts related to patriotic education, moral education, and specific materials related to anti-drug education (Zhang and Yao 2005). Generally speaking, these reading materials cover three areas: moral education, legal education, and inmates' code of conduct.

For moral education, new inmates need to study various selected moral textbooks or readings that aim to instil moral concepts and standards. The assumption behind these practices is that the drug users are morally defective. Some prison officers report that drug users are generally 'self-centred' (*ziwo wei zhongxin* 自我為中心), 'extremely selfish' (*jiduan zisi* 極端自私), lack compassion (*quefa tongqing xin* 缺乏同情心), and 'irresponsible' (*meiyou zeren gan* 沒有責任感) (J. Yang 2006; Zhang and Yao 2005, 237). Officials believe that through copying, reading, and memorizing classic moral textbooks, the new inmates' moral defects can be 'corrected' (*jiaozhi* 矯治) (J. Yang 2006; Zhang and Yao 2005).

One text that is commonly used is *Standards for Being a Good Pupil and Child*. It was written during the Qing dynasty (AD 1662–1722) based on the *Analects*. The general theme of the text is about the appropriate behaviours of a student. It includes different sub-themes like obeying parents and siblings, code of behaviour in daily life, and moral doctrines like 'be trustworthy' and 'love all equally' (Y. Li 2005, 69, 75).

Legal education, on the other hand, refers to the copying and recitation of those regulations and laws that are related to the new prison inmates' offences. For example, new inmates in compulsory isolation for drug rehabilitation centres would be given the Anti-drug Law; new inmates in detention centres would be given the Criminal Law. The core element of legal education aims at making the new inmates accept the official purposes of incarceration. This includes two important components. First, inmates are required to 'accept that they are guilty and wrong' (*renzui rencuo* 認罪認錯) and to develop the willingness to 'change from evil to good' (*gaixie guizheng* 改邪歸正). Second, they are required to recognize that prison is the place for them to do so. Different terms like 'education' (*jiaoyu* 教育), 'reform' (*gaizao* 改造), and 'salvation' (*wanjiu* 挽救) are used in different legal regulations to describe such purpose in different types of prisons (Ministry of Public Security 2011; State Council 1982; 1990).

The prison inmates' code of conduct refers to the internal prison regulations on how prison inmates should behave during their incarceration. These official regulations include 'essential regulations for inmates' (*zaiya renyuan jiben guifan* 在押人員基本規範), 'regulations governing inmates' daily lives' (*zaiya renyuan shenghuo guifan* 在押人員生活規範), and 'rules governing inmates' behavioural manners' (*zaiya renyuan wenming limao guifan* 在押人員文明禮貌規範). Sometimes these regulations are written right on the wall of the cell, and other times the mentor will give the new inmate a written copy of these regulations. One main core element in it is to teach the new inmates to behave in a 'civilized and polite manner' (*wenming limao* 文明禮貌). It usually covers different areas like the 'correct attitude' (*zhengque taidu* 正確態度), the code of conduct among inmates, and the code of conduct among inmates and officers. One example can be found in the 'inmates' code of conduct' stating that prison inmates should 'behave in a civilized manner (*juzhi wenming* 舉止文明), 'speak in a gentle manner' (*shuohua heqi* 說話和氣), and are not allowed to tell lies, swear, or 'make obscene gestures' (*zuo diji xialiu dongzuo* 做低級下流動作). Violent behaviour against other inmates is also officially forbidden (He and Zheng 2002). These types of regulations are sometimes not only written in documents but also made into posters put up on the walls of the cell, or sometimes written directly on the wall. Similarly, in the *Standards for Being a Good Pupil and Child*, it is said that 'cunning words, foul language, and philistine habits must be avoided at all cost' (Y. Li 2005). Other examples of these statements include 'spreading rumours about the wrongdoing of the others is a wrongdoing in itself' and 'if I use my power to make them submissive, their hearts will not be with me. If I convince them with sound reasoning, they will have nothing to object to' (Y. Li 2005).

After copying and reciting the materials, something that usually lasted for about two weeks, new inmates would be examined either by an officer or a more experienced inmate. The examiner would randomly select one document and require the new inmate to recite it. Those who failed to recite it correctly might be scolded and would then be asked to extend their admission training until they could thoroughly perform the tasks correctly.

It is quite common for prison officers to ask new inmates to copy, read, and memorize the above texts and regulations in Chinese prisons.[4] The assumption behind such practices is that through repetitive reading, writing, memorizing, and reciting, the new inmates can internalize the 'moral education', the 'legal knowledge', and the 'internal regulations' and thereby become better persons. 'Be civilized' is a value that is supposed to make the prison inmate a better person, if they can really internalize such values. There are debates in educational psychology about whether memorization and recitation really works in learning such deeds. One camp holds that memorization is a characteristic of the Asian Confucian learning approach. However, according to this line of thinking, memorization is a kind of passive learning that yields a poor outcome, and memorization and understanding are mutually exclusive (Purdie et al. 1996). Another line of thinking points out that outstanding Asian students can incorporate understanding into memorization through specific methods like 'attentive memorization' (Dahlin and Watkins 2000; Tran 2013). However, in former prison inmates' experiences of admission training, none of the prison officers provided any explanations whatsoever to the texts that

---

4. See, for example, Guangdong Prison Administration Bureau 2008; Judicial Department of Jiangxi Province 2012; Shanxi Prison Administration Bureau 2010; Sichuan Prison Administration Bureau 2011.

they had copied and recited. The only thing the new inmates were asked to do was to sit down, copy, read, and recite the texts word for word.

The former prisoners felt that the prison officers did not care whether they understood these texts and documents. Moreover, what they had learned from these texts was very often contradicted by what they had experienced during their incarceration. This again made the inmates aware of what they deemed to be the hypocrisy inside the prison system. While code of conduct, like being 'civilized', has been emphasized in many of the education materials, in the initiation ceremony as well as in their later lives in prison they had instead experienced many different 'uncivilized' humiliations and violence. While they were forced to read out loud different classical moral doctrines like those of 'being trustworthy', they were forced to lie about their true feelings about their drug use and instead recite the 'correct' official 'explanations'. Through the prisoners' initiation ceremony, the current experienced inmates established their power over the new inmates. Pain and power described the reality of everyday prison life rather than 'civilized behaviour'. The indignation over these facts of life in prison were so pronounced in my interviews and encounters with the former inmates that it prompted me to formulate my book along the lines of hypocrisy. The whole system seemed to be based on such experiences of clashes between ideals and reality in the prison context.

Prisoners' initiation ceremony/prisonization

If the prison authorities' initiation ceremony is aimed at creating obedient inmates who can be controlled by the officers, then the prisoner initiation ceremony is aimed at creating obedient 'cellmates'. Every new inmate would be allocated to a cell. In the detention centre and *qiangjie* the cell would be the place where new inmates would spend most of their time. In *laojiao* and *qiangge*, the cell is usually called 'living area' (*shenghuo qu* 生活區). This is the place where inmates go after their 'labour time'. Controlling the prison inmate is a core element of prison administration. One main strategy that Chinese prison authorities use to control the inmate is to make use of the old inmates to control the new inmates. The inmate authority in China is similar to the prison gang as described in the English-language criminological literature. However, what might be distinctive in China is that the prison authority actively mobilizes and appoints some inmates in the prison to control other inmates (something I will address in more detail in the next chapter). From the former prisoners' point of view, the prison officers implicitly agree to and intentionally turn a blind eye on the inmates' own initiation ceremony.

In Chinese prisons, each new inmate would be allocated to a cell with ten to thirty current prison inmates. In each cell, the 'dorm head' (*shezhang* 舍長) was responsible for the order of the cell. In return, the dorm head would be given extra privileges. However, if any disorder like gang fights were to occur in the cell, the dorm head would be penalized by various methods depending on the perceived severity of the disorder. This puts a lot of pressure on the dorm head during the period of arrival of the new inmates. With a severe lack of resources and knowledge about how to obtain the new inmates' obedience, the inmate authority organized their own version of prisonization that involved the use of both physical and non-physical violence. Previous studies have shown that the preoccupation of maintaining one's social status in the prison is an important factor that leads to prison violence (Connell and Farrington 1996; Ireland 2000; South and Wood 2006). In the case of the Chinese prison authority, 'maintaining social status' is indeed an important factor that encourages prison violence, but in addition to this the dorm heads' concern for 'avoiding penalization' further exacerbates the violence.

To secure better control over the new inmates, the inmate authority, led by the dorm head, very often organized some kind of initiation ceremony to establish power over the new inmates. In contrast to the officers' formal initiation ceremony at the arrival of the new inmates described already, the prisoners' initiation ceremonies are much less organized and vary widely among different cells in different prisons. They are also much more arbitrary and involve more physical violence. Each prison cell consists of its own order, including a social hierarchy, different responsibilities, and rights and privileges within the social hierarchy. In the inmates' words, this is 'inside-regulation' (*limian de guiju* 裡面的規矩). These regulations constitute the real power structure in a prison cell and are seen by current inmates as one of the main forces that keep the cells in order. The purpose of the inmates' initiation ceremony is to uphold the inmates' social hierarchy and institution regulations, and thereby stability and order in the cell. Many former prisoners identified three components in the ceremony: (1) the 'shock-and-awe ceremony', which is also called the 'spirit-breaking beating' (*sha wei bang* 殺威棒); (2) the 'inmates' trial' (*guotang* 過堂); and (3) a set of regulations governing daily life during the initiation ceremony.

Shock-and-awe ceremony

Different prison inmates perform different parts of this shock-and-awe ceremony. Inmates in each cell in all prisons have their own 'traditional' shock-and-awe ceremony. Some of these shock-and-awe ceremonies were very violent, while some were less violent. The violent type of initiation ceremony very often happened in the detention centre and in the *qiangjie*. Prison inmates seldom openly questioned the legitimacy of the ceremony. To use their own words, it is a 'rule that has been established for thousands of years' (*qiangu yilai de guiju* 千古以來的規矩). Modern Chinese governments have used 'tradition' as a stabilizing force to tame the potential instability brought about by the process of modernization (Bakken 2000). Similarly, prison inmates use 'tradition' as a force to tame newcomers, whom they see as a potential disruption to the established order of the cell. This tradition is taken for granted and performed. Different shock-and-awe ceremonies are usually carried out either on the first night when new inmates join the cell or during the morning after their arrival. Such practices are performed sometimes by one inmate, sometimes by several inmates, and sometimes by all of the inmates.

The *qiangjie* in Motai is notorious for the physical violence performed in the local shock-and-awe ceremony. Five former drug users whom I interviewed had been incarcerated in the *qiangjie* in Motai, which typically housed thirty prisoners per cell. When new inmates came to a new cell, a shock-and-awe ceremony called *guoban* (過板) would be performed. It usually goes as follows: Under the command of one current inmate, the new inmate is required to stand straight. Several inmates who are responsible for executing the shock-and-awe ceremony queue up in front of the new arrival, whom are each is required to beat with several blows to the front of the chest and several blows to the back. The number of blows ranges from one to fourteen. All three male former drug users said that they were beaten with elbows, and the two female former inmates said that they were beaten with both hands clasped. The new inmates are required to stand up against the wall, so that they cannot 'unload' the force of beating. Lee, a female former *qiangjie* inmate from Motai shared her experiences of *guoban* in the mid-1990s:

> Lee: We, all the newcomers, were put into one cell. All together eight old inmates were there. The four most powerful ones were responsible for beating us. Seven blows from the front and eight blows from the back. Every one of them [beat the new inmates with seven blows to the front and eight blows to the back]. My friend told me that I should not make any noise when I was beaten. The more noise I made, the harder they would beat me.
>
> Author: Did you make any noise?
>
> Lee: No, I kept my mouth shut [*yaojinyaguan* 咬緊牙關]. I was lucky. One of them [the powerful inmate] was my neighbour. . . . You can hear the dong-dong when they beat you . . . they intentionally want to dong you.[5]
> (Lee, interview 66, 2012)

Although all former prisoners in Motai had heard of stories about new inmates being beaten to death during the initiation ceremony, all of them had survived the *guoban*. It was certainly very painful, but the ceremony is not just about the pain inflicted on the new inmates; it is also about the new inmates' obedience to the unreasonable requests of the 'dorm head'. Yong, a male former *qiangjie* inmate in Motai told me a similar story:

> It's called 'to-be-a-newbie' [*zuo xinren* 做新人]. It's like the 'one hundred spirit-breaking beating' [*yibai sha wei bang* 一百殺威棒] in the famous classical novel *Water Margin* [*Shuihu zhuan* 水滸傳]. If you are a newbie, you have to be [beaten]. . . . If you scream, which is not allowed, they will beat you with ten blows instead

---

5. *Dong* (咚) is a Chinese onomatopoeia that Lee used to simulate the sound of beating.

of seven. You can't do anything about it. You grit your teeth and bear it. (Yong, interview 60, 2012)

Usually, the 'controllability' of a new inmate is determined by three factors. The first factor is his or her physical body size. A tall, buff, well-built new inmate is usually treated harsher than a short weak-looking one. A new inmate who looks stronger is perceived to be equipped with better combat ability and is therefore more threatening to the existing order in the cell. As one former drug user commented, the initiation ceremony is used to teach the new inmate that, in the cell, 'if you are a dragon you should coil up, and if you are a tiger you should crouch down' (*shi tiao long de panzhe, shi zhi hu de pazhe* 是條龍得盤著，是隻虎得趴著). 'Dragon' and 'tiger' here symbolize power. It means that no matter how powerful one is, through the initiation ceremony, one is modified to an inmate role that would obey the current inmates without questioning their authority. Another factor is the attitude shown by the new inmate during the initiation ceremony. Those who are seen as arrogant would be treated more harshly than those who show more respect to the current inmates.

In the classical Chinese novel *Water Margin*, when offenders arrived at the frontier of the country where they were banished, they would be beaten with one hundred blows of the 'spirit-breaking beating' so as to 'beat discipline into them' (Shi 2010, 103, 284; X. Wang 2011). Sidney Shapiro translates *sha wei* as 'spirit breaking', but it might be better understood as 'breaking down one's prestige'. As indicated by the name, the shock-and-awe ceremony, or the 'spirit-breaking beating', aims at breaking down the new inmates' previous identities that might threaten the order in the cell. Similar violent initiation ceremonies were performed in some detention centres in Zhiyang. One of these ceremonies is called *baotou cao* (抱頭操), in which the new inmates are required to squat with their hands on their heads. Under the command of the dorm head, inmates who are responsible for the violence would push the new inmate's head until it touches the ground. They would then beat and kick the new inmate until the dorm head gives a new command to stop.[6] Not all shock-and-awe ceremonies were as violence as *guoban* and *baotou cao*. According to my informants, shock-and-awe ceremonies in *laojiao* and *qiangjie* for female drug users usually involve less violence.

One example of it is when on the first night of new female inmates' arrival to their cell they would be required to take a bath in cold water in front of other current inmates. The 'cold bath' (*lenshui zao* 冷水澡) was again usually imposed

---

6. I have mentioned similar shock-and-awe ceremonies in my previous research, and I have obtained similar data during the fieldwork for this study: Shing Cheng, 'Fighting the White Monster: Three Stories from the Chinese Compulsory Detoxification Centre', in *Our Monstrous (S)kin: Blurring the Boundaries Between Monsters and Humanity*, ed. Sorcha Ni Fhlainn (Freeland, PA: Inter-Disciplinary Press, 2010); Cheng, 'Waging a Two-Front War: Inmates during Incarceration and Social Workers Working on Ex-Convict Rehabilitation in China' (MPhil thesis, University of Hong Kong, 2009).

under the command of the dorm head. Feng, a female former prisoner in Motai told me about her experiences of the 'cold bath':

> It was April. It was a bit cold. I put on a wool sweater. It was raining outside. They forced us to take a cold bath. . . . I had very long hair at that time. From head to feet, [I was] all wet. People were looking at you. It was cold outside, and there was no glass in the windows. The wind blew straight through the windows. I was so cold. [They found out that] there were some parts of me that were still dry. Then they forced me to splash water on every part of myself. If I didn't do it, they would splash water on me. It was the first day only, every newcomer needed to go through this process. Those were the 'inside rules'. (Feng, interview 62, 2012)

Cold baths might be ceremonial and did not cause much pain when it was performed in the summer, but they could be difficult in the cold winter. Moreover, the new inmates were forced to be naked and take the cold bath right in front of other current inmates. It certainly represented another 'obedience test' that aimed at degrading the new inmate and was meant to establish the power of the current inmates. This is how Xian, a female former prisoner in Zhiyang, commented on the inmates' initiation ceremony:

> You were the 'junior' [*xinbing* 新兵], so they wanted to pick on you. [They] asked you to do a cold bath to teach you a lesson. To show that they were the 'senior' [*laobing* 老兵] inmates. The officers would not do these things, but those inmates would. (Xian, interview 75, 2013)

Similar to the reasons given for *guaoban* in Motai, the reasons for the dorm head in Zhiyang to enforce cold baths was to demonstrate and reinforce personal power before the new inmates. Besides the shock-and-awe ceremony, some former prison inmates told me that within the first few days of their arrival to their cells the existing inmates organized an 'inmates' trial' (*guotang* 過堂). Again, it was a ceremony to enhance the dorm head's control of the new inmates.

The inmates' trial

Tang (堂) here refers to *gongtang* (公堂), which were law courts in dynastic China. The name also reflects some characteristics of *guotang*. First, it is a process that will put the new inmates under the scrutiny of the current inmates. Second, it shows an absolute power hierarchy between the new inmates—who are seen as defective offenders—and the current inmates. The new inmates have to answer whatever the current inmates ask, and the current inmates act as 'judges' who can exert their power over the new inmates.

Guotang can range from a small-scale incident involving only simple chatting between the current inmates and the new inmates to a comparatively large-scale 'trial' involving everyone in the cell. In a large-scale trial, one inmate acts as 'judge'. The judge asks several questions related to the new inmates' personal information like where they come from, the types of offences that they have committed, and how they committed these offences. The power hierarchy between the new inmates and the current inmates is demonstrated both by the requirement for new inmates to answer any questions the others ask and their body gestures. The new inmate was usually required to squat. He or she would then be surrounded by other inmates forming a circle with the judge standing at the front. All other inmates and the judge are either sitting or standing. This creates a scene where the current inmate is at the 'top' and new inmates are at the 'bottom'. Such a spatial difference defines a boundary between the powerful current inmates and the powerless new inmates. During the trial, the other inmates usually make some degrading comments. Some minor violence like slapping and kicking might also be involved. Sun gave me one example of such a conversation:

> Judge: Where did your [drug] money come from?
> New inmate: I used my own money.
> Another inmate: You are lying! Whom did you steal your money from?
> New inmate: I didn't steal from anyone
> Another inmate: Say it again, did you steal? [*Slapping the new inmate's face*]
> New inmate: No, I didn't . . . (Sun, conversations in a cafe, 2012)

According to an inmate who had been a 'judge' in a detention centre, there are three purposes of organizing this 'trial'. The first purpose is to teach the new arrivals who the boss is. This rationalization of the 'trial' is identical to Goffman's depiction of the 'obedience test' (Goffman 1968a). The second purpose is so that, through asking questions, the new inmate can be classified and thereby assigned to an appropriate role in the cell. This is especially the case in the detention centres where suspects and offenders of different types of crime are incarcerated. Different inmates are perceived to represent different levels of threat to the cell order. Usually, violent offenders are seen to be more threatening than non-violent offenders. The third purpose is simply for the old inmates to have a bit of fun. Life in detention centres and *qiangjie* is tough, especially during the time of the initiation ceremony, but once new inmates get used to prison life an overwhelming sense of boredom sets in. The 'trial' can establish and consolidate current inmates' power. Emotionally, by exerting power on the new inmates, current inmates can feel the satisfaction that they can hardly find elsewhere.

Food, work, and the initiation ceremony

Besides the shock-and-awe ceremony and the inmates' trial, sometimes new inmates in the first stage of their cell life are allowed fewer rights and assigned more duties than other inmates. These rights include access to resources like food, toilet paper, cigarettes, and clean clothes. They might also involve the right to speak, sit, and to go to the toilet. Among these, food is the most important issue when it comes to exerting power in the prison (Godderis 2006; Smith 2002). Sun told me about a practice called *sanqing liuban* (三清六半) performed in the detention centre, which literally means 'three empties, six halves'. It means that in the first three days of an inmates' arrival to the cell, he or she is not allowed to eat anything. In the six following days, he or she can only eat half of the food allocated. After the *sanqing liuban*, some inmates still need to give up some of their food to the current inmates.

Limiting and controlling one's food intake is said to be an effective disciplinary means (Smith 2002). Current inmates use hunger as a means to exert discipline, as well as a tool to break down the dignity of the new inmates. By limiting the new inmates' right to eat, current inmates demonstrate the existing power hierarchy in the cell, and at the same time remake the 'selves' of the new inmates.

According to former drug users, in particular heroin users, they did not suffer much from the first three days of hunger in the detention centre. The reason is that most drug users are suffering from withdrawal symptoms during the first few days of their incarceration. They have lost their appetite completely during this period. Some former drug users who have no experience in *sanqing liuban* told me that they did not eat anything, or very little in the first few days of their incarceration in the detention centres. However, although some former drug users reported that they had no appetite for about a week, others said that they had regained their appetite after three or four days. The last few days in *sanqing liuban* can be excruciating. One former drug user described her experience:

> We do not want to eat much when we take things [drugs], but then after a few days you feel very hungry. It's like you want to eat a lot. How would that amount [of food] be enough?

Hunger is only part of the suffering game. The new inmates were usually required to do different 'hard work' (*kuhuo* 苦活) in their prison cell. Xian told me this:

> [The dorm head] forced you to do everything—brushing the floors and cleaning the bed. Because you were the newbie, [they made you] work. [They would give you] less food. What could you do about it? Moreover, when we had just arrived there [in the prison], we were very uncomfortable [because of withdrawal symptoms]. These people had also experienced these things before [the shock-and-awe ceremony], but they [still did it because they were] 'cruel' [*canku* 殘酷]. Their qualities were really so bad. (Xian, interview 75, 2013)

Similar to the experiences from the official initiation ceremony, it is also the fact that they were forced to obey the existing rules and regulations that made the inmates feel pain and humiliation. However, from the dorm head's points of view, what they wanted was neither simply the extra food nor the work offered by the new inmates. What they wanted was indeed the new inmates' 'obedience' and subordination. Wang, a former dorm head, commented on such concerns:

Let's say this person was 'doing good' [*hun de hao* 混得好] outside [the prison]. If you asked him to do the cleaning work, he would of course feel he was losing face. Naturally, he did not want to do that. . . . However, if he broke the rules, how would I be able to manage [the cell] after that? . . . There were no other methods, people like us, we do not talk about 'reasons' [*daoli* 道理], we solved the problem by fighting. (Wang, interview 20, 2012)

The feeling of physical and psychological pain varies among former drug users. The level of physical and mental torture that the existing drug users imposed on new inmates also varied. According to former drug users who have participated in and conducted the initiation ceremony, there are several criteria that decide how much physical or mental torture that should be imposed on the new inmates. Individual preferences do play a role here. However, there is one general principle: the higher chances a new inmate might disrupt the existing cell order, the more torture would be imposed.

The Production of Hypocrisy

The section above reviews several main components of the official initiation ceremony and the prisoners' initiation ceremony. These initiation ceremonies, however, had produced hypocrisy on two levels. On the first level, in order to survive the prison environment, new inmates learned to lie about their own feelings and to 'perform well' when they were under the officers' gaze. The prison authority did provide different types of 'education' to the new inmates by providing paramilitary training, by forcing them to do the quiet-sitting, and by requiring them to write the autobiography, to copy, read, and recite different legal regulations, classical Chinese pieces of assumed morally uplifting literature, and political official doctrines. However, many former prisoners described this education as mere 'formalities' (*xingshi hua* 形式化). What they had learned from these processes were simply how to 'perform' or 'act' according to what the prison officers' wanted. During this process, the contradiction between what one actually thought and what one was required to say was also made explicit to the new inmates. One core element in the 'inmates' code of conduct' is to require the inmate to have a 'correct attitude'. According to a handbook published for detention inmates, a 'correct attitude' is interpreted as 'to give up evil and take up good' (*gaixie gui zheng* 改邪歸正). In many cases, new inmates do not agree with the idea that they are 'evil', nor did they feel that what they had done was morally wrong. However, during the writing of the 'autobiography' and the 'inmates' court', inmates were somehow forced to put themselves into the position of 'evil'. Through this process, inmates started to get used to a practice of differentiating between what they really think from what they *present* to the others in the prison. In other words, they learned a special form of hypocrisy.

This type of hypocrisy could still found in the later stage of their incarceration. Ying told me her experience when they had to receive some visitors in the prison:

> In 2003 some Americans came to visit our prison. They [the officers] taught us how to answer their questions. The Americans thought that we were not doing prison labour; they thought that we were doing exercises only. The prison officers taught us how to answer the questions. [If the Americans ask,] 'When do you wake up in the morning?' [We should answer,] 'I wake up naturally.' [If the Americans ask,] 'What do you eat for breakfast?' [We should answer,] 'Milk and bread.' [If the Americans ask,] 'Do you have any working quota?' [We should answer,] 'We do not have quota. We work if we want to work. We do not work if we do not want to work.' (Ying, interview 7, 2012)

Similarly, inmates in some prisons were required to write a 'happy diary entry' (*kaixin riji* 開心日記). No matter whether there was anything for them to feel happy about, they needed to write or make up some 'happy stories'. This was how Sansan described the happy diary:

> Some inmates wrote the truth: 'There was nothing to be happy about. [There was] only hate [*yuanhen* 怨恨] and only complaints [*maiyuan* 埋怨].' If you wrote something like that, the prison officer would come to talk to you. [The prison officer] would ask you, 'Why are you not happy?' It was a compulsory procedure. It was like they forced you to write that you were happy even if you were not happy at all.... If the prison officers found you for a talk, they would find you during working hours. If you [spent time] talking [with the officer], then you wouldn't have time to finish your working quota. Then you would be punished to perform the quiet-sitting, and after that you wouldn't write anything like that anymore. Everyone wrote things like 'I finished my work quota. I am very happy'; 'Today I ate pork in the canteen. I am very happy'; and 'Tomorrow it is Sunday. We can take a shower in the bathroom. I am very happy.' (Sansan, Interview 18, 2012)

Juan's words relate to the compulsory labour in the *laojiao* and *qiangge* regimes that I will come back to in the next chapter. The key question here is that again the inmates were forced to lie about their true feelings. On the one hand the inmates hated to be forced to lie about their feelings. On the other hand, it would be difficult for the prison officers to assess how well the inmate had been rehabilitated. While Bakken (2000) pointed out that the systematic production of hypocrisy and 'ways of lying' make the prediction of human behaviour impossible in that the system creates 'fake behaviour', it was the same in the prison context. The 'prison education' is clearly not effective in that the relapse rate still remains extremely high—ranging from 85 to 90 per cent (Cui 1999; Y. Lu 2009; Zhu et al. 2009). Another unintended consequence of this form of 'education' is that through reading the 'legal documents' and 'code of conduct', new inmates learned what was expected of them in the prison. This effect is similar to the effect of the party propaganda. It created expectations that cannot be fulfilled by their actual experiences. This connects to the second level of hypocrisy.

On the second level, much like in the experiences of police arrest, experiences from initiation ceremony had given the former prisoners the impression that the reality in the prison is completely different from that represented in the party propaganda. The core of both the officers' and the prisoners' initiation ceremony are physical pain and humiliation. In the official initiation ceremony, the prison officers' concern seemed to be more about 'prisonizing' the new inmates by destroying their previous identities and transforming them into obedient prison inmates. Similar to the media's portrayal of model prison officers, in legal regulations that govern different types of prisons, it is commonly stated that the ultimate purpose of incarceration should be to educate the inmate. In the new and old version of the Anti-drug Law, it is further stated that the purpose of *laojiao* and *qiangjie* is to help the inmates to be 'rehabilitated from drug addiction' (*jiechu duyin* 戒除毒癮) and to 'educate and save' (*jiaoyu he wanjiu* 教育和挽救) them. While the prison has been said to be a 'breeding ground for shame and humiliation' harmful to inmates' self-esteem and correction (Scheff, Retzinger, and Ryan 1989, 189), pain and shame play a crucial role in Chinese penal and educational philosophy.

Chinese educational, penal, and social control philosophy

Criminologist suggests that 'pain' is counterproductive to offender rehabilitation (Christie 1981). Physical torture is also criticized by international treaties and protocols like the UN Convention against Torture and the Istanbul Protocol.[7] However, in China it was believed that through forcing inmates to feel 'pain' and 'shame' they can learn to recognize that they are indeed problematic and therefore become motivated to rehabilitate themselves (X. Chen 2002). The same assumption is applied to the rehabilitation of 'drug addicts'. Here the idea of 'rehabilitation' is more about deterrence than 'education'. That means to teach the offender a lesson (*jiaoxun* 教訓) rather than simply 'teaching' or 'educating' the offender (Zhao and Ma 2005). All 'education' during the initiation ceremony inflicts a certain amount of intended pain on the new inmates. Many of the techniques used in the initiation ceremony can be traced back to the traditional educational, penal, and social control practices. The quiet-sitting has its roots in traditional Confucian, Buddhist, and Daoist practices. The origin of copying, reading, and reciting texts could be found in abundance in traditional Chinese pedagogical practices. Even the use of shock-and-awe ceremonies can be found in classical fiction and legends. Here the 'Chinese culture' is used as a 'toolkit' for modern purposes.

---

7. The Convention against Torture and Other Cruel, Inhuman or Degrading Treatment or Punishment is also commonly known as the UN Convention against Torture (UNCAT). UNCAT is against 'torture and other cruel, inhuman or degrading treatment or punishment throughout the world' (UN General Assembly 1984). The full name of the Istanbul Protocol is the Manual on Effective Investigation and Documentation of Torture and Other Cruel, Inhuman or Degrading Treatment or Punishment. This protocol was developed in 1999. The purpose of the protocol is to 'serve as international guidelines for the assessment of persons who allege torture and ill-treatment, for investigating cases of alleged torture and for reporting findings to the judiciary or any other investigative body' (UN 2004).

The public humiliation of inmates during the strip-search, the prolonged quiet-sitting in difficult bodily postures, the march-drilling, the *guoban*, and the inmates' trial, all these ceremonies were shameful and painful but were not just for the sole purpose of inflicting pain and shame as such; they were seen as *useful* pain and shame. Much like Foucault's description of the public executions during the *ancien régime* in France (1977), all these pains were displayed in public. The noise made from beating up new inmates, the display of naked bodies when new inmates were forced to take the compulsory cold bath and when the new inmates change into their uniforms, all these can be seen as displays of power so as to acquire general submission and deter potential troublemakers and put them 'in their place'. It is difficult to judge whether the prison officers truly believed in the 'educational' effect of such pain and shame inflicted on the new inmates or if they simply wanted to 'beat' the new inmates into submission, enjoying such beatings.

However, what most former drug addicts have experienced during the initiation ceremony gives them the impression that the officers who supervise their admission training were not interested in educating them, at least not educating them so that they could become better persons. As mentioned already, the experiences of former drug users in the initiation ceremony gave them the feeling of physical and mental pain. Many former prisoners reflect that their physical well-being and dignity were completely deprived during the period of incarceration.

The inmates' initiation ceremonies thus appeared to be more about controlling the inmate than 'educating' or 'saving' them. Violence played a core role in the power inmates' control of the new inmates. Prison violence is nothing unique to the Chinese prisons—it is more or less a universal phenomenon within prisons. However, the paradox between the official ideal of 'behaving in a civilized manner' and the reality of sheer violence might not be found as strongly in other prison systems. New inmates in Motai were being beaten up during the *guoban* ritual right in front of posters declaring that 'bullying is prohibited'. That same morning they would read out loud the 'inmates' code of conduct' that talks about acting in a 'civilized and polite manner'. By experiencing these on-the-spot contradictions between the 'front-stage ideal' and the 'backstage reality', new inmates learn the knowledge of 'talking about politeness' while feeling the practice of violence. This contradiction is further reinforced in their daily routines that not only make them the victims of violence but also perpetrators of violence. The system itself encourages and indeed propagates violence. When I asked Dage, a former inmate in a detention centre, whether he had beaten up new inmates during his incarceration. He told me, 'Yes. I do not have a choice. This is the traditional rule inside. You cannot choose not to beat up the newcomers. If you do not beat up the newcomers, you make yourself the enemy of everyone else in the cell' (Dage, interview 2, 2012).

Dage has taken the prison violence for granted. He was beaten up when he was a newly admitted inmate. He had seen and participated in the violent initiation ceremony many times during his incarceration. We can say that Dage, just like many other prison inmates, was prisonized to accept and learn the violent prison culture. Another former prisoner, Yang, shared a similar view. When I asked him whether beating up new inmates is a good or bad practice, he replied, 'Beating is actually better. Nothing can be accomplished without norms or standards (*meiyou guize bu cheng fangyuan* 沒有規則不成方圓)' (Yang, interview 76, 2013).

For Yang, beating up new inmates seems to be an effective way, if not the only way, to enforce norms and regulations in the cell. While inmates like Dage and Yang might see the violence inside the prison as unavoidable or necessary, other prisoners saw it as an evil practice.

Three interpretations of pain

Former prisoners interpreted their physical and mental pain in three main ways. The first interpretation was that both the officers and inmates who are responsible for the initiation ceremony were by nature bad. In the autobiography of prisoner scholar Victor Hassine, he states:

> By now I began to realize how fragile civilization was and how easily modern man could be reduced to the savagery of his prehistoric ancestors. Although we had TVs, radios, clothes, and a wealth of commercial goods, behaviourally we had regressed thousands of years backward on the social evolutionary scale. The new order was now the law of the jungle. (1996, 28)

In accordance with Hassine's remarks on prison lives, former drug users who believe in this type of interpretation demonized the officers and inmates who brought them the physical and mental pain. One typical remark of the former prisoners was that 'they do not treat you as a human being' (*bu ba ni dang ren* 不把你當人). One typical explanation from former drug users who held this interpretation was that the officers and other inmates wanted to satisfy their 'perverted desire' (*biantai de yuwang* 變態的欲望) (Sun, conversations, 2012).

The second interpretation suggests that some officers and inmates are good but that most of them are bad. These former drug users claim to have met some 'good officers' who really wanted to educate them and help them to become better persons during their incarceration. To them, these 'good officers' are exceptional and different from most of the other officers. However, their perceptions about the 'bad officers' and 'bad inmates' are basically the same as in the first type of interpretation.

The final interpretation is more nuanced and focuses on the practical dimension of the initiation ceremony. From this point of view, the officers or the inmates are neither 'good' nor 'bad'. They are just performing their duty. These former drug users believed that all the pain that the officers and inmates imposed on them stems from administrative purposes. To them, the ultimate purpose of the initiation ceremony is to control the new inmates. The initiation ceremony acts as a kind of 'awing rod' or 'prestige-breaking rod' to demolish the power and prestige of the new inmates so that they could be put under more effective control. The former drug users holding such views are typically those who had been in the position of the 'most powerful inmate in the cell'.

Concluding Remarks

In this chapter I have documented two levels of hypocrisy in the prison context. On the first level, the former prisoners were forced to 'act' and 'perform' according to official doctrine in front of the prison officers. Their 'acts' and 'performances' coincide with what Scott (1990, 35) has called the 'ritual of submission'. In this ritual, the inmates strategically act according to the official discourse so as to survive and advance through the system (Crewe 2007). Second, they were exposed to clear contradictions between the party propaganda and the actual day-to-day practices in the prison during the different initiation ceremonies. Although many of the practices in the initiation ceremonies are rooted in the traditional understanding of education and pain, the current use of these techniques seems to be more about controlling inmates. None of the former drug users suggested that the purpose of the initiation ceremony is for educating or saving the inmates. They either perceive the initiation ceremony to be for the purpose of satisfying the 'perverted desire' of the officers and inmates, or they see it as a means to put the new inmates under control. While they disagree with the claim that prison is used for education, they learn that to survive in the prison, especially in front of the officers, they have to present themselves as if they agree with the idea that 'prison is used for education'. All these could only be made sense of through what Goffman (1968a) called the 'obedience test'. The prison authority, as well as the inmate authority, forced the new inmates to act against the new inmates' own will so as to deprive them of pride, agency, and even basic human dignity.

I have also mentioned the role of the inmate authority as prison officers' assistants in maintaining cell order. In the last part of this chapter I allude to the existence of compulsory labour in Chinese prisons. The next chapter will examine how the relationship between the prison authority and the inmate authority and the role of compulsory labour further contribute to the formation of the system of hypocrisy.

5
Prison Authority and the 'Inmate Elites'

This chapter examines former drug detainees' experiences of everyday life in the prisons. I look specifically at the power relationship between the detention officers and the powerful inmates (whom I referred to as the 'inmate elites') in *laojiao/qiangge*. On the basis of their power relations, I argue that the prison officers' concerns for maintaining control and the pressure on making profit had far superseded the concerns for drug rehabilitation. This further added to the former prisoners' feelings of unfairness and injustice and more deeply entrenched the systematic hypocrisy.

In Chapter 3 I examined how police officers made use of drug users and drug dealers as hooks to manage and arrest other drug users. The strategy of 'using drug users to control drug users' was not only practised by the police; it was also widely used in the prison context. Previous literature has shown that prison officers sometimes acquire the assistance of some of the prison inmates in their daily prison management (Bosworth and Carradine 2001; Clemmer 1966; McCorkle and Korn 1954). Similarly, in Chinese prisons, different inmates are selected to be the prison officers' assistants. For the sake of simplicity, I generally called them the 'inmate elites'. 'Inmate elites' in China were directly appointed by the prison officers to assist in the daily prison operations in two main arenas: maintaining order and labour production. In return, the inmate elites were given more power and privileges than other prison inmates. The use of inmate elites can be risky for the prison management since it is often seen as contributing to 'prison bullies' or 'cell bosses' (*laotou yuba* 牢頭獄霸) (Feng 2012; Y. Lu 2009; Seymour and Anderson 1998; N. Zhou 2009). Despite the risk involved, and the call for the abolishment of the use of 'working offenders', such cooperation between the officers and the inmate elites still persists in China.

Through scrutinizing the power relationship between the prison officer and inmate elites, I want to highlight the prison officers' concern of order and management in the prison factory. In the following sections I will briefly review the existing literature related to the cooperation between prison officers and powerful inmates, followed by an examination of such cooperation in the Chinese prison context. The chapter ends by going back to the issue of the production of hypocrisy.

Inmate Power Hierarchies and Cooperative Relationship

The formation of inmate elites is related to two important issues often addressed in previous prison literature. The first issue is about the power hierarchy that exists among the prison inmates. The second issue is related to the prison officers' strategy of using powerful prison inmates in the daily management of the prison. In this study, I am not referring to the 'powerful inmates' in a general sense. By 'inmate elites', I am referring specifically to the prison inmates who are appointed by the prison officers to be in power. Existing prison literature has well documented different power hierarchies among prison inmates. The formation of such a power hierarchy is recognized to be affected by different individual, structural, and institutional factors (Akers 1977; Crewe 2012, 247; Schrag 1954; South and Wood 2006; Sykes 1958). These studies assume that individual prison officers usually do not have much influence over an individual prison inmate's power status in the prison. Instead, an individual inmate's status is usually determined by other structural and institutional factors. For example, Akers (1977) points out that the type of prison has strong influence on the type of prison inmates who can climb up to the top of the prisoner hierarchy. According to his study, treatment-oriented institutions are more likely to have prisoners who can lead democratically as prison leaders; while custodial prisons with their harsher environments are more likely to have 'tough, autocratic and harmful' inmates as prison leaders (Akers 1977, 383). Similarly, in a more recent study of a British prison, by seeing 'respectability' as a signifier of one's position in the prisoner hierarchy, Crewe points out that the respectability of a prisoner is affected by the 'intrinsic condition of prison life':

> As seemed appropriate in an environment of physical and social compression, appraisal respect was given to men who showed loyalty, sincerity, and respect for personal space and property, who dealt skillfully with prison staff, did not create problems for others, exhibited stoicism in the face of provocation, and upheld high levels of personal hygiene. (Crewe 2012)

Within the context of a particular type of prison, there are different factors that might affect an inmates' status in the power hierarchy. The type of crime the inmate has committed plays an important role here. Sex offenders, for example, generally remain at the bottom of the hierarchy (Sapp and Michael 1990; Trammell 2012). Other personal factors like how aggressive the prison inmate is, ability in physical combat, skills in developing favourable relationships with other inmates and officers, ability to develop trust, and ability to control the prison market also affect the prisoners' social status (Goffman 1968a; Goffman 1968b; Sykes and Messinger 1960; Trammell 2012). While these studies take institutional characteristics of the prison-like 'environment of physical and social compression' into consideration, the role of the prison authority in the determination of an individual prisoner's status in the prison hierarchy has generally been omitted. One can account for this omission by citing two factors. First, in recent studies (e.g., Crewe 2012), it is found that the power of the prison authority has dramatically diminished. It might be possible that prison authority nowadays, especially in the UK context, does not have enough power to influence a prison inmate's status. The second factor comes from the prison officers' tendency to appoint 'natural leaders' within the inmate community—that is, the status of an inmate is determined by how well the inmate's personal characteristics can be fitted into the structural and institutional conditions of the prison, disregarding the personal favour of the individual prison officer. However, admitting this argument overlooks the power status bump some prison inmates experience when they are appointed by the prison officers to control other inmates.

Using prison inmates to control prison inmates has been described in the classic monograph *The Prison Community*. In it, Clemmer (1966, ix–x) states that in facing the increasing work burdens the prison officers tend to 'enlist, unofficially, the aid of inmates themselves', while the inmate authority can enforce inmate codes that can 'help the administrators maintain general control over prisoners'. Similar observations have also been confirmed elsewhere (McCorkle and Korn 1954; Welch 2011). It rebuts the view that prison authority and the inmates are generally in an oppositional position (Crouch 1982; Goffman 1968a). In the studies of prison inmate codes, some have said that the inmates' code of behaviour is equivalent to the rejection of the prison administrative code of conduct. However, such an observation is based on the assumption that the inmate community is a single unit. Instead, the prison authority sometimes divides the inmate community into two main factions: the inmate authority and the remaining inmates. The relationship between the prison authority and the inmate authority is symbiotic instead of oppositional. The inmate authority provides assistances to the prison authority, whilst the prison authority offers the inmate authority rights and benefits.

One extreme depiction of this kind of relationship can be seen in the case of the *Kapos* in the Nazi concentration camps. *Kapos* were the concentration camp inmates appointed by the Nazi authority to control other inmates. They were depicted as cruel and selfish inmates who tortured other inmates in exchange for better food, alcohol, cigarettes, and other privileges (Kogon 1950; Levi 1989; Wolf 2007). A less extreme case can be found in the studies of Marquart and Roeruck (1985) on prison 'snitches'. In the studies on a pre-1984 British prison, they point out that the officially appointed snitches are one of the most powerful clusters in the inmate community. By 'snitches', they are referring to the inmates who are recruited by the prison officers to leak information about other inmates to the prison officers. Arguing against the popular perception to see the 'snitch' as the weakest, most disgraceful, and pathetic members among the prison inmates, they show that snitches are usually 'the most aggressive and feared inmates' (Marquart and Roebuck 1985, 217). Snitches, according to them, occupied some of the highest positions in the power hierarchy among the inmates. Although they do not point this out specifically, the 'snitch system' (Marquart and Roebuck 1985, 219–21) forms an internally hierarchical inmate authority that assists the prison authority to control all the inmates.

Officer-inmate cooperation

Clemmer (1966) identifies two institutional factors to explain the emergence of cooperative relationships between prison inmates and prison officers. First, as inmates always outnumber the prison staff, it is difficult, if not impossible, for the prison officers to keep the inmates under control without the help of the inmates themselves. Second, prison officers are given more and more duties to perform. Clemmer points out that the social expectations to the function of prison have been increased. Instead of only seeing it as a place to keep inmates quietly and securely confined, a conception marred by frequent outbursts of physical violence, riots, and prison escapes, new expectations have been added without reducing the existing expectations. These new expectations include the responsibility to engage inmates in 'production, housekeeping, maintenance, educational, and treatment activities while, at the same time, efficiently repressing them' (Clemmer 1966, ix). With all these new burdens, prison officers' available efforts in maintaining order are further limited.

Another possible reason for the use of prison inmates in maintaining prison order is that, especially in the Anglo-Saxon context, the increasing requirement of risk management in prison makes the officers shift part of the management duty to the prison inmates. By employing what Garland (2001) calls a 'responsibilization strategy', rehabilitation and maintaining order are now presented as not only the duty of the prison officers but also the duty of the prison inmates themselves (Bosworth and Carradine 2001). As reflected in previous studies, the prison officers and the powerful inmates very often maintain a relation of reciprocity so as to maintain order (Cloward 1960; Kalinich and Stojkovic 1985).

Maintaining order is likewise one of the most important tasks for Chinese prison officers. However, one main difference between the duties of the Chinese prison officers and that of the prison officers reviewed above is that the Chinese prison officers also need to supervise the entire running and profits of the prison factory. Chinese prison officers were required to maintain order as well as to watch over the profitability of the prison factory.

Compulsory labour in Chinese prisons

In 1960, in an interview with American journalist Edgar Snow, Mao Zedong claimed, 'Our prisons are different from the prisons of the past—our prisons are schools, factories or farms' (S. Wang 1999, 77). The ideology behind the contemporary Chinese use of compulsory labour as a means of correction can be traced back to the Marxist-Leninist ideology that offenders can be reformed through compulsory labour into socialist 'new men' (*xinren* 新人) (Williams and Wu 2004). The origin of the Chinese Communist system of labour reform can be found in the 1930s labour reformatories in areas under Communist control (V. Shaw 1998). Inmates at that time were forced to perform various types of labour for the local Communist authority. Such labour tasks included making products for the local government and the Red Army, repairing roads, building bridges, and transporting military supplies. This practice had been continued through World War II to the civil war and adopted in the new socialist state after 1949.

In post-Maoist China compulsory labour is still officially seen as one of the main strategies in re-educating and rehabilitating the inmate (Dutton 2005a; H. Fu 2005b). It is enforced in three types of prisons: 'reform through labour' (*laogai* 勞改), which was later officially called the 'prison' (*jianyu*); re-education through labour (*laojiao* 勞教), which was formally abolished in 2013; and the 'compulsory isolation for drug rehabilitation centres' (*qiangge* 強隔). All inmates in *laojiao* and *qiangge* were forced to perform different labour duties in the prison factory. It was also the prison officers' duty to supervise the compulsory labour. The contemporary use of compulsory labour in prison was said to serve three goals: (1) to segregate the inmates from the public, (2) to reform the inmates into 'new persons', and (3) to reduce future criminality (Du 2004). Similar principles are also applied in the use of compulsory labour in drug rehabilitation.

In China the use of compulsory labour in drug rehabilitation is termed as 'labour rehabilitation' (*kangfu laodong* 康復勞動). It is said to serve three purposes for drug rehabilitation in the custodial facilities. Firstly, it is believed that compulsory labour can provide physical training to the inmates, which is again beneficial to their rehabilitations (Z. Liu 2004). Second, it is claimed that compulsory labour can provide vocational training (*zhiye jineng peixun* 職業技能培訓) to the inmates so that the inmate can be better equipped for their later discharged lives (Bureau of Reform-through-labour; Ministry of Justice 2009; Z. Liu 2004; National People's Congress 2008). Third, the profit generated through compulsory labour can be used to subsidize both the daily operation of the prison and the resources and food provided to the prison inmates (Z. Liu 2004). The first two goals are about the education and reform of the inmates. They were repeatedly mentioned in the propaganda and different government reports. However, in most former prisoners' experiences, 'education' was not the real concern of the prison officers. Instead, many of them thought that making profit through compulsory labour is the real concern of the officers.

In the foregoing, I have shown that in the Anglo-Saxon context prison officers very often recruit some inmates to assist in the daily prison operations. I have also shown that Chinese prison officers are concerned with the order and stability of the prison, along with the daily operation of the prison factory. Similarly, inmate elites in China, unlike those mentioned in previous studies, need to assist the prison officers not only in maintaining order but also in operating the prison factory. In order to maximize the efficiency of the prison factory, many of the *laojiao* and *qiangge* imitate the bureaucratic structure of a real factory. This requires a large number of people to work in the 'managerial' level, which further increases the burden of prison officers in need of manpower. Under this constraint, prison inmates are selected to be the 'inmate elites' to fill up these managerial posts.

In the following section, I will document the power relationship between the prison officers and the inmate elites within a 'demand-supply' matrix (summarized in Table 5.1). I look firstly at what the prison authority demand from the inmate elites and how the inmate elites can fulfil the prison officers' needs. I will then look at what the prison officers can offer the inmate elites through a system of 'principled particularism', which is a control strategy used in Communist work units in which the authority secures the loyalty of a certain group of workers through rewarding them with bonuses, raises, and promotions (Bakken 2000; Walder 1986). I will soon come back to this control strategy in more detail.

Prison Officers' Demand and Inmate Elites' Offer: Maintaining Order

One of the most important functions that the inmate elites serve is to help the prison officers to maintain order in the cell and to keep the inmates under control. The self-governing of prison inmates is not something unique to China. One scholar studying life imprisonment in the prison at Graterford, Pennsylvania, states, 'If you ask any staff member or inmate who runs Graterford, the answer will always be the same: "The inmates run Graterford"' (Hassine 1996, 45). In China, prisoners' everyday life is spatially and temporally divided. In the presence of the prison officers, the prison cell become an 'officer-run space'; however, when prison officers are not there, the prison cell become an 'inmate-run space'. In the course of twenty four hours prison inmates spend much of their time with other inmates, when most prison officers are off duty late at night until early in the morning before the official 'roll call' (*dianming* 點名). To keep the prison inmates under control during this time, the prison officers need the help of the inmate elites. Inmate elites can function in three ways: to solve the problem of the lack of manpower, to resolve conflicts among prison inmates, and to enforce the prison officer's authority when no obvious rules are broken.

The lack of manpower: Formation of an 'inmate authority'

One main reason for the prison officers to recruit inmate elites is that prison inmates always outnumber the prison officers. It is especially the case when Chinese prisons are operated as custodial institutions, as well as production institutions. Short-staffing can be seen as an intrinsic problem faced by prisons all over the world. With the possible exception of some Scandinavian prisons (Pratt 2008), in most prisons the inmates almost always outnumber the prison officers (Clemmer 1966; Yang et al. 2008; Yang and Cheng 2012; Zheng 2006). According to Chinese official regulations, the effective operation of a prison requires a standard staff-to-inmate ratio of at least 1:5.6 (Z. Sun 2007; Yang and Cheng 2012). Regardless of how this ratio is formulated, a recent report states that the actual frontline staff-to-inmate ratio is much lower; usually ranging from 1:12.5 to 1:34 (Zhou and Wan 2008). A report in 2006 stated that the staff-to-inmate ratio in over 50 per cent of the *laojiao* was 1:12.5 or below (Zheng 2006). According to this report, because of the lack of manpower, an individual officer can work up to ninety hours a week. In former prisoners' experiences, in detention centres about one hundred inmates were guarded by about ten officers; in *qiangjie*, *laojiao* and *qiangge* there were usually about twenty prison officers to take care of about one to three hundred inmates. The problem of lack of manpower is even more severe during the night shift. According to the former prisoners, during the 'inmate-run time' there are usually not more than two prison officers on each floor where roughly one hundred to three hundred inmates were incarcerated. Although surveillance cameras were usually set up in each room, it was still impossible for the duty officers to watch over all the inmates, especially when there were some conflicts between the inmates. In order to solve this 'human resources' problem, one type of the 'prison elite'—the dorm heads—were recruited to act as the order enforcers of the prison cells.

The dorm head usually recruits several inmates to be his followers. With these 'followers', each dorm head forms a cell-inmate authority. Within one cell, there were one dorm head and at least three to four 'followers' to watch over about ten to thirty inmates. They were usually called 'followers of the dorm head' (*shezhang de ren* 舍長的人). Each of these 'followers' would be assigned duties: one responsible for the 'education activities' (*xuexi huodong* 學習活動), another responsible for the 'discipline' (*jilü* 紀律), and one responsible for the 'housekeeping' (*neiwu* 內務). By 'housekeeping', what is meant is the management of the financial accounts of each inmate and the hygiene of the cell. Each inmate had a financial account that he or she could use to purchase different goods. (I will return to the inmates' financial account later in this chapter.) The dorm head and his followers were generally called 'people in the front' (*qianmian de ren* 前面的人) or 'people at the top' (*shangmian deren* 上面的人).

In a *laojiao* team with three hundred inmates, there would be at least ten dorm heads and each of them would form different small power clusters within each cell. The power cluster became the quasi-guards who enforced rules and regulations. They were also the 'powerful inmates' that I have mentioned in the last chapter who enforced the 'inmates' initiation ceremonies'. On a day-to-day basis, they acted as the representatives of the prison officers to resolve conflicts among inmates through both violent and non-violent means.

Regulating the inmate's code and resolving conflict

According to the former prisoners, most of the time prison cells were peaceful and well regulated. However, on some occasions, individual inmates might get into conflicts. These issues were sometimes very minor. Lily, who was a dorm head, told me how a small conflict led to a big fight:

> I remember when two newcomers from Guiyang came to our cell. They were in a group of three: two locked up in our room and one locked up in the opposite room. It was okay in the beginning, but later everyone in our cell started disliking one of the newcomers. She acted as if she knew everything. It's like, if you said you were selling planes, she would say she made atomic bombs. She [talked as if she] knew everything. She just interrupted all conversations. Maybe she wanted to show that she was doing very good outside. Later, I forgot because of what, she had a quarrel with some other inmates. We [the inmate authority] did not join it, but then everyone below started to beat her up. The other new girl tried to stop it, but of course she couldn't do anything. (Lily, interview 3, 2012)

Another source of conflict could originate from the underground cell market. Underground markets exist in almost every prison where different legal and illegal goods are traded (Casella 2000; Crewe 2006; 2012; Gleason 1978; Goffman 1968a; Kappeler and Potter 2005; Sykes 1958). In the Anglo-Saxon context, this kind of underground trading of goods and services is usually controlled by prison gangs and informally permitted by the prison authority (Kappeler and Potter 2005). Similar to prisons internationally, in Chinese prisons, the open exchange of goods and resources are prohibited by the prison regulations. This forces all the trading between the inmates into an underground prison cell market. The prison officers usually could not legitimately control the illegitimate market in the prison. Different legitimate commodities like snacks, cigarettes and lighters, new prisoner uniforms, and illegitimate goods like pornographic pictures, alcohol, drugs, and mobile phones exist and are exchanged in the underground market.

The value of these goods varied in different prisons, and there was no standardized price assigned to each of them. It was even more complicated in the case of the Chinese prison, for the exchange of goods and services were not seen as 'trading' (*maimai* 買賣) only, but as an 'exchange of favours' (*zuo renqing* 做人情) and a cultivation of *guanxi* (關係). For example, in the re-education-through-labour centres in Motai in the 1990s, two cigarettes could be used to 'purchase' one day of labour duty. However, the two cigarettes were seen as a kind-hearted offer of the powerful inmate to give an opportunity to the poor inmate to earn two cigarettes. It also demonstrated that the 'poor inmate' who received the two cigarettes was under the protection of that powerful inmate. The involvement of *guanxi* in the prison market had made it far too complicated for the prison officers to get involved. Moreover, since officially this kind of exchange is forbidden in the prison, it is impossible for the prison officers to manage it. If the prison officers enforce the rules in the illegitimate market, the prison officer would be the one breaking the rules.

In the studies of the organized crime groups, it is said that they exist mainly because of the lack of reliable rule enforcers in both the legitimate and illegitimate market sphere. Instead of simply extorting the legitimate and illegitimate business owners, organized crime groups act as the rule enforcers who provide protection to both the sellers and buyers in the market (Chu 2000; Gambetta 1993). The role of the inmate authority is similar to the role played by these organized crime groups. Instead of only watching over the trading, however, the inmate authority also needed to comprehend the complicated *guanxi* between different inmates so as to resolve any conflict.

The enforcing prison officer's authority

Another condition in the prison that favours the establishment of an inmate authority is that the prison officers need someone to do the 'dirty work' in order to enhance their power authority, especially in the case when prison inmates harm their authority without obviously or explicitly breaking prison rules. Crewe (2007) stated that the prison officers in modern British prisons have lost much of their power. They have fallen from 'having been gods' and their 'power of life or death' has been eroded. The Chinese prisons, as reflected by the former prisoners, seem to be experiencing a similar change. According to inmates incarcerated in the 1980s and 1990s prison officers tend to use physical violence against the prisoners once their authority had been challenged. A report about the 'occupational crime' committed by Chinese prison officers shows that fewer and fewer prison officers were being accused of abusing the prison inmates when compared with the 1980s and early 1990s (Yang et al. 2008). According to the report, in those decades most of the 'occupational crime' committed by prison officers were 'the crime of physically abusing prison inmates' (*tifa nuedai bei jianguan renyuan zui* 體罰虐待被監管人罪) and 'homicide caused by negligence' (*guoshi zhiren siwang zui* 過失致人死亡罪). The report also states that instead of physically abusing the inmates, there are more and more 'corruption' cases occurring today. Although one might doubt the authenticity of the above research, according to former prisoners who had been incarcerated before and after 2000, prison officers nowadays are indeed less willing to employ physical violence when their authority is threatened (Yang, interview 39, 2012; Hang, interview 65, 2012). Yang told me,

> When I was there at that time, the ways in which the prison officers spoke and acted were all very rude. After I came out, it was totally different. [They now do] 'civilized enforcement' [*wenming zhifa* 文明執法] and 'civilized management' [*wenming guanjiao* 文明管教]. At that time, they [the prison officers] beat us severely. . . . They used electric batons and tied you up. It's a punishment, it's a murder. (Yang, interview 39, 2012)

Many prison officers in the 1980s and 1990 used physical violence to punish the inmates and to establish the officers' authority. However, those incarcerated after the new millennium seldom mentioned random physical violence imposed by prison officers on prison inmates. In their words, the prison officers are more 'formal' (*zhenggui* 正規). What they mean is that the prison officers usually need to exercise their physical violence within the framework of legal regulations, implying that they could only use physical force when they were physically threatened or when other inmates were physically threatened. Although these regulations are sometimes interpreted and manipulated, prison officers now generally need to perform their job according to them. Similarly, in a study of re-education through labour in China, Fu (2005a) reflects that in post-reform China making profits has become increasingly important for the prison authority. One result of this is that the prison officers are less willing to torture or punish the inmates, and instead focus on how to treat the inmates who can then help the prison factory generate more income in a less hostile manner. However, on certain occasions, some prison inmates may act in a way that might publicly threaten the prison officers' authority without breaking any rules. These acts include 'talking back' to the prison officers and making fun of the officers. The following scenario can best illustrate such a situation:

> A new inmate acted like a 'psycho' [*shenjing bing* 神經病] on the first night when she arrived in the prison cell. She shouted, screamed, and turned the prison cell into a mess. She threw her personal belongings at a prison officer. Such an act clearly had violated the authority of the prison officer. However, without directly breaking any rules in the prison, the prison officers could not find a legitimate reason to punish the troublemaker. Encountering this situation, the prison authority in the cell commanded other inmates to beat the new inmate up. When this incident transformed from an 'individual inmate acting crazily' to 'controlled prison violence', the prison officer came back with a stretcher and tied the new inmate up on it. (Cheng 2009)

This incident highlights the limitations of the power of the prison officer in using physical violence. When I heard about this incident, I imagined that the prison officer would summon other prison officers to come and beat up the new inmate. However, as reflected in this case, the prison officer actually needed to wait until certain regulations were broken, and only then could exercise physical power legitimately. The role of the inmate authority in this case was to protect the authority of the prison officers when the troublemaker had not obviously broken any regulation. Ironically, the more the prison officers follow the legal regulations, the more they need someone to do the dirty jobs for them. Similar observations can also be made in other aspects in China. For example, when police officers are increasingly required to comply with laws in exercising their power, there is a corresponding increase in the use of 'informal force' to do the 'dirty work'. Out there, 'municipal officers' or 'urban management officers' (*chengguan* 城管) are beating up unlicensed hawkers and smashing their stands; in the prison, the inmate authority is beating up the unruly inmates. In each instance, this 'informal force' is taking the dirty job of violence from the formal police officers and upholding a system of violence outside the formal rules.

What I have presented above is the power hierarchy among inmates within one cell and how the prison officers used the inmate elites to assist the operation of the cell. Above the cell level the prison officers organized a 'prison-level' inmate power hierarchy. Prison officers appointed different prison inmates to this prison-level power hierarchy. In a re-education-through-labour centre in Zhiyang, the most powerful inmate was called the 'manager' (*tongguan* 統管). He or she reported directly to the prison officers and had four to six 'administrators' (*guanli yuan* 管理員) under him or her. Each of these administrators was responsible for one main duty. These administrators include at least two 'production administrator' (*shengchan guanli yuan* 生產管理員) who were responsible for the labour activities, one 'discipline administrator' (*jilü guanli yuan* 紀律管理員) who was responsible for the enforcement of rules and regulations, and one 'housekeeping administrator' (*neiwu guanli yuan* 內務管理員) who was responsible for the hygiene in the cell room. Then there was the administrator of the financial account of all inmates and the 'education administrator' (*jiaoyu guanli yuan* 教育管理員) who was responsible for coordinating different education-related activities (see Figure 5.1). All dorm heads, with the assistance of their 'followers' (see Figure 5.2), reported to the 'administrators', although sometimes the dorm heads reported to the prison authorities directly.

Unlike the power hierarchy between the 'followers' whose power status was basically the same, the power of the two 'production administrators' was much greater than other administrators. This also linked to another important function of the inmate elites—to assist in the prison factory. In other words, the system on the inside of the prisons in many ways mimics the hierarchical structure outside the prison walls, with its cadres and administrators placed in different hierarchical positions of power.

Pressure in making profits

Starting from the Maoist period, Chinese prisons had long been used as correctional institutions, as well as factories to generate profit. However, similar to other public enterprises, the profit motive plays an increasingly important role in the post-socialist Chinese prison (Dutton 2005a; H. Fu 2005a; H. Wu 1992). In post-socialist China, criminal justice institutions have been given lower priority in government funding when compared to economic development. Government funding providing for the Chinese prisons has also declined (H. Fu 2005a). What makes it worse is that the economic reforms had made the prison industry less and less profitable. Seymour and Anderson (1998) convincingly argue that in general the Chinese prison enterprise system was not profitable, even if the enterprises helped cover the costs of the prison system. Fu (2005a) made similar observation in his study of a Chinese *laojiao* enterprise. Similarly, I found no evidence to show that the *laojiao/qiangge* institutions are profitable. On the contrary, reports show that the prison factories in China often suffer from deficits (Mou 2013; J. Zhang 2011; Zhou, Ma, and Xie 2013). According to Mou (2013), Chinese prison factories in 1983 were still profitable. However, in 1990, the state government already needed to pay ¥514 million to cover the financial losses in the whole prison industry. In September 1997, Chinese prison factories had outstanding loans totalling more than ¥9.1 billion and a debt-to-assets ratio of over 80 per cent (Mou 2013, 138). Although the number shown in the report is dubious and subject to manipulation, together with other recent studies in contemporary China, it does show that prison factories in today's market economy have many disadvantages in the competition with outside factories (He and Fu 2000; J. Zhang 2011; Zhou, Ma, and Xie 2013; Zhou and Zhou 2006).

To cope with the challenges, many prison officers tried to replicate the factory environment in the real world inside the prison factory as much as possible (H. Fu 2005a). The recent establishment of the 'prison enterprise group' (*jianyu qiye jituan* 監獄企業集團) can be seen as an example of such responses. One characteristic of the 'prison enterprise group' is that within the criminal justice system, they present themselves as a 'prison'. However, when they do business with their potential clients, they present the prison as a 'business company'. Indeed, many of the 'prison enterprise groups' are registered as 'companies' (*gongsi* 公司) or 'enterprises' (*qiye* 企業). This strategy had been used way back in the early period of economic reform. At that time, when prison officers went outside to talk business with their clients, they would present themselves as a 'company' instead of a 'prison' (H. Wu 1992). Prison staffs often operate with two business cards, one with a prison title and profession, and one with business titles only.

A whole new set of business enterprise logics like 'enterprise management' (*qiye guanli* 企業管理), 'equipment management' (*shebei nengyuan* 設備能源), 'technical quality' (*jishu zhiliang* 技術質量), 'cost control' (*chengben kongzhi* 成本控制), and 'supply and sales' (*gongying xiaoshou* 供應銷售) have infiltrated the daily operation of the prison enterprises. Here is how a prison enterprise in Inner Mongolia described itself in a local yearbook:

> We speed up the production and adjust the product mix. . . . Our motto is 'Our products are as good as our morality, the quality [of the product] is as important as our lives'. We have 'excellent quality, excellent delivery, and excellent management'.
> (Li, Shang, and Zhang 2012)

Although the above studies are about the official 'prison' (*jianyu*), they certainly shed light on the situation of *laojiao* and *qiangge*. In 2005 I met a factory owner who had used *laojiao* for their production. His company signed a contract with the *laojiao* authority. The factory provided all raw materials and technical supervision necessary for the production, and the *laojiao* provided the cheap human labour for the production process. The company paid the *laojiao* for the work, and the *laojiao* authority would pay the inmates who worked in the *laojiao* factory. Each inmate would be given about ¥300 to ¥400 per month for their work in the *laojiao* factory. However, the *laojiao* inmate might be punished if their products could not meet the quantity and quality requirement of the factory. After learning that some of the inmates were actually punished because of the production work, out of humanitarian reasons, the contractor stopped cooperating with that particular *laojiao*. According to the *laojiao* inmates, they had worked on many different products, including making paper boxes with the logo of KFC, making footballs with the logo of the FIFA World Cup (for the world football championship in South Africa in 2010), and other products like teddy bears, light-bulb stems, and ballpoint pens.

Similar to the prisons, the *laojiao* industry imitated not only the language but also the practices of private business for the purpose of promoting its business. It can be seen as a response to the increasingly competitive market outside the prison. Besides language, some prison factories replicate the human resources allocation system of a private factory. The human resources allocation of a prison factory can be seen as more complicated than that of either a normal prison or a normal factory. Since the prison authority needs to manage its manpower to keep the prison inmates under control as well as to manage the production cost effectively, production in the prison factory has become increasingly sophisticated. The process further increases the need of a more detailed division of labour among the inmates, including assigning prison inmates to perform managerial tasks. The concern for simultaneously maintaining order and keeping the factory operating effectively has exerted additional pressure to the already short-staffed prison authority.

Using an institution of re-education through labour, which specialized in the production of teddy bears in Zhiyang as an example (see Figure 5.3), two 'inmate elites' are appointed as the 'production administrators' responsible for the whole production process. Under them are three 'helpers'. One is responsible for keeping an inventory of the raw materials used for producing teddy bears. Another one is responsible for ensuring that the quality of the teddy bears meets the requirements of the buyers. The third is responsible for ensuring the fulfilment of the everyday production quota. A representative from the teddy bear company visits the prison factory to provide instructions to the 'administrators'. The company representative, usually called the 'instructor' (*shifu* 師傅), makes the final decision on whether the products meet their required quality.

All other inmates are divided into different production lines responsible for cutting out the pieces of cloth, sewing mouths and nose, sewing various seams, and stuffing cottons into the cloth. Within each of these production lines, there is at least one 'line head' who is responsible for both the quality and quantity of the final products. There are about three hundred inmates in that institution. I could not obtain data about how many officers there were in the prison. However, if it is comparable to the standard inmate-to-officer ratio provided by Zheng (2006), there would be about twenty-four prison officers. Within the 'production process', at least fifteen 'managerial persons' are needed. By taking the concern for disciplinary control and order maintenance into consideration, it is quite impossible for the prison to use more than 60 per cent of their officers in the production. This fact may explain why all these managerial positions were taken up by the inmates. These inmates become a part of the inmate authority, which is endowed with the power to manage other inmates in the labour process. Managing a prison, especially a 'prison enterprise', requires quite a bit of manpower. With a lack of prison officers, the formation of an inmate authority composed of inmates could effectively relieve such a problem.

Rewarding the inmate elites

We can see from the above discussion that the prison officers need help from the inmate elites so as to keep the prison cells in order, and to keep the prison factory in operation. In return, the prison officers provided the inmate elites with different powers and benefits. The tactics that the prison officers used to control and reward the inmate elites coincide with two traditional tactics that had been used by the Communist government to control and manage its populations—'organized dependence' and 'principled particularism'.

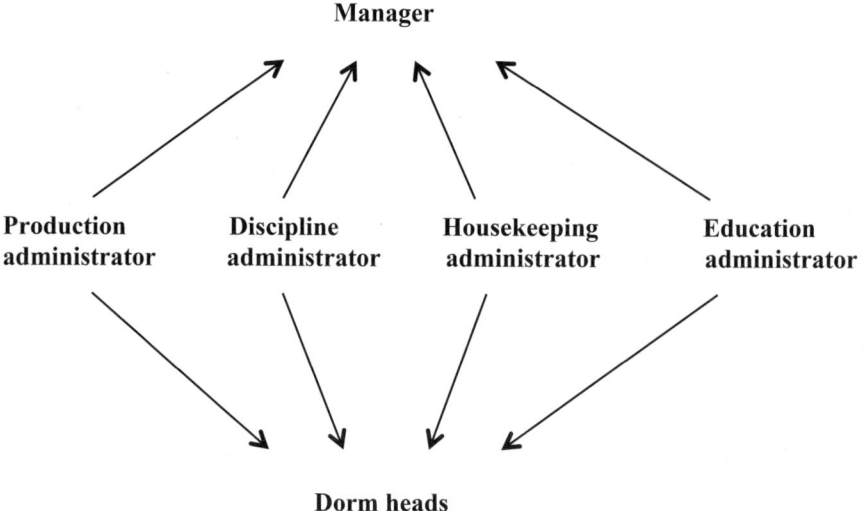

Figure 5.1: Prison-level inmate power hierarchy

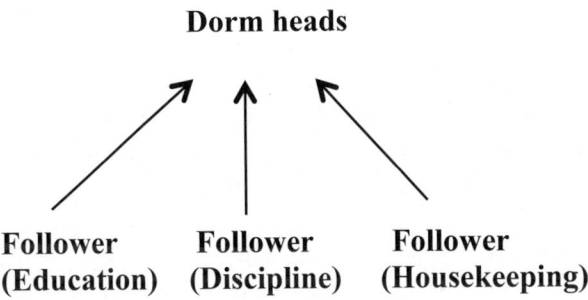

Figure 5.2: Cell-level inmate power hierarchy

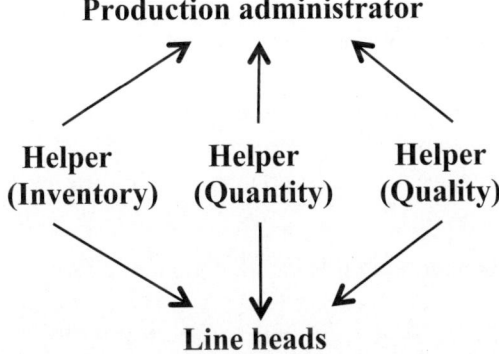

Figure 5.3: Production-line division of labour

'Organized dependence' and 'principled particularism'

In socialist China, 'organized dependence' and 'principled particularism' were two foundations of the control mechanism that the work unit (*danwei* 單位), cadres, and party leaders used to secure workers' obedience and loyalty (Bakken 2000; Lee 1999; Lee and Zhang 2013; Walder 1986). Organized dependence describes a structure in which the work-unit leaders and the party leaders monopolize the allocation of goods and services to the workers so as to make the workers totally dependent on the work unit for survival. Principled particularism describes a strategy where the work-unit leaders build up and mobilize networks of 'activists' (*jiji fenzi* 積極分子). 'Activist' refers to a minority of the populations who are loyal to the party and the work unit. They act as 'leaders' of other workers and assist the work-unit cadres in their daily management and control of other workers.

Under principled particularism, workers are evaluated according to their *biaoxian* (表現). *Biaoxian* is a Chinese concept which literally means 'to manifest', 'to display'. In practice, *biaoxian* is a blurred concept of individual worth which comprises a wide range of human qualities like one's attitude towards the prescribed norm and the concrete measurement of 'all kinds of little things'—for instance, an individual's fashion and make-up (Bakken 2000, 233, 260). Among diverse criteria, loyalty and conformity to the party is the most important. In other words, principled particularism is merit based. The strategy of 'principled particularism' is different from the strategy of 'using *guanxi*' (*la guanxi* 拉關係). While the personal tie is the most important aspect of *guanxi*, in 'principled particularism' one's ability to manifest one's loyalty and the ability to perform the assigned task is seen as the most important aspect in order to gain favourable treatment. Principled particularism and organized dependence are used in different kind of work units, as well as in different prisons.

In the prison context, the prison officers act as a cluster of leaders of the prison regime who control different resources in the prison. A prison is structured along the lines of 'organized dependence', and prison officers are in control of different material resources and an evaluation system of giving and reducing 'points'. With the control over these two resources, with principled particularism, the prison officers rewarded the inmate elites with special favours for their loyalty and services.

Merit points, early release, and principled particularism

'Merit points' (*fenshu* 分數) that an inmate obtains from the prison officers determine not only the inmate's living standard but also the length of time that he or she is required to stay in the prison. In China, prison officers have the discretionary power to extend or reduce the term of imprisonment. How to reduce the 'term of imprisonment' (*xingqi* 刑期) is the ultimate concern of most prisoners, according to the former prisoners I interviewed.

In the Chinese prison, there is a quota that limits the number of inmates who can get a commutation of their sentences (Yang et al. 2008). In other words, not all inmates who meet the criteria for commutation can have their legal penalties reduced. Instead, they need to compete for it by getting these points. Inmate authorities are usually given more 'points' than other inmates (S. Jiang 2002; Z. Zhang 2006), and thereby have better odds at securing a reduction in the length of their sentences. As mentioned, reducing the term of imprisonment is the most important concern of prison inmates. Prison officers rewarded the inmate authority through a preferential treatment in giving merit points. Prison inmates' term of imprisonment, especially those who were jailed for criminal offences in prison is determined by such a 'merit point system' (Ministry of Justice 1990). Former inmates who had been incarcerated in *laojiao* and detention centres also recall that there is a similar system there to determinate an inmates' terms of imprisonment.

In China prison inmates in general are classified into three categories according to how 'well reformed' they are. The best category is the 'well-reformed' inmates who are sometimes called the 'active reform elements' (*gaizao jiji fenzi* 改造積極分子) or the 'outstanding students' (*youxiu xueyuan* 優秀學員). The lowest-ranked group of inmates is sometimes given stigmatized descriptions like the 'the stubborn and dangerous elements who resist reform' (*kanggai wanwei fenzi* 抗改頑危分子) (Zhang and Qi 2006). Other inmates are usually in between. The well-reformed inmates are usually rewarded with reduced sentences, while the stubborn and dangerous inmates are subjected to an increase in their sentences. According to the experiences of the former prisoners, for an inmate sentenced to three years in *laojiao*, the maximum reduction of sentences that he or she can obtain is about three months.

In the Chinese prison system, according to former prison inmates, not all 'active reform elements' are inmate elites, but inmate elites very often make up most of what is described as the 'active reform elements'. In other words, prison officers can reward inmate authorities through either assigning more 'merit points' or by giving them a higher priority to be recognized as 'active reform elements'.

Resources, prison economy, and principled particularism

One main characteristic of the prison lives is the lack of different kinds of daily resources. These resources include a variety of free food, daily necessities, and cigarettes. The prison authority can provide the inmates with preferential treatment in terms of the allocation of these resources. Although starvation is no longer a problem faced by prison inmates in China today, the quality of free food is still very poor. Former prison inmates usually judge the quality of food according to the amount of meat and oil in their dishes. As Shan wrote in his prison diary:

> Thirteen pieces of meat in the bucket.
> No oil in the vegetable.
>
> Rice is always sufficient.
> Too many wolves, too little meat.
> My tummy is unlikely to be satisfied. (Shan, prison diary)

Among the five prisons where the former prisoners had been incarcerated, with the exception of one in Zhiyang, all provided a very limited variety of free food to the prison inmates. According to their experiences, within seven days a week, usually there will be two days that they can find some meat in their lunch and dinner. Most of their regular meals are rice with boiled vegetables. Similarly, other daily necessities like toothpaste, soap, and shampoo are usually not provided for free. However, in contrast to former times when all resources were provided by the prison authority, inmates today are usually allowed to buy snacks, extra food, and other better-quality daily necessities from a prison shop.

Hierarchy of goods in prison

One notable recent change in the prisoners' lives is the development of a prison economy in which daily necessities like toilet paper, toothbrushes, and soaps are no longer solely allocated by the prison authority but can be purchased in 'prison commissaries'. In Chinese prisons, inmates are not allowed to keep any cash. The 'money' that an inmate owns, the 'salary' that they earn, and their daily 'expenditures' are recorded in a financial account book called the 'big account' (*dazhang* 大賬), which is usually managed by the 'followers' and watched over by the 'housekeeping administrators'. With the income that they earn from labour, prison inmates can purchase a wide range of goods and better daily necessities of higher-quality brands from the 'prison supermarket' and the 'prison canteen'. In China cigarettes are only available in male prisons. Female prisoners usually need to purchase or obtain cigarettes through illegitimate channels. (This will be discussed in greater detail in the later section on 'turning a blind eye'.) Prison inmates can generate enough money to purchase all the basic daily necessities as long as they can finish their labour quota. Take a *laojiao* in Zhiyang for example, even the inmates who cannot meet the quota can survive by the free allocated food like rice and vegetable dishes provided by the prison authority. Those inmates who can meet their production quota can generate enough income to purchase a wide range of food provided in the prison canteen, which usually includes pork, beef, fish, and different vegetables and rice. As the former prisoners described it, the supermarket in the prison is much the same as the supermarket outside. While a normal prison inmate can generate enough income for survival, the 'inmate elites' are usually given even more 'salary' than other inmates. As Lily states:

> We [the inmate elites] do not eat those free foods [provided by the prison officers]. Those foods are only for the 'outsiders' (*waidi ren* 外地人) and those who are 'not able to do well' (*hunde buhao* 混得不好). . . . We only ate food that we bought from the shop. (Lily, conversations in a cafe, 2013)

While labouring in the socialist Chinese prison used to be only a 'burden' that prison inmates need to carry, prison inmates in the post-socialist prison are actively motivated to do labour so that they can consume more goods of better quality. That is especially the case when it becomes common for the inmate elites as well as other inmates to use the food they eat and the brand of goods they use to signify their power and status in the prison. Crewe (2012) points out that in UK prisons consumer possessions are important signifiers of status among prison inmates. Similarly, prison inmates in post-socialist China tend to use different consumer goods to demonstrate their identities as well as status. However, this privilege has become more than a new 'freedom' or 'option' for them; it is also a new responsibility and new burden. Powerful inmates like the inmate elites need to learn to consume certain types of foods and goods that fit their status, especially when they are in front of other inmates. Different consumer goods are divided into 'luxury' (*gaodang de* 高檔的), 'normal' (*putong de* 普通的), and 'pretty bad' categories (*bijiao cha de* 比較差的).

For example, in male prisons, cigarettes are divided into 'luxury' and 'pretty bad' only. The luxury one includes brands like *Zhonghua pai* (中華牌) and *Furong wang* (芙蓉王); the bad ones are cigarettes of brands like *Mudan* (牡丹) and *Da qian men* (大前門). The 'luxury' cigarette brand is only for the powerful inmates—or, in their words, the inmates who are 'doing well' (*hunde hao* 混得好)—while the ordinary (*putong de* 普通的) inmates smoke the 'bad' brands. Those who are 'doing badly' (*hunde buhao* 混得不好) either do not have enough cigarettes or need to share with others who 'do badly'. Consuming cigarettes in today's Chinese prisons is no longer only for the purpose of relieving craving but is also a strategy of 'impression management' (Goffman 1958). A former 'manager', Hui, told me that behind other inmates' backs, he smoked the bad cigarette brand. However, in front of other inmates, he sometimes not only needed to smoke the good cigarette but also to distribute the good cigarettes to other inmates who worked for him. Here the ownership, consumption, and distribution of certain brands of cigarettes had become a burden for the 'manager' in order to maintain his status.

One important characteristic of the 'hierarchy of goods' is that the 'luxury' brands are usually not legitimately purchasable in the prison. There was no place where the inmate could legitimately purchase *Zhonghua pai* cigarettes and *Furon wang* cigarettes. Similarly, since cigarettes were not sold or allowed in female prisons, all types of cigarettes would be regarded as 'luxury' goods in female prisons. Other examples of 'luxury' goods according to the former prisoners included pornographic magazines, portable MP4 players with downloaded pornography, alcohol, and mobile phones. Another study shows that even drugs were available inside the prison (Gao 2008). The rise of consumerism, or the so-called 'consumer revolution' (D. Davis 2000), in China seems to have also given the inmate elites further burdens in the consumption of higher-level goods.

Principled illegal particularism: Turning a blind eye

As a response to the inmate elites' need for luxury goods, as well as to reward the inmate elites, the prison authority very often intentionally turns a blind eye when the 'inmate elites' smuggle luxury goods into prison. Bentham (1995), and Foucault after him (1977), talked about the 'panopticon' which allows prison officers to see all the inmates without allowing the inmates to know whether or not they are being watched. 'Turning a blind eye' is exactly the reverse of the 'panopticon'. The prison officers intentionally ignored the misconduct of the inmate elites. It was a reward to the inmate elites, providing them the loopholes to smuggle 'luxury' goods that allowed them to climb up the prison hierarchy. In practice, inmate elites bought the luxury goods through someone who could frequently go in and out of the prison. As reflected by the former prison inmates, these people included the trash collectors who come in and out of the prison every day, the 'instructor' of the prison factory who came over to the prison occasionally to supervise the production process, and on a rare occasion the prison officers would themselves participate in this trade. 'Inmate elites' would ask their family members or friends to pay the bill outside the prison walls. The instructor or the trash collector would then smuggle the luxury goods into the prison. Hui, the former inmate elite, described his first attempt to buy cigarettes from the outside:

> We had a trash collector who came [to the prison] every day to collect the trash.... I told him to bring some cigarettes [to the prison] every day. We cannot do it openly. He would put the cigarettes into the trash bin. (Hui, interview 58, 2012)

After getting the cigarettes, Hui wanted to test whether he would be in trouble if some of the prison officers found out that he had smuggled goods into the prison. So he went to the office of one of the prison officers:

> On that night, I went into his office. A prison officer was playing a computer game. I put two packs of *Zhonghua* [中華] on his desk and said, 'I am leaving.' He looked at me and asked, 'What's the matter with you?' I left the office immediately without answering him. After ten minutes, he still had not summoned me. So I went into his office again. The two packs of cigarettes were gone... So these things cannot be said openly. [Only] heaven, earth, and he [the officer] knows.

In this case, Hui bribed the prison officers with *Zhonghua* cigarettes. However, as Hui said, the reason he did that was to test whether the prison officer would grant him the right to smuggle things into the prison. The prison officer rewarded Hui's services of managing the prison inmates by turning a blind eye to Hui's act. If principled particularism aims at securing the inmate elites' loyalty through preferential allocation of material resources, then the principled illegal particularism aims at securing the inmates' loyalty through the partiality, or perhaps we should call it 'flexibility' of rule enforcement. The similarity between principled particularism in general and the principled illegal particularism shown here is that they are both used to reward the inmate elites for their loyalty and services. The difference between them is that preferential treatment in economic resources can be officially justified by framing it as a 'legitimate reward', which is usually allowed by the prison regulations. We might say that in this case the prison officers reward the inmate elites by 'bending the rules'. However, when the prison officers intentionally turn a blind eye to inmate elites breaking rules, they are clearly acting against the prison regulations and in fact 'breaking the rules'.

Power and dignity

Prison inmates' daily lives are marked by frustration, dehumanization, degradation, shaming, and humiliation (Crewe 2012; Goffman 1968a; Scheff Retzinger, and Ryan 1989). Starting from the strip-searches, the training section for new inmates, to the daily interaction between the inmates and the prison officers, the prison inmates are systematically degraded and humiliated. But by endowing the power to the inmate authority, the prison officers allow the members in the inmate authority to regain their dignity by exercising power over other inmates. In addition to their power to allocate resources among inmates, inmate authorities are also given the power to evaluate other inmates. In the prison enterprise, the managers are allowed to walk around the 'production line' to supervise other inmates while other ordinary inmates are required to stay in the production line. In the daily evaluation of inmates, although prison officers are the ones who stand for the final decisions, the opinion of the dorm head does also play an important role. In one detention centre in Motai, each dorm head is required to hand in inmate evaluation reports to the prison officers. The evaluation reports are used as one crucial reference that determines which category an inmate is put into. Having all this power at hand, according to former prisoners, many inmates are more than willing to flatter or fawn over the dorm head. This usually gives the inmate authority a feeling of superiority.

'Prison officers: Inmate elites' reciprocity, corruption, and hypocrisy

What I have documented above is the power relationship between the prison authority and the inmate elites. The prison authority needed the inmate elites to relieve their lack of manpower, to resolve conflicts among inmates, as well as to exercise power when their authority was challenged. In return, the prison authority can provide the inmate authority with extra resources, shorter sentencing, and more power. The relationship between the prison authorities and the inmate authorities can be summarized in the following table:

The cooperative relationship between the prison officers and the inmate at first glance seems to have effectively maintained the order of the cells and the operations of the prison factories. However, to most former prisoners, it was seen as unfair and unjust. Similar to the use of drug dealers and drug users as 'hooks', the use of inmate elites in prison could be understood in the context of the party's 'united-front tactics'. Many of the former prisoners and news reports referred to these inmate elites as 'prison bullies'.[1] Instead of protecting the inmates from these 'prison bullies', the prison officers actually cooperated with and rewarded them.

---

1. I presented a paper about the 'inmate elites' in a conference organized by the Asian Association for Substance Abuse Research in 2013. In the Q&A session, a lawyer started his question by teasing me, 'Whatever terms you are using, you are basically saying "prison bullies".' The audience burst out laughing, and I saw many in the audience, who were mainly composed of scholars, police officers, and prison officers coming from mainland China, nodding their heads while they were laughing.

Table 5.1 The cooperative relationship between the prison officers and the inmate elites

	Prison officers	Inmate elites	
Need	Manpower	Forming an 'inmate authority'	Offer
	Maintaining order of the prison cells and resolving conflicts among inmates	Controlling the prison inmates and resolving conflicts	
	Enforcing officers' authority when no obvious rules are broken	The use of violence to enforce prison officers' legitimacy	
Offer	Extra 'salary' and turning a blind eye to the illegitimate market	Extra resources that can demonstrate their power	Need
	Reduction of the terms of imprisonment	Reduction of the terms of imprisonment	
	Power	Dignity	

The cooperative system encouraged the inmate elites to maintain order through violence and other illegitimate means through the tacit consent of the prison officers. In addition, the prison officers were actually rewarding the inmate elites even though the inmate elites sometimes used illegitimate means to control other inmates. Last, the prison officers intentionally turned a blind eye when the prison elites tried to obtain luxury goods through illegitimate means. After all these experiences with the collusion between prison officers and inmate elites, most of the former prisoners strongly rejected the party-government's 'front-stage' talk about the model exemplary prison officers; instead, they saw the prison officers doing things in the completely opposite way. Their experiences also told them that the prison officers were actually 'self-interested', and a lot more concerned about controlling the inmates and making profit for themselves personally than in educating them.

In my survey of the twenty-eight former prisoners, when I asked them what they regarded as the single most important concern of the prison officers, ten (36 per cent) of them said that the prison officers' primary concern was 'enforcing discipline' (*jilü* 紀律), while the majority, sixteen (57 per cent), named 'reaching the production quota' as the most important. Only two of them (7 per cent) said that 'educational activity' was the most important task of the prison officers. None of them thought that the prison officers wanted to actually educate them to become better persons through the compulsory labour.

Educational activities did exist in *laojiao* and, especially, in *qiangge*. Both the 'education administrator' and the cell 'followers' needed to organize different education activities. In *laojiao*, one example of these education activities was the writing of the 'happy diary' that I mentioned in the last chapter. Other educational activities included watching 'anti-drug propaganda videos' (*jindu xuanchuan pian* 禁毒宣傳片), submitting writings to the internally circulated prison newspaper, and occasionally attending lectures organized by the prison officers. In the *qiangge* in Zhiyang, inmates needed to attend a lecture every Monday night and Wednesday afternoon. However, their burden of compulsory labour was still enormous. Sansan, a former prisoner from Qiangge, told me,

> They did not reduce the 'work target' [*gongzuo zhibiao* 工作指標]. It was still very high. We were already under big pressure. Now they add 'learning' pressure on us too. We really could not stand it.... Now it was double pressure. You have to finish the labour. It was directly related to the food you could eat and your quality of life there.... We very often took naps during the lecture. If you could not finish the 'labour target', you would [be punished by] sitting in the lobby on a stool for one hour when every other inmate went back to rest in their room. (Sansan, interview 18, 2012)

Many prison officers and former prisoners shared Sansan's point of view: labour was still the main concern. The 'production target' in *qiangge* had definitely been reduced compared to the 'production target' in *laojiao* in the early 2000s. At that time inmates needed to work twelve to fifteen hours a day. Many former *laojiao* inmates told me that during the peak season they were only allowed to sleep for two to three hours a day. The *qiangge* today indeed provided more 'education' to the prison inmates. However, by looking into the cooperative relationship between the prison officers and the inmate elites, I would argue that the pressure of maintaining order and making profits in the prison factory was still the major concern of the prison officers.

Concluding Remarks

In this chapter, I have explored former prisoners' experiences of incarceration. I examined specifically the relationship between the prison officers and prison inmates who were appointed by the prison officers as members of the 'inmate elites'. In prison studies, the relationship between the prison officers and inmates has generally been held to be antagonistic rather than cooperative (Cohen and Taylor 1972; Goffman 1968a), though other studies have indeed shown that prison officers sometime acquire assistance of some of the prison inmates in their daily management of the prison (Bosworth and Carradine 2001; Clemmer 1966; McCorkle and Korn 1954). Viktor Frankl, a former inmate in the Nazi concentrated camps, described *Kapos*, the concentration camp inmates who were appointed by the Nazi officers to control other inmates: 'Often they were harder on the prisoners than were the guards, and beat them more cruelly than the SS men did' (Frankl 2006, 4). According to former prisoners' experiences, it was similar in the Chinese prison. It is quite true that the people who were assigned to be dorm heads were more violent than the prison officers. However, as I have tried to demonstrate, that was one of the main reasons why they were appointed to be dorm heads in the first place—they could resort to discretionary violence to maintain order when the prison officers' hands were tied by the regulations. Maintaining order is possibly the ultimate concern of all prison officers. In China, in addition to maintaining order, the prison officers also need to operate the prison factory. Mao was quite right that prison in China was a 'school' and a 'factory'. In official propaganda, compulsory labour had been said to be for the purpose of education and vocational training. Shaw (1998, 4) notes in his study of Chinese prison that labour is 'a secondary goal' but 'primary activity'. However, the reality experienced by the former prisoners was that 'profit making' is the 'primary goal' and the 'primary activity'.

In accordance with their experiences of 'hooking' and the 'initiation ceremony', former prisoners very clearly saw the reality of the backstage during their incarceration. Instead of seeing model prison officers who sacrifice their own interest to save the drug addicts, they saw the cooperation between the prison officers and the inmate elites, the implicit authorization of the use of violence, the legal and illegal particularism that favour the inmate elites, and the enormous pressure of compulsory labour. None of these issues matched the rosy party propaganda. The former prisoners again saw the system of hypocrisy hide behind the beautiful phrases of party propaganda.

To many first-timers, being discharged from prison should be looked forward to as the end of their nightmare. Many prisoners were looking forward to a new life after their discharge, while at the same time they would worry about whether their identities as a 'former prisoner' or 'former drug user' would be exposed. The next chapter will examine former prisoners' experiences of post-discharge life. Again, the backstage behaviour of the local police officers had shown them the opposite picture from that portrayed in the party propaganda. The concern for surveillance and control of former prisoners and former drug users had in many cases exposed former prisoners' stigmatized identities.

6
Post-discharge Reintegration and Surveillance

The former prisoners experienced and participated in the hypocritical system both when they were arrested and during their incarceration. Their experiences after they were released from prison further reinforced their perceptions that the system was indeed breeding hypocrisy more than anything else. While the party propaganda always suggests that the police officers and the local government cadres strive to save the former prisoners, the former prisoners I met and interviewed strongly suggested that the reality was the completely opposite. To them, the local government and police officers had no interest in 'rehabilitating' or 'saving' them. Instead, they did many things that had not only prevented their reintegration but had also brought them shame and humiliation. While former prisoners often blame the police officers' behaviour for their suffering, this chapter frames their experience in a more general context of the policing of 'targeted populations' (*zhongdian renkou* 重點人口). In China, all former prisoners, including those discussed in this study, are categorized as 'targeted populations'. Different policies are made to manage, control, and obtain information about such 'targeted populations'. Since most of these former prisoners were incarcerated because of drug use, many of these control techniques are concerned with the control of former and current drug users. In the following, with the example of four control techniques, I will demonstrate how the concern for control hijacks the concern for education and reintegration and destroys the police's image of 'benevolent saviours'.

'Targeted Populations'

The policing of former prisoners in China can be understood under the broader context of the Chinese government's surveillance of its population, and particularly of the control of the mentioned 'targeted populations'. Local police officers in China are supposed to monitor the entire population within its jurisdiction. However, since it is impossible for the police officers to monitor each and every resident, they prioritize surveillance of the most 'threatening' category of 'targeted populations'. These populations are defined as people who potentially threaten state security and public order. According to official doctrine, they should be governed with special attention (Ministry of Public Security 2012; F. Wang 2004). The establishment of such population categories is not an invention of the Chinese communist government. One of its earlier forms can be found in the Guomindang period. This population category was then called 'special residents' (*tezhong renkou* 特種人口). During the Republican period, these special residents were mainly underground communists. The Communist government continued to use such categories for control purposes after its takeover of China. In 1950 the 'special resident' category was divided into two types. The first type included Guomindang members, 'counter-revolutionaries', and landlords. The second consisted of criminals like thieves, drug users, and prostitutes. The term 'targeted population' was officially adopted in 1953 (H. Wang 2011). In the early days, especially during the Cultural Revolution, targeted populations were mainly defined in political terms. According to Mao's political theory, there were two types of contradictions: contradictions between the people and the enemies and contradictions among the people. The first type of contradictions was seen as antagonistic, the second as non-antagonistic. The idea was that common criminals could be won back through rehabilitation, while the first category of political enemies mainly had to be eliminated (Mao 1965).

The Regulations on Targeted Population Management (*Zhongdian renkou guanli gongzuo guiding* 重點人口管理工作規定) from 1998 is the most recent regulation I could find concerning this matter. The current regulation defines targeted-population management in a simpler 'crime control' manner, although the 'political' aspect still plays a role in selecting people 'under surveillance'. It is just that the political aspect is toned down compared to the days of Maoist rule. The aims of such regulation are stated as 'preventing, uncovering, and fighting crimes; educating, managing, and rehabilitating "rule breakers" (*weifa renyuan* 違法人員) and "law breakers" (*fanzui renyuan* 犯罪人員); and maintaining social stability' (Ministry of Public Security 1998). Targeted populations today include people suspected of 'threatening state security' (*weihai guojia anquan* 危害國家安全), people suspected of 'serious criminal offences' (*yanzhong xingshi fanzui huodong* 嚴重刑事犯罪活動), people who might potentially 'make trouble' (*naoshi* 鬧事), and those 'taking violent revenge' (*xingxiong baofu* 行兇報復). The regulation also mentions ex-inmates from prisons and re-education-through-labour institutions who have been released for less than five years, and finally drug users in general (Ministry of Public Security 1998). Although the list consists of all different types of populations, in practice targeted populations currently consist mainly of former prison inmates and drug users (Hou 2009). There are different types of surveillance of former prisoners in practice. One commonality among these surveillance techniques is that they all, to a certain degree, expose the former prisoners' stigma to their surroundings, a practice that has brought them nothing but continuous unbearable shame and humiliation.

Goffman divided stigma into 'discreditable' stigma and 'discredited' stigma (Goffman 1968b, 5). A stigma is 'discreditable' if it can be concealed. A stigma would be 'discredited' if the stigma is visible or known to the people around the stigmatized person. All former prisoners I met had discreditable stigma, and they wanted to keep this stigma away from their social surroundings. However, different surveillance techniques had often turned their discreditable stigma into a discredited stigma in their social surroundings. In other words, the surveillance techniques exposed former prisoners' stigma to the public gaze.

In the following sections, I will examine four types of surveillance techniques. These four types were selected because they were the ones that were mentioned most frequently by the former prisoners. They included embarrassing and shaming types of 'home visits', 'compulsory urine tests', and the enforcement of 'drug users' online registrations'.

Home Visits (*Jiafang* 家訪), 'Help Education' (*Bangjiao* 幫教), 'Background Information' (*Modi* 摸底), and Shame

According to the regulation, local police officers are required to visit former prisoners and conduct regular background investigations. They are required to be in control of various information like where the former prisoners live, current addresses, nicknames, appearances, financial status, associations, and daily activities. Local police officers are required to do home visits to the former prisoners in their jurisdictions regularly. This kind of visit has two official aims. The first is information collection as described by the existing regulations. Another one is said to be for the rehabilitation of the former prisoners. The Chinese expression for this type of information collection and control is *modi paicha* (摸底排查). *Modi* means to understand one's background information, and *paicha* means to investigate each and every one of the population group. Through visiting and talking with the former prisoners, their family members, and neighbours, police officers collect and update the data.

The second purpose for home visits is for the rehabilitation of the former prisoners. In Chinese, the term they use for such kinds of rehabilitation is 'help education' (*bangjiao* 幫教). *Bang* means 'to offer help' and *jiao* stands for 'to educate'. Help education in real-life practice is usually a heart-to-heart talk between the police officer and the former prisoners. Police officers usually ask them about their adaptation to post-release life to see if they have any difficulties in dealing with issues like their relationship with their families and progress in job-hunting. There are different kinds of stories in the mass media about how the local police officers rehabilitate the former prisoners. The story of Qing who saved the drug addict (in Chapter 2) is only one of the many of these repeatedly told stories that are characterized by a repeated storyline.

The story starts with a person who has broken some law or regulations. That person is either 'bad' or 'miserable' and has 'wrong values' until he or she meets a good police officer. This good police officer then sacrifices his or her own good to educate and convince this person to change his or her values and way of life. Then this 'bad' or 'miserable' person becomes good again. We recognize this storyline from the 'cautionary tale' in Chapter 2.

In practice the police officer did come to do home visits and talk to the former prisoner, sometimes he or she even talked to their family members and neighbours. Such visits, from the experience of former prisoners, can be very unpleasant. One former prisoner, Yanzi, told me a story about an unpleasant home visit:

> I was not at home at that time. My neighbour told me that eight police officers had come to my place. Two police cars were parked outside my block. They could not find me because there was nobody at home. Then they knocked on the door of my neighbour and told him that I was a drug user. They had given a phone number to my neighbour and told him to call them if he saw me later. These uniformed police officers and the police cars caught the attention of more than thirty bystanders. You can imagine how I felt at that time when my neighbour told me this. (Yanzi, interview, 2012)

The whole setting of this story is like a scenario in a typical crime movie: Two police vehicles stop in front of a building. Eight brave armed and uniformed police officers get out of the police car and run upstairs towards a door. Such a scenario in a crime movie is usually about police busting a dangerous mafia group, not one single former drug addict inmate. Being targeted in front of their family members and neighbours clearly brings much shame and humiliation to former inmates. To the former prisoners, there was nothing about education in such a scenario, and these police officers were not at all concerned about the well-being of the former inmate. Of course the former offenders do not want to expose their stigmatized identity as 'former drug user' to their neighbours and families. However, what the police officers do in such cases is equivalent to a public announcement of the former inmate's stigma. It has turned the discreditable stigma into a discredited stigma in front of everyone. The stigma thus becomes visible to everyone, taking the form of a public shaming process.

It is also true that some of the neighbours of the former prisoners already knew that they were former drug users. However, in such cases, the home visit could send an erroneous message to their neighbours that the former prisoner has relapsed. Many of the former prisoners were very sensitive about how other people might perceive them. Some of them believed that people around them were looking down on them because of their previous experiences. Caixia, a girl who had been jailed for using heroin, knew that many of her neighbours knew about her previous experiences. This is a part of our conversation:

> Caixia: Our type of people is very sensitive. One of my neighbours got a baby. Everybody wanted to hug the baby, but I wouldn't do that. I'm afraid that they [her neighbours] might be afraid of me. I'm afraid that they might reject me in their heart. . . . The children in our neighbourhood very often play in different neighbours' homes. Sometimes their parents

would chit-chat to my mother. However, whenever I came back home, they would stay a while and find an excuse like 'I need to cook' or 'I need to dry the blankets' and then leave.

Author: Do you really think that it is because of you or maybe because they really needed to cook?

Caixia: It was because of me. . . . Maybe in their eyes I am still a drug user. They do not trust you. They just do not trust you.' (Caixia, interview, 2013)

It was not clear whether the neighbours of Caixia were really afraid of her or looking down on her. However, clearly she cared very much about how she was perceived in the eyes of her neighbours. She also told me that she had tried to make her life 'normal' by finding a proper job and quitting drugs. However, when a band of police officers came knocking on her door, spreading her stigma about drug use to everyone standing around, no matter whether she had relapsed into drug use, her neighbours would really believe that she had. While many other former prisoners like Caixia are very sensitive about how they are perceived by their neighbours, the appearance of uniformed police officers would destroy not only their image within the neighbourhood but also their dignity. Instead of taking care and educating the former inmate, this shaming process of putting her in the 'public gaze' had the exact opposite effect from aiding and educating her.

One interesting phenomenon that some of the former prisoners emphasized was that the police officers very often came to do home visits before the international anti-drug day. This apparently repetitive and ritual behaviour on the part of the police also made the former prisoners feel that the reason for the police officers' 'visits' was not done out of reasons of education or even control. Rather, this was the reflection of a bureaucratic routine to improve the police's own performance record. This is how Xian talked about how she was caught during a regular home visit,

It was the anti-drug day. You know people like us who have these records. These days they [the police] have a quota. I knew that they would come to find me sometime before that day. I left home and found somewhere to live for few days, just because I was afraid. I thought that they would not come on that day itself, so I went back home. I didn't expect they would come on that day, but they did, and they caught me. (Xian, interview, 2013)

Xian thought that the reason for the police to come to do the home visit on that international anti-drug day was precisely because it *was* the international anti-drug day. This is a day when the police have to 'prove' their performance, in campaign-style manner, as Chinese policing usually operates. Her impression was not only caused by the fact that the police came on that day, but also because of her previous experiences of being 'hooked' (see Chapter 3). The mindless shaming is pointless from a rehabilitation point of view and can only be understood rationally as a procedure of a management system far removed from any rehabilitative logic. In fact, this bureaucratic procedure is more about management (*guan*) than about education (*jiao*). This also clarifies that the 'system of hypocrisy' is not first and foremost about 'good' or 'bad' police officers but is part of a systematic clash between two different systems and entirely different rationalities, making the 'culture' of hypocrisy into a 'system' of hypocrisy devoid of any personal motivation of the different police officers.

Similarly, if the home visit brings the former prisoners shame within their home environments, the surprise drug test humiliates them everywhere. In the next section I will explain how the drug test operated as yet another process of public shaming.

The Drug Test

In China local police officers are required to conduct regular 'drug tests' (*xidu jianche* 吸毒檢測) on former prisoners incarcerated for illicit drug use (National People's Congress 2008). These police officers are responsible for the populations within certain administrative areas (Pan and Lü 1999). Many of the former prisoners would have personally known these police officers in their home places. Different cities might have different concrete policies regarding how many times the local police officers should conduct drug tests on these former prisoners. For example, in Zhejiang, local police officers are required to conduct at least twelve urine tests with each of these former prisoners within the first three years after they are discharged (Zhejiang Province 2008). Some former prisoners claimed the actual number was even higher, while some others said that the actual number was lower. In some cities the police officers conduct such drug tests with the help of the local cadres or social workers; in other cities they did it themselves. The most common way of drug testing, according to the former prisoners, is the 'urine test' (*niaojian* 尿檢). In their experiences, the police officers sometimes conduct surprise inspections. Sometimes it was done during the home visits; sometimes it was done on other occasions. Former prisoners are not against the practice of 'drug tests' per se. But they are against what they called the 'unregulated urine test' (*bu guifan de niaojian* 不規範的尿檢). These unregulated urine test usually do not happen during the regular surprise inspection at home. Rather, they very often were performed when former prisoners were 'caught' by police officers outside their home environment. This is related to the establishment of a nationwide drug user control system that I will come back to later in this chapter.

In my interviews, the former prisoners have talked about the 'good' police practices and the 'bad' police practices in doing the drug test, although most of them talk more about the 'bad' police practices. These different practices have also helped them to differentiate the 'good' police officers from the 'bad' police officers. The major criterion that the former prisoners used to distinguish the 'good' from the 'bad' is whether the police officers had consciously protected them from exposing their stigma.

The 'good' police officers are those who tried to protect the former prisoners from exposing their stigmatized identity. This type of police officers, according to the former prisoners, is not only aware of the protection of their identity but also willing to sacrifice their own good in order to do so. The 'bad' police officers are those who exposed their stigma to the surrounding people and at the same time did so for self-interest. Hua gave an example of good police officer:

> Do you know how lucky I was . . . ? When they [the police officers] came, I was doing business with a couple. They wanted to order a wedding cake and the woman was very picky. One police officer came to ask me, 'What is your name?' I asked him back, 'What's going on?' He said, 'It's all right, [let's wait until] you finish your business.' They were in uniform. They parked their car outside the shop and waited for like three hours when I was doing the business. The [woman] asked me about many different issues. I needed to call the head office for many of her requests. The width, the length, the colours, she wanted everything to be done according to her requests. We talked for like three hours, a bit less than three hours. They [police officers] had waited for me for three full hours. (Hua, interview, 2012)

Although the police officers came in their uniforms and in their police car, Hua still felt that she was 'lucky'. She felt that these police officers were the good ones. From her point of view, the police officers could have caught Hua right in front of her customers. They did not have to wait for those three hours, but they were willing to sacrifice their time to wait until Hua finished her business so as to minimize the harm done to her. Mirroring the images of the model police officers in the party propaganda, these police officers sort of sacrificed their own good for Hua's. That might explain why Hua and many other former prisoners who knew her experiences thought she had met some good police officers. One important feature of their perceptions is that they all thought Hua was 'lucky' (*yunqi hao* 運氣好) to have met these good police officers. It also implies that from their point of view, most of the police officers are not as good as those whom Hua had met. Indeed, most of the former prisoners' experiences with the 'drug test' were a lot worse.

Many of the former inmates told me stories about police officers who came to accost them in a public area. These police officers, according to the former prisoners, did not care about whether the act would expose their stigmatized identities. Most important, the former prisoners thought that these police officers did the 'drug test' for their own self-interest, like meeting a quota or merely getting 'their job done' without concern for the alleged 'offender'. As mentioned, most of their 'bad' experiences with the drug test happened when they travelled to another administrative region. While the local police officer and the former prisoners very often known each other well, the police officers in other administrative regions usually know nothing about the former prisoners. Whenever former prisoners use their identity cards in a place, the respective local police officer would be informed. Behind it is a nationwide management and control system specifically targeting any person who has been officially recorded as a 'drug addict'.

The Drug User Management and Control System

In 2006 the Chinese Public Security Bureau established a 'drug user information database' (*xidu renyuan xinxi shuju ku* 吸毒人員信息數據庫) and a 'dynamic management and control system' (*dongtai guankong xitong* 動態管控系統) to keep track of the current status of former and current drug users who had been caught for using illicit drugs. In 2013, 2.47 million current and former drug users were recorded in the system (Office of China National Narcotics Control Commission 2014). Chinese scholars suggest that one of the main obstacles in drug rehabilitation is that these drug users are very often 'highly mobile' (*liudong xing da* 流動性大) and hide from the public (J. Li 2004; G. Sun 2007; Xue et al. 2011). *Liu* (流) in Chinese has a connotation of 'drift' and 'flow', which is often connected to a more general fear of modernity and unpredictability (Bakken 2000). *Liu* is working against control, stability, and predictability, and is thus treated with a lot of suspicion. The deviant, the unlawful, and the irregular are seen as a danger to general stability, and the police are basically caring about questions of stability rather than the well-being of the 'unstable'. The loss of control of the drug users is used to explain their high relapse rate (J. Li 2004; G. Sun 2007; Xue et al. 2011). The reason for the establishment of the 'database' and the 'control system' is to address this problem. Information about all current and former drug users known by the police, all inmates in compulsory drug rehabilitation centres, and all drug addicts in the detention centres are recorded in the database. In practice, according to the former prisoners, their experiences with the 'control system' were sometimes a lot worse than being in an information collection system.

In the experiences of the former prisoners, this 'control system' had put their personal information into the nationwide database. Whenever they are required to show their 'identity card' (*shenfen zheng* 身份證) in places like motels, Internet cafes, roadblocks, and airports in mainland China, the local police officers would be alerted and come to make them take a drug test. This can sometimes be a very humiliating process since very often several police officers would come in their uniforms and 'catch' the former drug users. The worst cases happened when the former inmates 'refused to cooperate'—they would rapidly be handcuffed and humiliated in several ways. The official regulations authorize police to use 'compulsory' (*qiangzhi* 強制) measures if the person 'refuses to undergo the test' (*jujue jiezhou jiancha* 拒絕接受檢查) (National People's Congress 2008). Neither the definitions of 'refuse' nor 'compulsory' are clearly stated. Lili told me how that system works in real life:

> On a highway checkpoint, a police officer stopped a coach for a routine check. He got on the bus and there were a group of men on the bus. He collected everyone's ID cards and checked them with a portable ID scanner. The scanner gave a warning notice when he started scanning the first ID card. To his surprise, the scanner gave warning notice not only on the first ID card, but also on each of the other ID cards. A guy on the bus joked, 'Here you are with a coach of criminals.' He explained to

the police that they were on their way back from a prison. They all were discharged from that prison, well rehabilitated, and now working in a job-placement centre [*jiuye jidi* 就業基地]. They went to the prison again on that day to conduct a 'help education' session for the current inmates there. (Lili, interview, 2012)

Lili kept giggling when she told me this story. This is the experience of her friend, and I also laughed after listening to this story. However, Lili also hinted that the whole scene could have been very different. If there had been only one former prisoner on the bus, the scene would have been very embarrassing, and that former prisoner would feel tremendous pangs of shame. Many former prisoners are afraid of going to another city because they might be checked and frisked by the police officers at the roadblock, or the police officers would come after the former inmate checks into a motel. One former drug user, Qin, expressed her fear of such a possible scenario in her diary in 2010:

> Because of my good performance, I became the purchasing manager of the company. It was originally a good thing because I could learn new knowledge and skills . . . , but I do not know whether I was lucky or unlucky to get this job. They arranged a training trip for me. I tried to put it off but they insisted that I had to go. My colleagues thought that I acted very weird. Any other person would love to go, because you can go on a trip and work at the same time. I was arranged to share a room with a colleague. What if the police come after I check in with my ID card? Will she believe that I have quit drugs for eight years? What if she tells the company about it? What if our bus is stopped at a police roadblock? So many people will be on the bus. How should I explain it to them? It's too difficult! (Qin, diary entry, 2010)

Qin's diary entry expresses a fear that is constantly haunting many former prisoners. Other former prisoners' stories also informed me that many of their experiences of being checked are not as funny as Lili's story. Indeed, what we can see behind this story is the big database in which the information of these former prisoners is recorded, and the process of the ID check has led to the public humiliation of many a former prisoner. A local NGO report shows that in Yunnan, among the people who have been forced to do drug test because of the 'control system' (n=105), 14.3 per cent of them were handcuffed before the drug test, and 38.1 per cent of them reported that they were 'treated in uncivilized ways' (*bu wenming duidai* 不文明對待) (Xue et al. 2010). The same report shows that in Guangxi 45.2 per cent of people who have experienced the 'control system' (n=84) were handcuffed when they were caught by the police before the drug test, and 40.5 per cent reported that they were 'treated in uncivilized ways'. In this report, the ways that the police officers conduct the drug test are divided into those that are 'civilized' (*wenming* 文明) and 'uncivilized' (*bu wenming* 不文明). This categorization also echoes what the former prisoners called the 'good' police practices and the 'bad' police practices. Here are some examples of what the former prisoners called the bad practice. These 'bad practices' have not only affected the life opportunities of the former prisoners but also triggered their anger towards the outside society. Lili shared another experience of her friend:

> My friend used his ID card to check in at a cyber cafe. He had just come back (from the prison). His ID card was connected to the local police station, and he was caught. He was jailed for nine hours (in the local police station). They made him do the drug test three times. All negative. They then let him go. The police officer said to him before he left, 'You can escape this time, but I will for sure catch you next time.' (Lili, interview, 2012)

What we can see in this story is that the former prisoners suffered from this 'control system'. Their suffering does not only come from being incarcerated for long hours, repeated drug test, or the provocative words of that police officer; it also comes from their feeling of the loss of hope and the violation of their original expectations upon release from the prison. One diary entry of Bing vividly reflects such a contradiction between hope and frustration. It was one week after his discharge from prison:

> On 8 November, with my hope for a better life, I jumped on the train to this new city. My cousin introduced me to a boss of a logistic company here. I went to that city and checked into a motel. I called the boss, and he said that we could meet at five in the afternoon. So I went out to have lunch. It was about four when I finished. I went back to the motel. I didn't realize that the three people behind me were coming for me. When I opened the door, they burst into my room and told me they were from the local police station. They pinned me down on the bed. They searched my luggage and found nothing there. They then tied me up with my belt and sent me to the police station. When we were in the police station, they didn't even ask anything. They took all my cash and told me to take off my shoes and socks. They locked me in a room. I was so angry. 'I didn't break any law. On what grounds do you lock me up?' I said. One hour later, a police officer came to make me do the urine test. Without telling me the result, they locked me up again. At around twelve, the police came to make me do another urine test for 'new drugs' again.[1] Then they asked me to squat in the corner of the jail barefoot... until about two in the morning, [when] the police gave me back my things and told me, 'You can leave now.' I said it was midnight and I didn't know the way. I asked them to drive me back [to the motel]. They rejected me. I was angry, but left the police station. I called the boss the next day, he told me he could not come and see me. ... I later found out that he asked the motel counter, and the staff told him I was arrested by the police. He then went to the police station and the police told him I had a 'history of drug use' [*xidu shi* 吸毒史]. So he decided not to have me in his company. (Bing, diary entry, 2010)

Bing's experiences had again pointed out the two important effects of the 'control system' to the former prisoners. First, the 'control system' had directly

---

1. 'New drugs' (xinxing dupin 新型毒品) in China refers to club drugs like MDA, MDMA, and Ketamine (Xia et al. 2009).

affected their life opportunities. While some former prisoners reflected that they were fired because their stigmatized identity was exposed, many of them actually gave up different opportunities to get jobs or promotions so as to avoid the shame and humiliation that might have followed from the exposure of their identity. The identity as 'former prisoner' and 'drug user' is clearly stigmatized. The former prisoners would avoid any incident that could expose their identity as 'drug users'. Almost all the former inmates said that they did not want to expose their previous identity to their colleagues or bosses. The 'control system', however, put them in the potential danger of exposing their identity. Business trips, training trips, and travelling—the former prisoners feel they cannot participate in any of these activities. They always need to find different excuses to reject the invitation and sometimes reject the promotions that require these types of travelling or other activities. The former prisoners expected that they would be humiliated, rejected, or even fired if their identities were exposed.

Second, the way in which the police officers had handled their cases made them feel like they were still treated as criminals or prisoners; something that had destroyed their hopes of having a new life with dignity. These former prisoners had experienced how it was like to be arrested and incarcerated. They could still remember the painful feeling of lost dignity when they were under custody and being dominated by the prison officers and the powerful prison inmates. Being released from prison is supposed to symbolize freedom from these devastating feelings. However, the drug test had brought them back to the scenario that they were supposed to be freed from. They felt like they were not trusted. They were still treated as criminal suspects. They still did not have the rights that normal people should have. Bing received no explanation from the police officers and was forced do what he was told to do. That is the life of an 'eternal prisoner', not that of a free person. It produces frustration and anger.

The 'home visit' and 'control system' were two of the most common stories told when I asked the former prisoners about their current lives. Their anger against the police officers continued to exist after they were released from the *laojiao*. Their experiences of 'hooking' told them that the police had no interest in helping or saving them. Their experiences with the control system had further confirmed such perceptions. This had further contributed to the formation of the 'hypocritical system' in China. The police officers who exposed the former prisoner's stigmatized identity to his neighbours and the police officers who forced Bing to do the drug test stand in stark contrast to the benevolent police officers of cautionary tales in the media who 'sacrifice their own selves in order to save and educate the drug users'. Police officers are supposed to treat former prisoners like 'victims' as portrayed in the propaganda. Many former prisoners asked me, 'Are we not supposed to be patients? Are we not also victims?' Clearly under the 'control system' they were treated as suspects, if not criminals, instead of being treated as victims.

Revocation of Drug Users' Driver's Licences

The 'control system' is a result of the party's concern for control. The former prisoners are believed to be highly mobile and therefore dangerous and in need of tighter controls. If the 'control system' is an attempt to tighten the government and police's control over the populations of former prisoners or drug users, the new laws in 2012 regarding the revocation of drug users' driver's licences would aim at the eradication of potential drug users from the road. The problem of traffic accidents resulting from 'drug-driving' (*dujia* 毒駕) had rarely been reported as a problem before 2009. Beginning in 2009 more and more of these cases were reported in newspapers. Compared to 2009, in 2010 the number of reported cases of drug-driving increased sixfold (Zhu et al. 2010). This number, however, may not so much show the actual increase in one year as the heightened attention to the problem by the police force. In 2012 a new regulation was issued by the Public Security Bureau to target drug-driving (Ministry of Public Security 2012). According to this regulation, the driving licences of all people who were listed in the 'drug user information database' will be suspended. Moreover, all people who are listed as 'drug users' (*xidu renyuan* 吸毒人員) will not be allowed to apply for a driver's licence. By the end of 2013, 24,000 former or current drug users' driver's licences were revoked. Three thousand former or current drug users' applications for driver's licences were rejected (Office of China National Narcotics Control Commission 2014). This regulation was implemented after I had come back to Hong Kong following the first round of my fieldwork in 2012. The number might not be very high and not all the former prisoners whom I had met were affected by this policy. However, some of these former prisoners' lives were severely disrupted by this policy.

Shan made his living by driving an 'unlicensed taxi' (*heiche* 黑車) after he was discharged from the prison. He could earn up to ¥10,000 per month. One day he drove me to his house to give me his prison diary. On the way, he told me the following story:

> My ex-wife bought me this car after I was discharged from the prison. I am lucky when I compare myself with others. At least I have a car and can make my living. I have nothing to complain about. This job is a bit risky, though. It is an unlicensed taxi after all. I need to hide from the traffic police. I want to apply for a job in a taxi company. Although I will earn a lot less, like around ¥5,000, my life will be more stable. (Field notes 2012)

When I arrived at Shan's house, he showed me many pictures of his ex-wife. He felt indebted to his ex-wife who left him after he had relapsed so many times. More than once he told me, 'This car is a gift from my wife.' His car symbolized his ex-wife's blessings to his post-discharge life. Driving is more than Shan's way of making a living; it also symbolizes his ex-wife's expectations and his hope for a new life. I lost contact with Shan after I went back to Hong Kong. According to one of his friends, not being able to become a taxi driver, he went on to work as an unlicensed driver. He was, however, caught for unlicensed driving, and his car was confiscated. Among all the former prisoners I have met, Shan is the only one who was caught after the implementation of the new regulation. Among my survey with twenty-eight former prisoners, only six were affected by the regulation, but sixteen of them thought that it is a problematic regulation. Besides the immediate effect of being deprived of the rights of driving, one of the most important impacts of the new regulation is that it has become the signal to former prisoners that the government does not care about their livelihood. To them, it has become evident that the party propaganda is hypocritical. In 2013 I was invited by a former prisoner to join a QQ chat group in which people were in the midst of a long discussion about the revocation of former drug users' driver's licences. One entry read:

> The government department is the one that takes the lead in discrimination.... Talk in one way and do things in another way.... They said that all government officers should not discriminate the discharged drug users... and (talk about) help education and job placement.... If the government do not trust us who have had a drugs history, how can you expect other people to trust us? I have gone through all these difficulties to find a job and reintegrate into society, now you again pushed us to the dead end. (QQ entries 2013)

Another entry read:

> I think only if a hero comes to blow up the government department, then someone might notice. Whoever does that I will bring flowers to his grave every year. (QQ entries 2013)

The first former prisoner had expressed his view about the hypocrisy of the system in his entry. To him, the government should do what it has said—that is, take the lead in protecting former drug users. However, his reality was totally opposite. The second entry had clearly shown the anger of the former prisoner not only towards the police officers but towards the government or the party in general. In this chat group there are many entries about the Communist Party (*Gongchandang* 共產黨). From March 2013 to June 2014, among eighty-seven entries mentioning the term *Gongchandang*, seventy-five were negative comments. Some of these negative comments blame the party for their suffering. One of the entries stated, 'The Communist Party doesn't want us to be alive.' Another wrote, 'Does the motherfucking Communist Party want to give us any room for survival at all?'

These types of entries specifically target the new regulation. To them, this law is made by the Chinese government, and in their view the party should thus be responsible for the negative influences of the law on the former prisoners. Targeting the new regulation, some former prisoners express their view that the party is hypocritical. One said, 'The Communist Party said we should reform, but how? Now l lost my driver's licence! How can I reform, my friend?' Another one said, 'Communist Party's law only sounds good on the surface... pathetic!'

Facing this system of hypocrisy, many other comments express the feeling of helplessness, since it was almost impossible for them to overtly resist the party. For example, one wrote, 'This is the Communist Party's land, the Communist Party is the "law".' Another wrote, 'Sigh, it's so pathetic, what can we do? We are under the Communist Party's rule.' Yet another wrote, 'What we can do now is only grumbling on the Internet, we are living under the oppression of the Communist Party.' This type of entries has gone beyond the new regulation and expressed former prisoners' view on how the party rules in general. These entries include comments like 'The Communist party has been thoroughly corrupted (*lan dao guzi li qu le* 爛到骨子裡去了),' and 'The Communist Party is so fucking dark (*tai tama heian* 太他媽黑暗).' There are even more rude comments about the party not fit for presentation here.

Concluding Remarks

All former prisoners are put into the category of targeted populations in China. Different systems and policies are established to enhance the government's control. Although there are also regulations and policies regarding the education and rehabilitation of former prisoners, what we can see from this chapter is that the concern for education and rehabilitation seems to be overridden by the concern for control. The control of former prisoners and former drug users operates under a bureaucratic system that has almost nothing to do with education. Police officers, like mindless robots operating within the bureaucracy, were required to fill in forms about the updated information about the former prisoners. They were required to respond to the warnings given by the 'dynamic management and control system'. They were required to revoke the former drug users' driver's licences. They work within and according to the system. Whether the surveillance tactics would expose former prisoners' 'stigmatized identities' is not a concern of the system and completely irrelevant to the management of the former prisoners. Unlike the shaming methods involved in the prison initiation ceremony, the humiliation and shaming brought about by the 'home visit', the surprise drug test, and the drug user management and control system could better be seen as the unintended consequences of the system of control. However, from the former prisoners' point of view, it was not a matter of whether the police officers intentionally exposed their stigmatized identities. It was that both the police officers and the state-imposed control system *do not care* about exposing their identities.

Again, former prisoners' experiences of post-incarceration life showed them that those stories in the media about how the model police officers save the drug users were mere hypocrisy. Their experiences in post-discharge life not only reconfirm that the police are acting in hypocritical ways but have also made some of them view the entire party-state as a hypocritical entity. These issues came up over and over again during the interviews and talks I had with the former drug user inmates. From the former prisoners' experiences we can see that the concern for education or reform has been devoured by the concern for control. While former prisoners' lives are constrained by the surveillance of a nationwide control system, they cannot find what the party or government has done to help them to reintegrate into society.

7
Conclusion

When I presented my idea about the discrepancies between the propaganda and the former prisoners' experiences at an academic conference in 2013, someone in the audience commented:

> I do not know if you had read about it, but in psychology, we know that criminals tend to blame the police officers and the prison officers so as to make themselves feel better. What's the problem with that?

This argument resonates with the neutralization thesis. It was not clear whether the commentator just wanted to test me or if he was blaming the former prisoners for 'rejecting the rejector', thus belittling the former prisoners' complaints (McCorkle and Korn 1954). On another occasion, a scholar asked me, 'What's so special about former prisoners hating police officers? I would be surprised if they did not.' Both statements above have pointed out a taken-for-granted 'natural facts of life' (Garfinkel 1964, 225) argument held by many people; that criminals and former offenders hate those enforcing the law. The whole matter is regarded as self-explanatory. It is as simple as the fact that 'the rat hates the cat'. However, looking at this question from a humanitarian, or even a rehabilitative, perspective, former prisoners have suffered both physically and mentally from their experiences. First comes the physical pain they suffer during incarceration. Then the humiliation and shaming they suffer from the day they were arrested will often follow them throughout life. From the perspective of 'rehabilitation', as Sherman (1993) indicates, the feelings of injustice and unfairness are counterproductive to offender rehabilitation. It is difficult to imagine how the former prisoners can be 'reformed' through these processes. In a speech delivered in the House of Commons as far back as 1910, a young Winston Churchill announced, 'The mood and temper of the public in regard to the treatment of crime and criminals is one of the most unfailing tests of the civilization of any country' (cited in Eady 2007, 264).

While Churchill's later life may not always have reflected that of a reformer, the quote has become part of his legacy, and may have been inspired by the famous British prison reformer John Howard (1726–1790) who strongly advocated a humane and rehabilitative prison system instead of an inhumane, punitive, and non-rehabilitative system. This quote emphasizes the basic humanistic idea of rehabilitation, an idea the Chinese party and state claims they subscribe to in their propaganda. However, the prisons that the former prisoners experienced were the opposite: inhumane, punitive, and non-rehabilitative.

Moreover, as Garfinkel (1964) reminds us, it is essential for social scientists, and particularly sociologists, to detect the essential features of socially recognized 'familiar scenes' and relate them to dimensions of social organization. It is important for sociologists, again according to Garfinkel, to 'produce reflections through which the strangeness of an obstinately familiar world can be detected'. While I would agree that it might be normal for the former prisoners to dislike the police officers and the prison officers, I do find such 'strangeness' behind their narratives. It is the failure of rehabilitation; a clear commonality in their complaints is that they criticize the police and prison officers for being 'self-interested', and it is common for inmates to see the whole system as one based on sheer hypocrisy. I have tried to capture these attitudes of the former inmates I interviewed. On the one hand, this study treats the former prisoners' complaints as important in their own right and, on the other hand, sees these complaints as a 'window' through which the failure of a rehabilitative system and a broader system of hypocrisy can be revealed (Bauman 1993; Xu 2010).

The Failure of Education and Rehabilitations

In party propaganda, both the police officers and the prison officers have been portrayed as important components in the education and rehabilitation of the former or current drug users. However, what the former prisoners had experienced in the prisons and after their discharge was the complete opposite of what had been propagated, and their daily life was instead full of physical torture, humiliations, and lies.

As reflected by the names of the prisons—'*re-education* through labour' and 'compulsory isolation for drugs *rehabilitation* centres'—re-education and rehabilitation are presented as, and are supposed to be, the essence of imprisonment. Former prisoners' narratives have, however, presented a completely different picture and brought us to the dark side of the system. What we can see from chapters 4 and 5 is that the prisons are inhumane and have failed to deliver a system of rehabilitations. To many former prisoners, their experiences of imprisonment were simply about *physical* and *mental torture*. Former prisoners were physically tortured during the prolonged 'quiet-sitting', the 'march-drilling', the violent inmates' initiation ceremonies like *guoban* and 'cold baths', and their prolonged compulsory labour. They were also mentally tortured when they were humiliated during the 'strip-search', and when they were forced to follow the degrading paramilitary etiquette. Instead of 'education' or 'rehabilitation', shaming and humiliation have become the core features of imprisonment in China.

While it was suggested that the Chinese government used both disintegrative and reintegrative shaming to rehabilitate the offenders (X. Chen 2002), the former prisoners' experiences of incarceration and post-discharge life told us that they had been shamed *dis*-integratively instead of *re*-integratively (Braithwaite 1989). Braithwaite shows that official sanctions usually result in shaming without the efforts of reconciling the offender with the community. He called this process 'disintegrative shaming' (Braithwaite 1989, 55). In this process, formal sanction becomes a degradation ceremony that shames the *offenders* and transforms the labels into master status. Through this process, offenders are excluded from the support from their families, schools, and the wider community. This also increases the attraction of these labelled offenders to criminal subcultural groups that are more likely to provide social support for crime. Braithwaite, however, suggests that shame can also be used to reconcile offenders to the community. He calls this kind of shaming 'reintegrative shaming' (Braithwaite 1999, 55). This is an informal mediation that starts by community disapproval of the offenders' *act* but is followed by gestures of reacceptance into their original community. Gestures of reacceptance can be everything from a smile that symbolizes forgiveness to a lengthier ceremony that is aimed to 'decertify' the criminal as deviant. With this process in place, it would be less likely for the offenders to develop a negative self-perception.

According to Braithwaite's definition, the shaming that the former prisoners in this study had experienced in prison and after they were discharged was clearly disintegrative. It was the *prison inmates* themselves, instead of their *acts*, that were shamed. They were humiliated, degraded, and deprived of their basic human dignity. There was also no 'gesture of reacceptance' in the experiences of the former prisoners. Their comment that 'they do not treat us as a human beings' has clearly shown their experiences of disintegrative shaming in the prison. Similarly, in Chapter 6 I have shown that they were still humiliated by the system after they were discharged. The unpleasant home visit, the surprise drug test, and the nationwide 'control system' in many cases exposed the former prisoners' stigmatized identity to the public and put them into embarrassing and humiliating situations. Perhaps different from the case in *laojiao/qiangge*, the continued shaming and humiliation after release may or may not be intended. However, the pain brought to the former prisoners was similar.

Moreover, the prison inmates do not learn anything other than mere survival strategies through the incarceration system. As seen in Chapter 4, during incarceration, instead of being rehabilitated, the former prisoners learned to talk and behave as if they were rehabilitated. Instead of learning the ways of 'becoming a better person', the prisoners learned the 'ways of lying' (Bakken 2000). In order to survive the system, prison inmates learned how to overtly perform self-criticism through both the writing of 'autobiographies' and 'inmates' trials'. The inmates had learned how to be hypocritical so as to survive the painful and inhumane prison environment. What we can see here is that the 'prison' system has broken its promise of rehabilitation. It has also created a type of humiliation that goes against the basic human dignity of the inmates.

Propaganda and Moral Expectations

Besides the failure of rehabilitation, another important implication we can derive from the former prisoners' narratives is that the 'system of hypocrisy' is formed by the discrepancy of party propaganda, on the one hand, and the practical reality, on the other hand. The party propaganda about the model police and prison officers seems to be working well, until the former prisoners encounter the police and prison officers in real life. It is clear from my conversations with the former inmates that they all *expected* the police and the prison officers to possess at least some qualities portrayed in the propagandistic tales of heroic and upright helpers. In other words, the morally upright and sacrificing officer was a tale internalized by the inmates before incarceration. The reality came crashing down on them only when they were arrested and during their time in jail. During my interviews I encountered persons who still felt betrayed and lied to, people who had seen the contrast between propaganda and reality, and who had begun to see the whole system as one based on sheer hypocrisy.

It might be common for former prisoners or former offenders in most contexts to be afraid of or to dislike the police and prison officers. However, it might not be common for them to blame the police officers and prison officers for being 'self-interested' and see such behaviour as an 'immoral' quality. In other contexts, in modern-day China, as elsewhere, by saying someone is 'self-interested' one may not even imply a criticism, since every person is expected to be somehow 'self-interested'. As Adam Smith (1937, 14) wrote in *The Wealth of Nations*, 'It is not from the benevolence of the butcher, the brewer, or the baker that we expect our dinner, but from their regard to their own interest.' Here, whether 'self-interested' is moral or not is less important than whether it can contribute to effective economic performance. Of course, this is a far cry from the Maoist 'we' of collectivism and self-sacrifice, but still may be expected in today's China. Similarly, in criminology, there are many concerns about people's perceptions about 'police performance' (Cao et al. 1996; Cheurprakobkit 2000; Weitzer and Tuch 2005). Seldom, however, is there any concern about whether people think the police officers are 'self-interested'.[1] When the former prisoners in this study complained that the officers were 'self-interested', they demonstrated their moral expectations towards both the police officers and the prison officers: to serve in the interest of the drug users and the prison inmates.

---

1. There are a wide variety of studies about 'police ethic/morality' in its own right. These studies are more about the content of that ethic or morality. However, the focus in this study is about how people, particularly former prisoners, perceive what 'moral' means, how such moral expectation is created, and why these expectations were not met in the reality.

One of the origins of such a moral expectation, I would argue, is the moralistic tales of party propaganda.

As I mentioned in Chapter 2, through party propaganda, the images of different model police and prison officers were distilled down to the everyday life of the general public. Similar to what Xu (2012) called the 'political performances', the stories of the models can be seen as the state's 'theatrical performance' or 'impression management' strategy (Goffman 1958). In the propaganda, the images of different model officers were carefully tailored to portray them as either the 'hero' or the 'saviour'. The core moral quality, as reflected in the propaganda, is the spirit of 'self-sacrifice'. One might argue that it is in the Chinese culture that people put emphasis on 'collectivism' and despise 'individualism', that there is a culture in which 'self-sacrifice' is glorified, and 'selfishness' is disgraced (Bakken 2000; X. Chen 2002). However, as Bakken (2000) reminds us, 'Chinese culture' is not a static but a malleable entity. The Chinese Communist Party selects and propagates specific cultural norms—the 'exemplary norms'—for the purpose of maintaining stability. 'Self-sacrifice' for the collective good is one of these selected norms of exemplary behaviour. In this context, the norm becomes a 'super-social norm', one that is propagated, managed, and enforced rather than being a product of a living culture. The purpose of the propaganda is to educate and to enhance the 'moral legitimacy' of the party-government (B. Xu 2012). The logic behind the propaganda is that through propagating the images of models, first, the public can learn from the models by imitating these models (Bakken 2000); second, the public can accept the image of the models as they are presented and at the same time connect these images to the image of the party-state and thereby enhance the moral legitimacy of the party-state (C. Jiang 2001; B. Xu 2012; R. Yan 2004). Through this repetitive and imitative process, people will gradually internalize such moral norms in themselves. At least so goes the methodology of party propaganda.

The 'Hideous Reality'

This theory of how propaganda is supposed to work, however, often fails to operate in the expected ways, depending on the experiences of the people who are subject to this propaganda. Much like in Scott's analysis (1990) on 'public transcripts', the effect of propaganda, as demonstrated by former prisoners' narratives, is very different from what the party-state would expect. Instead of simply accepting the ideology behind the propaganda, the former prisoners form expectations according to the propaganda. That is not to say that the former prisoners' expectations are exactly the same as what has been propagated. No former prisoners would expect officers to sacrifice their lives for the good of the public, but they do expect officers to work for the good of the drug users—to 'fight the evil drug dealers', and to 'save the drug users'. However, with their real-life experiences with the police and the prison officers, no former prisoner thinks that the reality is even close to the stories in the propaganda.

As Chapters 3 to 6 have shown, the logic that governs the day-to-day practices of the local police and prison officers are completely irrelevant to the logic behind the making of the propaganda. In Chapter 3 I have shown that under the state bureaucracy, the police officers are assigned with the duty to meet certain performance criteria, in our case typically an arrest quota. The use of 'hooks' is a convenient tactic for the police officers to meet the arrest quota. However, to the former prisoners, this was evidence that the police officers were not interested in 'educating' or 'saving' them. Instead, they saw it as collusion between the police officers and drug dealers and other drug users. Besides meeting the arrest quota, the police officers are also required to control and manage information about the former prisoners and former drug users. The requirements are imposed bureaucratically and these requirements have nothing to do with 'heroically fighting the drug dealers' or 'saving the drug users'. These are structural requirements of a police bureaucracy, and as Weber has pointed out, the original meaning of bureaucracy is 'that which is not human'. It has little to do with kindness and morality and the heroic tales about how the self-sacrifice of the officers aids the drug user.

Similarly, the prison officers are required to maintain order in the prison environment. They are also assigned to operate the prison factory efficiently. The concern for order and effective operation of prison the factory has superseded the concern for education. Throughout their encounters with the police and prison officers, the inmates saw the cooperation between the officers, the so-called hooks, and inmate elites. They were also constantly shamed and humiliated throughout the process of incarceration, and this humiliation continued even after they were discharged. Although shaming has been one important component in traditional Chinese education and reform philosophy, the former prisoners did not see the police officers or the prison officers as having the intention of 'educating' or 'saving' them.

This confrontation of myth and reality is particularly acute when the former prisoners' stigmatized identities are exposed by the 'management and control system'. Former inmates continue to be harassed years after their release, and together with policies like the revocation of drug users' driver's licences, the former prisoners are constantly reminded that the police officers do not care about their 'rehabilitation or reintegration'. In many ways, what the former inmates instead experienced is a continuous process of shaming and humiliation. This continuous type of shaming is disintegrative rather than reintegrative.

When former prisoners criticized the police officers and the prison officers, very often they were also criticizing the 'Communist Party'. The term 'Communist Party' was sometimes used interchangeably with the terms 'police officers' and 'prison officers'. While the former inmates were complaining about the officers, they were also complaining about the 'party'. This again goes back to the party propaganda, and comes back at the party as distrust and hatred rather than as trust and love for the party as prescribed in the propaganda.

The 'Models' and the Communist Party: A Double-Edged Sword

In Chapter 2 I have shown that in the propaganda about model police and prison officers the two were always subtly linked to the party-government. By showing the models as morally upright, the propaganda also bolsters the idea that the party-state is morally upright. The main purpose of this strategy is to enhance the authority and the legitimacy of the party-state (C. Jiang 2001; B. Xu 2012; R. Yan 2004). This strategy, however, can be seen as a double-edged sword. If the performance of the local police and prison officers can fit into what has been described in the propaganda, the party-state's image and thereby its moral legitimacy might be enhanced. However, if the reality is opposite to what has been portrayed, the party's image might actually be threatened. From the former prisoners' perspectives, they were not convinced that the party-state is as good as the model officers in the propaganda. Instead, they connected the behaviours of the police officers and the prison officers to the party-state. While the former prisoners criticized the police officers and the prison officers as being 'self-interested', they also criticized the party-state for being hypocritical. They saw the propaganda as what the party-state had 'said', and they saw the behaviour of the police officers and the prison officers as what the party-state had done.

In the last part of Chapter 6, I have mentioned that the former prisoners express their grievances with the party through an online chat group. Their complaints are not only targeting the revocation of drug users' driver's licences. Instead, it should be seen as a result of a whole series of life experiences—of being arrested, incarcerated, as well as of a range of experiences from their post release lives. Although the former prisoners I met might not have been as angry as those in the chat group, it is clear that they see the whole party-state as being hypocritical. My analysis has also shown that the system itself is indeed hypocritical, especially when it presents the 'front stage' of propaganda and the 'backstage' of the actual practices to the former prisoners. Such a contradiction, I would argue, possibly threatens rather than enhances the party-state's legitimacy.

The Demise of Exemplary Models and Ideological Resistance

Brady (2008) seems to have overestimated the power of the modern party propaganda in her monograph *Marketing Dictatorship*, and she may also have underestimated Chinese audiences' ability to resist the propagated ideology. As demonstrated by former prisoners' experiences, instead of accepting the party-propagated ideology as reflected in the exemplary models, Chinese audiences have the ability to scrutinize the propaganda and compare such propaganda with their real-life experiences. On 5 March 2013, which was the national 'learn from Lei Feng day' (*xuexi Lei Feng jinian ri* 學習雷鋒紀念日), three movies about the exemplary model Lei Feng were released in Nanjing. They turned out to be so unpopular that many theatres were not able to sell even one ticket (Levin 2013). When I talked about this movie with a former prisoner, she said that Lei Feng is now more of a joke in China since his complete 'selflessness' is so unrealistic in the modern society. It seems that the power of the national 'models' is now far weakened from what it used to be. Brady (2008) makes a point out of how propaganda is renewed and strengthened in the new millennium, but in terms of 'model learning' this seems not to be a case where propaganda has achieved such success. Maybe this is also a question of which audience one looks at since the former inmates seemed to have internalized the tales of heroic and self-sacrificing officers *before* their experiences of incarceration.

In 2014 when I was formulating my thoughts about the system of hypocrisy, I discussed the idea with a group of research students coming from Mainland China. None of them was surprised by the fact that the party-state presented itself in a way that was completely different from reality. Propaganda about different 'models' was so prevalent that it had become a part of their lives. While nobody actually believed in traditional models like Lei Feng, the power of the new types of 'normal people' models like the model police officers is still functioning (Ding and Li 2010). These 'normal people', much like the traditional models, are portrayed as 'exemplary models'. However, as I have demonstrated, the power of these 'exemplary models' no longer functions according to the will of the party-state. The party propaganda has in fact created an idealism that cannot be realized in real life. More importantly, model police and prison officers are only two out of many other types of 'models' propagated on state-controlled media on a day-to-day basis. While 'normal' citizens do not have many chances to see the 'backstage' of the criminal justice system, they do have chances to see the 'reality' in other arenas. With reference to former prisoners' experiences, it would also be reasonable to believe that other audiences can also see the hypocrisy behind the propaganda of certain exemplary models. Another possible consequence of the existence of such hypocrisy is the diminishing effect of the credibility of state propaganda in general. In the 2010s one joke has become popular on the Internet:

> Question: Why does the *National News Broadcast* [*Xinwen lianbo* 新聞聯播] have the most expensive television commercial time slot?
> Answer: Because businessmen know that those who like to watch the *National News Broadcast* are those who can be easily fooled. (Baidu 2014)

When I browse the Chinese online search engine Baidu (百度), this joke can be found on over 35,000 web pages. In *Jokes and Their Relation to the Unconscious*, Sigmund Freud (1976) points out that jokes allow people to avoid 'censorship' and express what would otherwise be prohibited to express. Jokes can also be seen as a 'looking glass' through which the perceived reality can be revealed in a slightly distorted way (Zijderveld 1982). The *National News Broadcast* can be seen as one of the main mass-media outlets through which different stories of the 'models' were told, and different tales of party propaganda is being broadcast. What this joke can reveal is the possible effect of the system of hypocrisy—the loss of credibility of the party propaganda and the ability of the Chinese audiences to resist the party-indoctrinated ideology. It was clear that the former prisoners in this study lost their trust in the party propaganda after they experienced the failing 'rehabilitation' system. It would, however, require further research to see if audiences in other arenas would also resist the party propaganda in similar ways when their experienced realities run contrary to the propaganda.

Appendix: Basic Information of the Former Drug Detainees

| Name | Gender | Area of residence | Age | Experience of incarceration | | | Had been an inmate elite |
				Qiangjie	*Laojiao*	*Qiangge*	
Ai	F	Zhiyang	40–49	✓	✓		
Bang	M	Zhiyang	40–49	✓	✓		✓
Bao	F	Zhiyang	20–29	✓	✓		
Caixia	F	Zhiyang	30–39	✓		✓	
Dage	M	Zhiyang	20–29				✓
Feng	F	Motai	40–49	✓	✓		✓
Fu	F	Zhiyang	40–49	✓	✓		✓
Gu*	F	Motai	30–39				
Hang	M	Motai	40–49	✓	✓		
Hangqi	F	Motai	50–59	✓			
Hao	M	Zhiyang	40–49	✓	✓		
Hai	M	Zhiyang	30–39		✓		
Hua	F	Zhiyang	30–39	✓	✓		
Huang	F	Zhiyang	30–39	✓	✓		
Huangpu	M	Zhiyang	50–59	✓		✓	
Hui	M	Zhiyang	40–49	✓	✓	✓	✓
Jim	M	Zhiyang	20–29	✓	✓	✓	✓
Jing	F	Zhiyang	50–59	✓	✓		✓
Juan	F	Zhiyang	30–39	✓	✓		✓
Kaopu	M	Zhiyang	20–29	✓	✓		✓
Keke	F	Zhiyang	20–29	✓		✓	✓

* I did not obtain detailed personal information about this former drug user.

Name	Gender	Area of residence	Age	Experience of incarceration			Had been an inmate elite
				Qiangjie	Laojiao	Qiangge	
Laoda	M	Zhiyang	50–59	✓	✓		
Lee	F	Motai	40–49	✓	✓		
Lili	F	Zhiyang	40–49	✓	✓		✓
Ling	F	Zhiyang	30–39	✓	✓		✓
Mei	F	Zhiyang	40–49	✓	✓		
Mushi	M	Zhiyang	40–49	✓	✓		✓
Ping	F	Zhiyang	20–29	✓		✓	
Qiang	M	Zhiyang	30–39	✓			
Qing	F	Zhiyang	50–59		✓		
Sansan	F	Zhiyang	30–39	✓	✓		✓
Shan	M	Motai	40–49	✓	✓		
Shufang	F	Zhiyang	30–39	✓	✓		✓
Sun	M	Zhiyang	40–49				
Tian	F	Zhiyang	30–39	✓	✓		
Ting	F	Zhiyang	20–29	✓		✓	✓
Wang	M	Zhiyang	30–39	✓	✓		
Xian	F	Zhiyang	30–39	✓	✓		
Xiao	F	Zhiyang	20–29	✓		✓	✓
Yan	F	Motai	40–49	✓	✓		
Yang	M	Zhiyang	50–59	✓	✓		✓
Yanzi	F	Zhiyang	50–59	✓	✓		✓
Ying	F	Zhiyang	20–29	✓	✓		
Yong	M	Motai	40–49	✓	✓		
Zheng*	M	Motai	30–39				
Zhong*	F	Motai	30–39				

* I did not obtain detailed personal information about this former drug user.

Chinese Glossary

bu shi ren 不是人	are not human beings
daqiang 大牆	great wall
daxue sheng 大學生	university student
gong 宮	palace
guanfang de hua 官方的話	official languages
guanxin women qunti deren 關心我們群體的人	the one who cares about us
jiafang	home visits
jianyu 監獄	prison
kaixin wan 開心丸	happy pill
kanshou suo 看守所	detention centre
ketao hua 客套話	courtesy
laodong gaizao 勞動改造	reform through labour
laodong jiaoyang 勞動教養	re-education through labour
liaojie 了解	understand
limian 裡面	inside
mei renxing 沒人性	inhuman
menmian 門面	lip service
mofan renwu 模範人物	model figures
mofan 模範	model
qiangzhi geli jiedu suo 強制隔離戒毒所	compulsory isolation for drug rehabilitation centre
qiangzhi jiedu suo 強制戒毒所	compulsory drug rehabilitation centre
shuo yitao zuo yitao 說一套，做一套	say things in one way and do things in another

tanxin 談心	heart-to-heart talk
xiao hunhun 小混混	little gangster
xinli xue boshi 心理學博士	PhD in psychology
xuwei 虛偽	hypocrisy
yiban ren 一般人	ordinary people
zhengchang 正常	normal
dang de houshe 黨的喉舌	the mouthpiece of the party
guangming mian 光明面	bright side
yin'an mian 陰暗面	dark side
chengji 成績	achievements
quedian 缺點	shortcomings
xinwen ziyou 新聞自由	freedom of the press
qi bujiang 七不講	seven things that are not to be talked about
zhengfu gongguan xue 政府公關學	government-public relations
zhen shan mei 真善美	truth, good, and beauty
weixin 威信	authority and credibility
zhefu de liliang 折服的力量	power to secure people's submission
gongchandang yuan 共產黨員	Communist Party members
ziwo xisheng 自我犧牲	self-sacrifice
qiongxiong ji'e 窮凶極惡	extremely fierce and vicious
fengkuang 瘋狂	mad
guiji duoduan 詭計多端	tricky
laojian juhua 老奸巨猾	shrewd and crafty
fuyu wankang 負隅頑抗	desperately fight against the police
nanmen lijian zhan dumo 南門利劍斬毒魔	The Southern Sword Slaying the Drug Devil
fenbugushen 奮不顧身	risk one's life
chongfeng xianzhen 衝鋒陷陣	charge towards the battle
shusi bodou 殊死搏鬥	life-and-death battle
kaocha 考察	investigation
zhanyou 戰友	comrades-in-arms
Mian dui mian 面對面	one-to-one

Chinese Glossary

sheshen wangsi 捨身忘死	risk one's life
feiqin wangshi 廢寢忘食	working days and nights almost without sleeping and eating
zuiren 罪人	sinner
fanlan chengzai 泛濫成災	inundate
weihai qinshi 危害侵蝕	endanger and erode
ba shengsi zhi zhi duwai 把生死置之度外	ready to sacrifice one's own life
zuoren yishen zhengqi, weiguan yichen bu ran 做人一身正氣，為官一塵不染	be upright as a person, be clean as an officer
guan 官	state government/official
yingyong bodou 英勇搏鬥	fight heroically
wuxian zhongcheng 無限忠誠	boundless loyalty
ji'e ru chou 嫉惡如仇	hatred for evil
yingyong wuwei de geming jingshen 英勇無畏的革命精神	fearless revolutionary spirit
chonggao qinghuai 崇高情懷	noble quality
haoran zhengqi 浩然正氣	awe-inspiring righteousness
Renmin jingcha 人民警察	People's Police
yinyou 引誘	seduce
wuru qitu 誤入歧途	gone astray
lao baixing 老百姓	the people
qinren 親人	family members
kaidao ta 開導她	straighten her out
milu de haizi 迷路的孩子	children who lost their way
shisheng 師生	teachers and students
pengyou 朋友	friends
qingchun 青春	youth
qingchun nianhua 青春年華	time of youth
ganlian 幹練	competent
suihe 隨和	easy-going
shengkai de xiangrikui 盛開的向日葵	blooming sunflower
kuxingseng 苦行僧	ascetic monk
yange yaoqiu ziji 嚴格要求自己	strict with oneself

xingfu kuaile 幸福快樂	happiness
wanjiu shengming 挽救生命	saving lives
wanjiu linghun 挽救靈魂	saving souls
putong ren 普通人	normal persons
Hunan Weishi 湖南衛視	Hunan Television
Pingmin yingxiong 平民英雄	*Heroic Civilians*
diaogou 釣鉤	hooking
daibu 逮捕	arrest
zhua 抓	catch
yanda dupin fanzui 嚴打毒品犯罪	fight drug crime
jingfei yijia 警匪一家	police and criminals come from the same family
xingfa 刑法	criminal law
Jindufa 禁毒法	anti-drug law
juliu 拘留	detention
youhuo zhencha 誘惑偵查	enticement detection
xianren 線人	informants/line
yongjian 用間	using spies
lianluo yuan 聯絡員	liaison personnel
zhi'an ermu 治安耳目	security eyes and ears
paichu suo 派出所	local police station
zerenqu minjing 責任區民警	district police
zhengzhi wending 政治穩定	political stability
zhi'an wending 治安穩定	social stability
hongse ermu 紅色耳目	red eyes and ears
rexin zhian gongzuo de qunzhong 熱心治安工作的群眾	civilians who are enthusiastic in maintaining social security
lüse ermu 綠色耳目	green eyes and ears
huise ermu 灰色耳目	grey eyes and ears
gaixie guizheng 改邪歸正	rehabilitated
zhencha xianren 偵查線人	investigative line
teqing 特情	special agent
po'an lü 破案率	crime-cracking rate

Chinese Glossary

ban'an shuliang 辦案數量	number of cases handled
po da'an lü 破大案率	big crime–cracking rate
jihui tigong xing 機會提供型	providing-opportunity type
fanyi youfa xing 犯意誘發型	provoking-criminal-intention type
yaokou 窯口	drug den
tong 同	commonality
zhuanye sushi 專業素質	professional quality
yangzhe 養著	feed
po du'an 破毒案	cracking drug crime
shoujie xidu renyuan 收戒吸毒人員	catching and rehabilitating drug user
gongan ju 公安局	security bureau
dianming piping 點名批評	named and criticized
xian gongan ju 縣公安局	county security bureau
renmin 人民	people's
jingcha 警察	police
zhengfu 政府	government
gongchandang 共產黨	Communist Party
zhengfu de ren 政府的人	government people
bu ba ni dang ren 不把你當人	do not treat you as a human being
diwo maodun 敵我矛盾	enemy-and-me
renmin neibu maodun 人民內部矛盾	conflicts among the people
shequ jiedu 社區戒毒	community-based drug treatment
xingzheng juliu 行政拘留	administratively detained
ziran liaofa 自然療法	natural therapy
yanjiao 煙教	drug reform
shejiao 社教	social reform
xingzheng chufa cuoshi 行政處罰措施	administrative detention penalty
qiangzhi xing jiaoyu yiliao cuoshi 強制性教育醫療措施	compulsory education and treatment measure
jiemu shijian 節目時間	show time
dui renge de wuru 對人格的侮辱	insult to basic human dignity
xinshou jixun 新收集訓	admission training
guodu jiaoyu 過渡教育	transitional education

yanguan qi 嚴管期	strict-control period
xinshou qu 新手區	the newcomers' district
xingwei jiaozhi 行為矯治	correction of acts
sixiang jiaozhi 思想矯治	correction of thoughts
wu guding 五固定	five regularities
jiao 教	to educate
xingwei xiguan ji bu zhengchang 行為習慣極不正常	have extremely abnormal behaviours and habits
bujiang weisheng 不講衛生	pay no attention to hygiene
meiyou limao 沒有禮貌	impolite
landuo sanman 懶惰散漫	lazy and idle
guifan yanxing 規範言行	regulate what one says and how one behaves
bucao 步操	marching drill
doufu bei 豆腐被	*tofu* blankets
guangbo cao 廣播操	radio callisthenics
biaoxian 表現	performance
jingzuo fansi 靜坐反思	quiet-sitting and self-reflection
jing 靜	quiet
an 安	stability
xiushen 修身	self-cultivation
dao 道	truth
zhishan 至善	ultimate good
canwu rendao 慘無人道	cruel and inhuman
mei renxing 沒人性	inhumane
biaoyan 表演	acting
zizhuan 自傳	autobiography
huiguo shu 悔過書	remorse letter
zixing 自省	self-reflection
xing 省	reflection
Lunyu 論語	*The Analects*
ri san xing wu shen 日三省吾身	reflect on oneself every day

Chinese Glossary

jian xian siqi yan, jian buxian er nei zixing ye 見賢思齊焉，見不賢而內自省也	reflect on oneself when encountering un-virtuous people to see if one had made the same mistakes as the un-virtuous people
Dizi gui 弟子規	*Standards for Being a Good Pupil and Child*
Ba rong ba chi 八榮八恥	Eight Honours and Eight Disgraces
Jiedu sanzi jing 戒毒三字經	*Drug-Rehab Three-Character Classic*
xueyuan xingwei guifan 學員行為規範	inmates' code of conduct
ziwo wei zhongxin 自我為中心	self-centred
jiduan zisi 極端自私	extremely selfish
quefa tongqing xin 缺乏同情心	lack compassion
meiyou zeren gan 沒有責任感	irresponsible
jiaozhi 矯治	corrected
renzui rencuo 認罪認錯	accept that one is guilty and wrong
jiaoyu 教育	education
gaizao 改造	reform
wanjiu 挽救	salvation
zaiya renyuan jiben guifan 在押人員基本規範	essential regulations for inmates
zaiya renyuan shenghuo guifan 在押人員生活規範	regulations governing inmates' daily lives
zaiya renyuan wenming limao guifan 在押人員文明禮貌規範	rules governing inmates' behavioural manners
wenming limao 文明禮貌	civilized and polite manner
zhengque taidu 正確態度	correct attitude
juzhi wenming 舉止文明	behave in a civilized manner
shuohua heqi 說話和氣	speak in a gentle manner
zuo diji xialiu dongzuo 做低級下流動作	make obscene gestures
shenghuo qu 生活區	living area
shezhang 舍長	dorm head
limian de guiju 裡面的規矩	inside-regulation
sha wei bang 殺威棒	spirit-breaking beating
guotang 過堂	inmates' trial

qiangu yilai de guiju 千古以來的規矩	rule that has been established for thousands of years
yaojinyaguan 咬緊牙關	kept my mouth shut
zuo xinren 做新人	to-be-a-newbie
yibai sha wei bang 一百殺威棒	spirit-breaking beating
Shuihu zhuan 水滸傳	*Water Margin*
shi tiao long dei panzhe, shi zhi hu dei pazhe 是條龍得盤著，是隻虎得趴著	if you are a dragon you should coil up, and if you are a tiger you should crouch down
baotou cao 抱頭操	squat with one's hand on the head and be beaten
lenshui zao 冷水澡	cold bath
xinbing 新兵	junior
laobing 老兵	senior
guotang 過堂	inmate's trial
gongtang 公堂	law courts in dynastic China
sanqing liuban 三清六半	three empties, six halves
kuhuo 苦活	hard work
canku 殘酷	cruel
hun de hao 混得好	doing good
daoli 道理	reasons
xingshi hua 形式化	formalities
kaixin riji 開心日記	happy diary entry
yuanhen 怨恨	hate
maiyuan 埋怨	complaints
jiechu duyin 戒除毒癮	rehabilitated from drug addiction
jiaoyu he wanjiu 教育和挽救	educate and save
jiaoxun 教訓	teach the offender a lesson
meiyou guize bu cheng fangyuan 沒有規則不成方圓	nothing can be accomplished without rules or standards
bu ba ni dang ren 不把你當人	do not treat you as a human being
biantai de yuwang 變態的欲望	perverted desire
laotou yuba 牢頭獄霸	bullies among inmates
xinren 新人	new men

Chinese Glossary

laogai 勞改	reform through labour
laojiao 勞教	re-education through labour
qiangge 強隔	compulsory isolation at drug rehabilitation centres
kangfu laodong 康復勞動	labour rehabilitation
zhiye jineng peixun 職業技能培訓	vocational training
dianming 點名	roll call
shezhang de ren 舍長的人	followers of the dorm head
xuexi huodong 學習活動	education activities
jilü 紀律	discipline
neiwu 內務	housekeeping
qianmian de ren 前面的人	people in the front
shangmian de ren 上面的人	people at the top
maimai 買賣	trading
zuo renqing 做人情	exchange of favours
tifa nuedai bei jianguan renyuan zui 體罰虐待被監管人罪	the crime of physically abusing prison inmates
guoshi zhiren siwang zui 過失致人死亡罪	homicide caused by negligence
wenming zhifa 文明執法	civilized enforcement
wenming guanjiao 文明管教	civilized management
zhenggui 正規	formal
shenjing bing 神經病	psycho
chengguan 城管	urban management officers
tongguan 統管	manager
guanli yuan 管理員	administrators
shengchan guanli yuan 生產管理員	production administrator
jilü guanli yuan 紀律管理員	discipline administrator
neiwu guanli yuan 內務管理員	housekeeping administrator
jiaoyu guanli yuan 教育管理員	education administrator
jianyu qiye jituan 監獄企業集團	prison enterprise group
gongsi 公司	companies
qiye 企業	enterprises
qiye guanli 企業管理	enterprise management

shebei nengyuan 設備能源	equipment management
jishu zhiliang 技術質量	technical quality
chengben kongzhi 成本控制	cost control
gongying xiaoshou 供應銷售	supply and sales
shifu 師傅	instructor
danwei 單位	work unit
jiji fenzi 積極分子	activists
la guanxi 拉關係	using *guanxi*
fenshu 分數	merit points
xingqi 刑期	term of imprisonment
gaizao jiji fenzi 改造積極分子	active reform elements
youxiu xueyuan 優秀學員	outstanding student
kanggai wanwei fenzi 抗改頑危分子	the stubborn and dangerous elements who resist reform
dazhang 大賬	big account
waidi ren 外地人	outsiders
hunde buhao 混得不好	not able to do well
gaodang de 高檔的	luxury
putong de 普通的	normal
bijiao cha de 比較差的	pretty bad
hunde hao 混得好	doing well
jindu xuanchuan pian 禁毒宣傳片	anti-drug propaganda videos
gongzuo zhibiao 工作指標	work target
zhongdian renkou 重點人口	targeted populations
tezhong renkou 特種人口	special residents
Zhongdian renkou guanli gongzuo guiding 重點人口管理工作規定	The Regulations on Targeted Population Management
weifa renyuan 違法人員	rule breakers
fanzui renyuan 犯罪人員	law breakers
weihai guojia anquan 危害國家安全	threatening state security
yanzhong xingshi fanzui huodong 嚴重刑事犯罪活動	serious criminal offences
naoshi 鬧事	make trouble
xingxiong baofu 行兇報復	taking violent revenge

modi paicha 摸底排查	information collection and control
jiafang 家訪	home visits
bangjiao 幫教	help education
xidu jiance 吸毒檢測	drug tests
niaojian 尿檢	urine test
bu guifan de niaojian 不規範的尿檢	unregulated urine test
yunqi hao 運氣好	lucky
xidu renyuan xinxi shuju ku 吸毒人員信息數據庫	drug user information database
dongtai guankong xitong 動態管控系統	dynamic management and control system
liudong xing da 流動性大	highly mobile
liu 流	drift
shenfen zheng 身份證	identity card
qiangzhi 強制	compulsory
jujue jiezhou jiancha 拒絕接受檢查	refuses to undergo the test
jiuye jidi 就業基地	job-placement centre
bu wenming duidai 不文明對待	treated in uncivilized ways
wenming 文明	civilized
bu wenming 不文明	uncivilized
xinxing dupin 新型毒品	new drugs
xidu shi 吸毒史	history of drug use
dujia 毒駕	drug-driving
xidu renyuan 吸毒人員	drug users
heiche 黑車	unlicensed taxi
lan dao guzi li qu le 爛到骨子裡去了	thoroughly corrupted
tai tama heian 太他媽黑暗	fucking dark
xuexi Lei Feng jinian ri 學習雷鋒紀念日	learn from Lei Feng day
Xinwen lianbo 新聞聯播	*National News Broadcast*

References

Adler, Patricia, and Peter Adler. 1987. *Membership Roles in Field Research*. Newbury Park, CA: Sage.
Adorjan, Michael, and Wing Hong Chui. 2014. 'Aging Out of Crime: Resettlement Challenges Facing Male Ex-Prisoners in Hong Kong'. *The Prison Journal* 94 (1): 97–117.
Akers, Ronald. 1977. 'Type of Leadership in Prison: A Structural Approach to Testing the Functional and Importation Models'. *The Sociological Quarterly* 18 (3): 378–83.
Baidu. 2014. 'Why does the National News Broadcast have the most expensive television commercial time slot?'. Baidu. Accessed 25 June 2018. https://zhidao.baidu.com/question/1303457139624745219.html?qbl=relate_question_0&word=%CE%AA%CA%B2%C3%B4%D1%EB%CA%D3%A1%B6%D0%C2%CE%C5%C1%AA%B2%A5%A1%B7%CA%B1%B6%CE%B5%C4%B9%E3%B8%E6%CA%C7%D7%EE%B9%F3%B5%C4.
Bakken, Børge. 2000. *The Exemplary Society: Human Improvement, Social Control, and the Dangers of Modernity in China*. Oxford: Oxford University Press.
Bakken, Børge. 2010. 'China, a Punitive Society?' *Asian Journal of Criminology* 6 (1): 33–50.
Bakken, Børge. 2013. *Disease and Crime: A History of Social Pathologies and the New Politics of Health*. London: Routledge.
Barnes, John Arundel. 1994. *A Pack of Lies: Towards a Sociology of Lying*. Cambridge: Cambridge University Press.
Bauman, Zygmunt. 1993. *Modernity and the Holocaust*. Cambridge: Polity Press.
Becker, Howard. 1954. 'Field Methods and Techniques: A Note on Interviewing Tactics'. *Human Organization* 12 (4): 31–32.
Becker, Howard. 1963. *Outsiders: Studies in the Sociology of Deviance*. New York: Free Press.
Beijing People's Broadcasting Corporation. 2014. 'The Beijing Municipal Public Security Bureau, Compulsory Treatment Management Centre, Foundation Work Department, Community Supervision Unit, Deputy Chief Xiao Jianfeng'. 28 April. Beijing: Beijing Spiritual Civilization Construction Committee [Beijing jingshen wenming weiyuanhui bangong shi]. Accessed 3 July 2014. http://zt.bjwmb.gov.cn/2014/20140501/lmfc/t20140428_570764.html.
Bentham, Jeremy. 1995. *The Panopticon Writings*. London: Verso.
Billingsley, Roger, ed. 2009. *Covert Human Intelligence Sources: The 'Unlovely' Face of Police Work*. Sherfield-on-Loddon, UK: Waterside Press.
Bosworth, Mary, and Eamonn Carradine. 2001. 'Reassessing Resistance: Race, Gender and Sexuality in Prison'. *Punishment and Society* 3 (4): 501–15.

Bourdieu, Pierre. 1984. *Distinction: A Social Critique of the Judgement of Taste*. Cambridge, MA: Harvard University Press.
Brady, Anne-Marie. 2008. *Marketing Dictatorship: Propaganda and Thought Work in Contemporary China*. Lanham, MD: Rowman & Littlefield.
Brady, Anne-Marie, ed. 2012a. *China's Thought Management*. New York: Routledge.
Brady, Anne-Marie. 2012b. 'State Confucianism, Chineseness, and Tradition in CCP'. In *China's Thought Management*, edited by Anne-Marie Brady, 57–75. New York: Routledge.
Braithwaite, John. 1989. *Crime, Shame, and Reintegration*. Cambridge: Cambridge University Press.
Bureau of Reform through Labour; Ministry of Justice. 2009. 'Research Report on Perfecting Drugs Treatment and Rehabilitation Work'. *Justice of China [Zhongguo sifa]* 1: 51–54.
Cai, Dao. 2013. 'Jingju xianren jiemi: ke huo weiwen jin duo yongyu zhenpo dupin an' [Police informant's review: Condolence money is mostly used in cracking drugs crime]. Sina, 12 March. Accessed 18 March 2013. http://news.sina.com.cn/c/sd/2013-03-12/161626509338.shtml.
Caldwell, Morris G. 1956. 'Group Dynamics in the Prison Community'. *Journal of Criminal Law, Criminology, and Police Science* 46 (5): 648–57.
Cao, Liqun, James Frank, and Francis Cullen. 1996. Race, community context and confidence in the police. *American journal of police*, 15(1): 3–22.
Cao, Liqun, Jihong Zhao, and Steve Van Dine. 1997. 'Prison Disciplinary Tickets: A Test of the Deprivation and Importation Models'. *Journal of Criminal Justice* 25 (2): 103–13.
Casella, Eleanor Conlin. 2000. '"Doing Trade": A Sexual Economy of Nineteenth-Century Australian Female Convict Prisons'. *World Archaeology* 32 (2): 209–21.
Chen, Juan. 2007. 'Jidu yingxiong Luo Jinyong yu qizi: Tiegu yao jinghui rouqing ying zhen'ai' [Heroic drugs fighter Luo Jinyong and his wife: Man of iron honours his police badge, his tenderness shows true love]. *People's Daily*, 3 June.
Chen, Lei 2011. 'Teqing zhencha lifa wenti yanjiu' [Study on the legalization of special agents]. *Xingshi fa pinglun* [Criminal law review] 29: 515–37.
Chen, Xiaoming. 2002. 'Social Control in China: Application of the Labeling Theory and the Reintegrative Shaming Theory'. *International Journal of Offender Therapy and Comparative Criminology* 46 (1): 46–63.
Chen, Xiaoming. 2004. 'Social and Legal Control in China: A Comparative Perspective'. *International Journal of Offender Therapy and Comparative Criminology* 48 (5): 523–36.
Chen, Yu. 2008. 'Problems and Indications: Drugs Rehabilitation under the Perspective of Labelling Theory'. *Chinese Journal of Drug Abuse Prevention and Treatment* 14 (3): 185–87.
Chen, Zhonghua. 2013. 'Zhibiao paiming zhengxian wancheng renwu tiqian' [Compete for quota ranking: Complete the mission in advance]. *Nanfang fazhi bao*, 20 November.
Cheng, Shing. 2009. 'Waging a Two-Front War: Inmates during Incarceration and Social Workers Working on Ex-Convict Rehabilitation in China'. MPhil thesis, University of Hong Kong.
Cheng, Shing. 2010. 'Fighting the White Monster: Three Stories from the Chinese Compulsory Detoxification Centre'. In *Our Monstrous (S)kin: Blurring the Boundaries Between Monsters and Humanity*, edited by Sorcha Ni Fhlainn, 15–28. Freeland: Inter-Disciplinary Press.

Cheurprakobkit, S. 2000. 'Police-Citizen Contact and Police Performance Attitudinal Differences between Hispanics and Non-Hispanics'. *Journal of Criminal Justice* 28(4): 325–36.

China Network Television. 2012. 'Face to Face: Vanguard in Fighting Drugs'. 24 June. Accessed 26 March 2013. http://big5.cntv.cn/gate/big5/news.cntv.cn/program/mianduimian/20120625/100184.shtml.

Chinese News Weekly. 2012. 'Yunnan Mengzi meinian 30 wan jiang jingfang xianren zuigao jiangjin 15,000 yuan' [Yunnan Mengzi awards 300,000 yuan to police informants annually, the highest bonus is 15,000 yuan]. http://www.chinanews.com/fz/2012/11-16/4333642.shtml.

Chinese Police Network. 2014. 'Hard Strike on Soccer Gambling During the World Cup'. Xinhua News Agency, 15 June. Accessed 27 June 2014. http://news.sina.com.cn/c/2014-06-14/223730361968.shtml.

Christie, Nils. 1981. *Limits to Pain*. Oxford: Martin Robertson.

Chu, Yiu Kong. 2000. *The Triads as Business*. New York: Routledge.

Clemmer, Donald. 1951. 'Observations on Imprisonment as a Source of Criminality'. *Journal of Criminal Law & Criminology* 41 (3): 311–19.

Clemmer, Donald. 1966. *The Prison Community*. New York: Holt, Rinehart, and Winston.

Cloward, Richard A. 1960. 'Social Control in Prison'. In *Theoretical Studies in Social Organization of the Prison*, edited by Richard Cloward et al., 20–48. New York: Doubleday.

Cohen, Albert. 1955. *Delinquent Boys*. Glencoe, IL: Free Press of Glencoe.

Cohen, Stan, and Laurie Taylor. 1972. *Psychological Survival: The Experience of Long-Term Imprisonment*. Harmondsworth, UK: Penguin.

Colquitt, Joseph A. 2004. 'Rethinking Entrapment'. *American Criminal Law Review* 41: 1–49.

Connell, Anne, and David P. Farrington. 1996. 'Bullying among Incarcerated Young Offenders: Developing an Interview Schedule and Some Preliminary Results'. *Journal of Adolescence* 19 (1): 75–93.

Conrad, Peter, and Joseph W. Schneider. 1980. *Deviance and Medicalization: From Badness to Sickness*. St Louis: Mosby.

Cooley, Charles H. 1922. *Human Nature and the Social Order*. New York: Charles Scribner's Sons.

Coomber, Ross. 1996. 'Vim in the Veins—Fantasy or Fact: The Adulteration of Illicit Drugs'. *Addiction Research* 5 (97): 195–212.

Coomber, Ross. 1997. 'The Adulteration of Drugs: What Dealers Do to Illicit Drugs, and What They Think Is Done to Them'. *Addiction Research* 5 (4): 297–306.

Craik, Jennifer 1994. *The Face of Fashion: Cultural Studies in Fashion*. New York: Routledge.

Crewe, Ben. 2006. 'Prison Drugs Dealing and the Ethnographic Lens'. *Howard Journal* 45 (4): 347–68.

Crewe, Ben. 2007. 'Power, Adaptation and Resistance in a Late Modern Men's Prison'. *British Journal of Criminology* 47 (2): 256–75.

Crewe, Ben. 2012. *The Prisoner Society: Power, Adaptation, and Social Life in an English Prison*. New York: Oxford University Press.

Crouch, B. M. 1982. 'Sex and Occupations Socialization among Prison Guards'. *Criminal Justice and Behavior* 9: 159–76.

Cui, Min. 1999. *Dupin fanzui: Fazhan qushi yu ezhi duice* [Drugs offences: Trends and control strategies]. Beijing: Jingguan jiaoyu chubanshe.
Dahlin, Bo, and David Watkins. 2000. 'The Role of Repetition in the Processes of Memorising and Understanding: A Comparison of the Views of German and Chinese Secondary School Students in Hong Kong'. *British Journal of Educational Psychology* 70: 65–84.
Das, Jacky. 2008. *Psychopathic Traits in Dutch Adolescent Offender and Community Samples*. Wageningen, Netherlands: Posen & Looyen.
Davis, Deborah. 2000. *The Consumer Revolution in Urban China*. Berkeley: University of California Press.
Davis, Fred. 1994. *Fashion, Culture, and Identity*. Chicago: University of Chicago Press.
Denzin, Norman K. 1970. *The Research Act: A Theoretical Introduction to Sociological Methods*. Chicago: Aldine.
Deutsche Welle (Chinese version). 2013. 'Zhu xuanlü shengji: Wu bugao hou yinglai qi bujiang?' [Upgrading the 'main melody': 'Seven not to be talked about' after the 'five not to be done'?]. 10 May. Accessed 1 July 2014. http://www.dw.de zh/主旋律升级五不搞后迎来七不讲/a-16802727?&zhongwen=simp.
Dikötter, Frank. 2002. *Crime, Punishment and the Prison in Modern China*. Hong Kong: Hong Kong University Press.
Dikötter, Frank, Lars Laamann, and Zhou Xun. 2004. *Narcotic Culture: A History of Drugs in China*. Hong Kong: Hong Kong University Press.
Ding, D. Y., and Z. J. Li. 2010. 'Changes in Model Figures: Changes in Mainland Chinese Moral Education Textbooks for Primary School Students'. *Hong Kong Teachers' Centre Journal* 9: 1–8.
Dostoevsky, Fyodor. 1951. *Crime and Punishment*. Translated by David Magarshack. London: Penguin.
Du, James J. 2004. *Punishment and Reform: An Introduction to the Reform-through-Labor System in the People's Republic of China*. Hong Kong: Lo Tat Cultural.
Duan, Xizhong, and Xuchu Wen, eds. 1960. *Zhuge Liang Reader*. Beijing: Zhonghua shuju.
Dutton, Michael R. 1992. *Policing and Punishment in China: From Patriarchy to 'the People'*. Cambridge: Cambridge University Press.
Dutton, Michael R. 2005a. 'A Question of Difference: The Theory and Practice of the Chinese Prison'. In *Crime, Punishment, and Policing in China*, edited by Børge Bakken, 103–40. Lanham, MD: Rowman & Littlefield.
Dutton, Michael R. 2005b. 'Toward a Government of the Contract: Policing in the Era of Reform'. In *Crime, Punishment, and Policing*, edited by Børge Bakken, 189–234. Lanham, MD: Rowman & Littlefield.
Eady, D. 2007. 'Prisoners' Rights since the Woolf Report: Progress or Procrastination?' *The Howard Journal of Crime and Justice* 46(3): 264–75.
Fan, B., G. Wang, and Y. Lei. 2007. 'Jingcha gongong guanxi weiji chuzhi fanglue' [Methods to deal with police public relations crisis]. *Gongan yanjiu* [Police studies] 8: 74–80.
Farrall, Stephen, Mike Hough, Shadd Maruna, and Richard Sparks, eds. 2011. 'Introduction: Life after Punishment: Identifying New Strands in the Research Agenda'. In *Escape Routes: Contemporary Perspectives on Life after Punishment*, 1–21. Oxford: Routledge.
Feng, L. 2012. '"Shiwufan" guanli zhong cunzai de wenti ji duice fenxi' [Problems faced in managing the 'working offenders' and its solution]. *Fazhi yu shehui*: 201–2.
Foucault, Michel. 1977. *Discipline and Punish: The Birth of the Prison*. London: Allen Lane.

Frankl, Viktor. 2006. *Man's Search for Meaning*. Boston: Beacon Press.
Freud, Sigmund. 1976. *Jokes and their relation to the unconscious*. Harmondsworth: Penguin.
Fromm, Erich. 1973. *The Anatomy of Human Destructiveness*. New York: Holt, Rinehart, and Winston.
Fu, Hualing. 2005a. 'Punishing for Profit: Profitability and Rehabilitation in a Laojiao Institution'. In *Engaging the Law in China: State, Society, and Possibilities for Justice*, edited by N. J. Diamant, S. B. Lubman, and K. J. O'Brien, 213–30. Stanford, CA: Stanford University Press.
Fu, Hualing. 2005b. 'Re-education through Labour in Historical Perspective'. *The China Quarterly* 184: 811–30.
Fu, Jianfeng. 2004. 'The Life of Professional "Lines"'. *Nanguo zaobao*, 26 February.
Fu, Jianfeng. 2007. 'Chinese Professional "Line": Find a Living on the Edge of a Blade'. *Nanfang zhoumo*. Accessed 23 February 2018. http://www.infzm.com/content/9865.
Gambetta, Diego, 1993. *The Sicilian Mafia: The Business of Private Protection*. Cambridge, MA: Harvard University Press.
Gao, Huan. 2008. *Women Heroin Users in China's Changing Society*. New York: Routledge.
Garfinkel, H. 1964. 'Studies of the Routine Grounds of Everyday Activities.' *Social Problems* 11 (3): 225–50.
Garland, David. 2001. *The Culture of Control: Crime and Social Order in Contemporary Society*. Chicago: University of Chicago Press.
Gleason, Sandra. 1978. 'Hustling: The "Inside" Economy of a Prison'. *Federal Probation* 42 (2): 32–40.
Godderis, Rebecca 2006. 'Dining in: The Symbolic Power of Food in Prison'. *Howard Journal of Criminal Justice* 45: 255–67.
Goffman, Erving. 1958. *The Presentation of Self in Everyday Life*. Edinburgh: Social Sciences Research Centre, University of Edinburgh.
Goffman, Erving. 1968a. *Asylums: Essays on the Social Situation of Mental Patients and Other Inmates*. Harmondsworth, UK: Penguin.
Goffman, Erving. 1968b. *Stigma: Notes on the Management of Spoiled Identity*. Harmondsworth, UK: Penguin.
Gordon, Kim. 1995. 'Farewell Cultural Revolution, Hello Box Rebellion'. *Independent*, 10 October.
Gottfredson, Michael R., and Travis Hirschi. 1990. *A General Theory of Crime*. Stanford, CA: Stanford University Press.
Greer, Steven. 1995. 'Towards a Sociological Model of Police Informant'. *The British Journal of Criminology* 46 (3): 509–27.
Gu, Yankui. 2003. *Hanzi yuanyuan zidian* [The dictionary of the origin of Chinese word]. Beijing: Huaxia chubanshe.
Guangdong Prison Administration Bureau. 2008. 'Qingyuan jianyu juxing daxing *Di zi gui* beisong bisai' [Qingyuan Prison organized a large scale reciting *Di zi gui* tournament]. Accessed 2 July 2013. http://www.gdjyj.gd.gov.cn/news_view.jsp?NewsIndex=1007.
Guangming Daily. 2009. 'Quanguo jingye fengxian mofan houxuan ren' [Candidate of the national devoted model figures]. 19 June. Accessed 1 July 2014. http://www.gmw.cn/01gmrb/2009-06/19/content_936884.htm.
Han, Xu. 2009. 'Xingshi susong zhong xianren zuozheng wenti yanjiu' [The use of 'lines' to bear witness in criminal cases]. *Zhongguo xingshi fa zazhi* [Criminal science] 3: 86–93.

Haney, Craig, Curtis Banks, and Philip Zimbardo. 2004. 'A Study of Prisoners and Guards in a Simulated Prison'. In *Theatre in Prison: Theory and Practice*, edited by Michael Balfour, 19–34. Portland, OR: Intellect.

Hassine, Victor. 1996. *Life Without Parole: Living in Prison Today*. Los Angeles: Roxbury Publishing Company.

He, Quansheng, and Tong Zheng. 2002. *Kanshousuo zaiya renyuan falü zhishi duben* [Textbook of basic legal knowledge for detention inmates]. Beijing: Zhongguo renmin gongan daxue chubanshe.

He, Z. M., and X. Y. Fu. 2000. 'Qian lun jianyu qiya baituo kunjing de kenengxing xuanze' [Possible choices for prison enterprises to relief its difficulties faced]. *Journal of Hunan Economic Management College* 4: 13–14.

Homel, Ross J. 1988. *Policing and Punishing the Drinking Driver: A Study of Specific and General Deterrence*. New York: Springer-Verlag.

Hong Kong Police Force. 2014. 'Expenditure of Rewards and Special Services'. Hong Kong: Hong Kong Police Force. Accessed 4 July 2014. http://www.police.gov.hk/ppp_tc/09_statistics/cs_rss.html.

Hou, J. J. 2009. 'Guanyu zhongdian renkou shehui hua guanli de jidian sikao' [Thoughts on socialized management of key population]. *Journal of Fujian Police Academy* 23 (5): 31–35.

Hu, Wenzheng. 2002. *Lunyu Reading*. Shanxi: Shanxi guji chubanshe.

Hu, Yaobang. 1985. *Guanyu dang de xinwen gongzuo: Zai zhongyang shujichu huiyi shang de fayan* [On the party's journalism work: Speech in the secretariat of the Central Committee]. Beijing: Renmin chubanshe.

Innes, Martin. 2010. '"Professionalizing" the Role of the Police Informant: The British Experience'. *Policing and Society: An International Journal of Research and Policy* 9 (4): 357–83.

Ireland, Jane L. 2000. '"Bullying" among Prisoners: A Review of Research'. *Aggression and Violent Behavior* 5 (2): 201–15.

Irwin, John, and Donald R. Cressey. 1962. 'Thieves, Convicts and the Inmate Culture'. *Social Problems* 10 (2): 142–55.

Jia, Zhenjun. 2010. 'Jiangzhi geli jiedu zhong de kunjing yu chulu' [Problems and countermeasures of compulsory isolation detoxification]. *Zhongguo yaowu lanyong zazhi* [Chinese journal of drug dependence] 19: 406–9.

Jiang, Chuntang. 2001. 'Woguo zhengfu gongguan de xianzhuang yu zhanwang' [Present and future of the government public relations in our country]. In *Zhengfu xingxiang tansuo* [Exploring government image], edited by Chuntang Jiang. Beijing: Zhongguo guoji guangbo chubanshe.

Jiang, Shiqiang. 2002. 'Jianyu ganjing zhiwu fanzui yufang duice' [On prevention of occupational crime committed by prison officers]. *Renmin jiancha* [People's procuratorial monthly] 6: 24–25.

Jones, Richard S., and Thomas J. Schmid. 2000. *Doing Time: Prison Experience and Identity among First-Time Inmates*. Stamford, CT: JAI Press.

Judicial Department of Jiangxi Province. 2012. 'Wosheng jianyu xitong caiqu wuxiang cuoshi guanche luoshi "jianyu fuxing renyuan xingwei guifan"' [Our province adopts five measures to implement 'prison inmates' behavioural regulations']. 2 July. Accessed 2 July 2013. http://www.jxsf.gov.cn/2012/7/2/espvgnoldcj.shtml.

Kalinich, David B., and Stan Stojkovic. 1985. 'Contraband: The Basis for Legitimate Power in a Prison Social System'. *Criminal Justice and Behavior* 12 (4): 435–51.

Kappeler, Victor E., and Gary W. Potter. 2005. *The Mythology of Crime and Criminal Justice*. Long Grove, IL: Waveland Press.

Kogon, Eugen. 1950. *The Theory and Practice of Hell: The German Concentration Camps and the System Behind Them*. London: Secker & Warburg.

Kozinet, Robert. 2002. 'The Field behind the Screen: Using Netnography for Marketing Research in Online Communities'. *Journal of Marketing Research* 39: 61–72.

Kubrin, C. E., and E. A. Stewart. 2006. 'Predicting Who Reoffends: The Neglected Role of Neighbourhood Context in Recidivism Studies'. *Criminology* 44: 165–97.

Lai, Tung-kwok. 2010. 'Legco: Acting Secretary for Security's Speech on Removing the Item of "Expenditure of Reward and Special Services"'.Information Services Department, Hong Kong, 21 April. Accessed 4 July 2013. http://www.info.gov.hk/gia/general/201004/21/P201004210267.htm.

Lan Yi District Police Office. 2012. 'Shequ minjing ruhe zuodao ercong muming' [How to make district police officers see and hear clearly?]. Xinzhou Shi: Lan Yi District Police Office. Accessed 27 June 2014. http://www.xzgabmfw.gov.cn/police/public/showinfo.aspx?id=201305121046380857O109.

Lee, C. K. 1999. 'From Organized Dependence to Disorganized Despotism: Changing Labour Regimes in Chinese Factories'. *The China Quarterly* 157: 44–71.

Lee, C. K., and Yonghong Zhang. 2013. 'The Power of Instability: Unraveling the Microfoundations of Bargained Authoritarianism in China'. *American Journal of Sociology* 118 (6): 1475–508.

Lemert, E. M. 1995. 'Secondary Deviance and Role Conceptions'. In *Deviance: A Symbolic Interactionist Approach*, edited by Nancy J. Herman, 111–13. Walnut Creek, CA: AltaMira Press.

Leung, Beatrice. 2005. 'China's Religious Freedom Policy: The Arts of Managing Religious Activity'. *The China Quarterly* 184: 894–913.

Levi, Primo. 1989. *The Drowned and the Saved*. London: Abacus.

Levin, Dan. 2013. 'In China, Cinematic Flops Suggest Fading of an Icon'. *The New York Times Chinese*. Accessed 25 June 2018. https://cn.nytimes.com/china/20130313/c13leifeng/zh-hant/dual/.

Li, Jianhua. 2004. 'Dangqian woguo jiedu gongzuo mianlin de tiaozhan' [Challenges faced by drugs rehabilitation in China nowadays]. *Zhongguo yaowu lanyong zazhi* [Chinese journal of drug dependence] 13: 224–26.

Li, Shuo. 2009. 'Laojiao minjing ruhe shiying qiangzhi geli jiedu gongzuo yanjiu' [How does *laojiao* police adapt to works in compulsory isolation for drugs rehabilitation]. *Jingguan wenyuan* 4: 72–73.

Li, Yuxiu. 2005. *Di Zi Gui: Guide to a Happy Life*. Toowoomba, Australia: Pure Land Learning College Association.

Li, Yuzhi, Yi Shang, and Haifeng Zhang. 2012. *Baotou Statistic Yearbook*. Beijing: China Statistical Publishing House.

Liao, Yiwu. 2013. *For a Song and a Hundred Songs: A Poet's Journey through a Chinese Prison*. Boston: Houghton Mifflin Harcourt.

Lin, Lin. 2011. 'Jianchi jiushi liliang' [Persistence is the key to strength]. *People's Daily*, 22 June.

Lin, Zao'en. 1991. 'Chang qing jing jin shilue' [Translation of Chang qing jing jin]. In *Ling bao zhen wei ye tu*, edited by H. Tao. Beijing: Zhonghua shuju.

Liu, Changwu, and Kang Li. 2014. 'Dufan yi duping jianfei wei xuetou youren xidu' [Drug dealers use 'lose weight' as gimmick to seduce people to take drugs]. *Dahe Daily*, 27 June.

Liu, L. 2017. 'Re-Education through Labor'. *The Encyclopedia of Corrections*. Hoboken: John Wiley & Sons, Inc.

Liu, L., and W. H. Chui. 2016. 'Chinese Culture and Its Influence on Female Prisoner Behavior in the Prisoner-Guard Relationship'. *Australian & New Zealand Journal of Criminology*. doi:10.1177/0004865816679685.

Liu, Qiang, Ju Wang, and Qunfei Zeng. 2014. *Chikuang dufan diaoru zishe xianjing* [Crazy drug dealer falls into his own trap]. *Legal Daily*, 12 June. http://www.legaldaily.com.cn/police_and_frontier-defence/content/2014-06/12/content_5590424.htm?node=23298.

Liu, Rong. 2005. 'Jingzuo yu lixuejia de weixue xiushen' [Analysis of sitting in meditation for cultivating moral character]. *Shandong tiyu xueyuan bao* [Journal of Shandong Institute of Physical Education and Sports] 21: 51–53.

Liu, Zhimin. 2004. 'Duiyu laodong kangfu jiedu de jidianjianyi' [Several suggestions regarding the use of labour in drug rehabilitations]. *Zhongguo yaowu lanyong zazhi* [Chinese journal of drug dependence] 13: 233–34.

Long, Y. 2010. 'Huifu xing sifa zai woguo de shixing fenxi" [The analysis of implementation of restorative justice in China]. *Yichun xueyuan xuebao* [Journal of Yichun College] 32: 80–88.

Lu, Jiali. 2012. 'Zhenxin wanjiu yinjunzi ta shi qingsheng nü wei jiemei' [Treat the public as 'kinsfolk' and win the public praise: Wholeheartedly rescuing the 'drug addict' she sees her as her sister]. *Huaxi dushi bao*, 12 June.

Lu, Xiuli. 2013. 'Song Lina: An Acre of Dreamland, Planting Spring Breeze'. *Honghe ribao*, 8 May. Accessed 29 May 2014. http://cnepaper.com/hhrb/html/2013-05/08/content_5_1.htm.

Lu, Y. 2009. '"Laotou yuba" chansheng yuanyin ji duice' [The reason of the formation of prison bullies and the solution to it]. *Jiancha ribao* [Procuratorial daily] 31 May.

Luo, Yongyuan. 2006. '500 Young People Become Security "Eyes and Ears" in Train Station'. *Qingnian bao*, 19 March.

Ma, Tao. 2000. 'Youhuo zhencha zhi hefaxing fenxi' [On the legitimacy of enticement detection]. *Chinese Criminal Science* 5: 69–72.

Machiavelli, Niccolò. 2006. *The Prince*. Translated by W. K. Marriott. PublicLiterature.Org. Online e-book.

Makkai, Toni, and John Braithwaite. 1994. 'Reintegrative Shaming and Compliance with Regulatory Standards'. *Criminology* 32 (3): 361–83.

Manning, Peter, and Lawrence Redlinger. 1977. 'Invitational Edges of Corruption'. In *Drugs and Politics*, edited by Paul E. Rock, 261–78. New Brunswick, NJ: Transaction Publishers.

Mao, Zedong. 1965. *On Contradiction*. Beijing: Foreign Languages Press.

Marquart, James W., and Julian B. Roebuck. 1985. 'Prison Guards and "Snitches": Deviance within a Total Institution'. *The British Journal of Criminology* 25 (3): 217–33.

Maruna, Shadd. 2001. *Making Good: How Ex-Convicts Reform and Rebuild Their Lives*. Washington, DC: American Psychological Association.

Maruna, Shadd. 2004. 'Desistance from Crime and Explanatory Style: A New Direction in the Psychology of Reform'. *Journal of Contemporary Criminal Justice* 20 (2): 184–200.

Maruna, Shadd, Thomas P. Lebel, Nick Mitchell, and Michelle Naples. 2004. 'Pygmalion in the Reintegration Process: Desistance from Crime through the Looking Glass'. *Psychology, Crime & Law* 10 (3): 271–81.

Maruna, Shadd, and Kevin Roy. 2007. 'Amputation or Reconstruction? Notes on the Concept of "Knifing Off" and Desistance from Crime'. *Journal of Contemporary Criminal Justice* 23 (1): 104–24.

Mathiesen, Thomas. 1990. *Prison on Trial: A Critical Assessment*. London: Sage Publications.

Matza, David. 1964. *Delinquency and Drift*. New York: Wiley.

Mauer, Marc. 2005. 'Thinking about Prison and Its Impact in the Twenty-First Century'. *Ohio State Journal of Criminal Law* 2: 607–18.

McConville, Mike, Satnam Choongh, Pinky Choy Dick Wan, Eric Chui Wing Hong, Ian Dobinson, and Carol Jones. 2011. *Criminal Justice in China: An Empirical Inquiry*. Northampton, MA: Edward Elgar.

McCorkle, Lloyd W., and Richard Korn. 1954. 'Resocialization with Walls'. *Annals of the American Academy of Political and Social Science* 293 (1): 88–98.

McCoy, Clyde, Shenghan Lai, Lisa Metsch, Xue-Ren Wang, Cong Li, Ming Yang, and Yulong Liu. 1997. 'No Pain No Gain, Establishing the Kunming, China, Drugs Rehabilitation Center'. *Journal of Drug Issues* 27 (1): 73–85.

Meachum, Larry. 2000. 'Prisons: Breeding Grounds for Hate?' *Corrections Today* 62: 130–32.

Mears, Daniel P., Eric A. Stewart, Sonja E. Siennick, and Ronald L. Simons. 2013. 'The Code of the Street and Inmate Violence: Investigating the Salience of Imported Belief Systems'. *Criminology* 51 (3): 695–728.

Mills, C. Wright. 1959. *The Sociological Imagination*. New York: Oxford University Press.

Ministry of Justice. 1990. *Sifa bu guanyu jifen kaohe jiangfa zuifan de guiding* [Ministry of Justice's regulations related to the evaluation, rewarding and punishment of offenders].

Ministry of Public Security. 1991. *Zhonghua renmin gongheguo kanshou suo tiaoli shishi banfa* [PRC regulations on the implementation of law on detention centre].

Ministry of Public Security. 1998. *Zhongdian renkou guanli gongzuo guiding* [Regulations regarding the management of the targeted population].

Ministry of Public Security. 2002. *Gongan bu guanyu gaige he jiaqiang gongan paichu suo gongzuo de guiding* [Ministry of Public Security's decisions about reforming and strengthening the work of the local police station].

Ministry of Public Security. 2011. 'Gongan jiguan qiangzhi geli jiedu suo guanli banfa' [Regulations on the management of compulsory isolation for drugs rehabilitation centre].

Ministry of Public Security. 2012. 'Gongan bu guanyu xidu renyuan jiashi jidongche guanli de tongzhi' [Public Security Bureau's notice on the strengthening of the management of drugs driving].

Morwood, J., and J. Taylor, eds. 2002. *The Pocket Oxford Classical Greek Dictionary*. Oxford: Oxford University Press.

Mou, J. 2013. 'Xin Zhongguo jianyu lingdao guanli tizhi de liubian ji shexiang' [Changes and hypothesis in the management system of the new Chinese prisons]. *China Prison Journal* 5: 136–40.

Mulder, Eva, Eddy Brand, Ruud Bullens, and Hjalmar van Marle. 2011. 'Risk Factors for Overall Recidivism and Severity of Recidivism in Serious Juvenile Offenders'. *International Journal of Offender Therapy and Comparative Criminology* 55 (1): 118–35.
National People's Congress. 2006. *Zhonghua renmin gongheguo zhian guanli chufa fa* [Law of the People's Republic of China on penalties for administration of public security].
National People's Congress. 2008. *Zhonghua renmin gongheguo jindu fa* [Anti-drug Law of the People's Republic of China].
National People's Congress. 2013. 'Criminal Procedure Law of the People's Republic of China'. National People's Congress.
Neuman, W. Lawrence. 2004. *Basics of Social Research: Qualitative and Quantitative Approaches*. Boston: Pearson.
O'Brien, Kevin J. 2013. 'Rightful Resistance Revisited'. *The Journal of Peasant Studies* 40 (6): 1051–62.
O'Brien, Kevin J., and Lianjiang Li. 2006. *Rightful Resistance in Rural China*. Cambridge: Cambridge University Press.
Office of China National Narcotics Control Commission. 2010. *Zhongguo jindu baogao* [Annual report on drugs control in China].
Office of China National Narcotics Control Commission. 2011. *Zhongguo jindu baogao* [Annual report on drugs control in China].
Office of China National Narcotics Control Commission. 2013. *Zhongguo jindu baogao* [Annual report on drugs control in China].
Office of China National Narcotics Control Commission. 2014. *Zhongguo jindu baogao* [Annual report on drugs control in China].
Olin, Lloyd E. 1956. *Sociology and the Field of Corrections*. New York: Russell Sage Foundation.
Pan, Guanyuan, and Yanjing Lü, eds. 1999. *Gongan paichusuo minjing gongzuo shouce* [Handbook of People's Police's work in police stations]. Beijing: Falü chubanshe.
Pang, X. M., and He, G. R. 2010. 'Ruyu leiji yue 20 nian hou ren busi huigai "wujingong" renyuan kai jiaoche qu qiaodao' [Remorseless five-time recidivist stealing from cars]. *Modern Life Daily*, 15 June, p. 8.
Paternoster, Ray, and Shawn D. Bushway. 2009. 'Desistance and the "Feared Self": Toward an Identity Theory of Criminal Desistance'. *Journal of Criminal Law & Criminology* 99 (4): 1103–56.
People's Daily. 2007. 'D25 Yin Chunrong'. 1 September. Accessed 26 June 2018. http://paper.people.com.cn/rmrb/html/2007-09/01/content_18490304.htm
People's Daily. 2010. 'Guangzhou haiguan shouhu pingan Yayun' [Guangzhou Customs guarding the safety of the Asian Games]. General Administration of Customs of the PRC, 10 November. Accessed 1 July 2014. http://www.customs.gov.cn/customs/302249/302425/358862/index.html.
Potenberg, Daniel L. 1963. 'The Police Detection Practice of Encouragement'. *Virginia Law Review* 49 (5): 871–903.
Pratt, John. 2008. 'Scandinavian Exceptionalism in an Era of Penal Excess, Part I: The Nature and Roots of Scandinavian Exceptionalism'. *British Journal of Criminology* 48: 119–37.
Purdie, Nola, John Hattie, and Graham Douglas. 1996. 'Student Conceptions of Learning and Their Use of Self-Regulated Learning Strategies: A Cross-Cultural Comparison'. *Journal of Educational Psychology* 88 (1): 87–100.

Qianjiang Evening News. 2009. '100 wei xin Zhongguo chengli yilai gandong Zhongguo renwu houxuan ren shiji' [Candidates of the 100 individuals who moved the Chinese people]. 20 July.

Quetelet, Adolphe. 1984. 'Adolphe Quetelet's Research on the Propensity for Crime at Different Ages'. Abstract. Translated by Sawyer F. Sylvester. National Criminal Justice Reference Service. https://www.ncjrs.gov/App/Publications/abstract.aspx?ID=94009.

Ritchie, Jane, and Jane Lewis. 2003. *Qualitative Research Practice*. London: Sage.

Ritzer, George. 2008. *Sociological Theory*. New York: McGraw-Hill.

Robinson, Martin. 2013. 'Police Forces Pay £25 million to Informants and Nearly Half Is Spent by London's Met'. *Daily Mail*, 18 June. Accessed 4 July 2014. http://www.dailymail.co.uk/news/article-2343764/Police-forces-pay-25million-informants-nearly-half-spent-London-s-Met.html.

Rosenfeld, Richard, Bruce A. Jacobs, and Richard Wright. 2003. 'Snitching and the Code of the Street'. *British Journal of Criminology* 43 (2): 291–309.

Sampson, Robert J., and John H. Laub. 1993. *Crime in the Making: Pathways and Turning Points through Life*. Cambridge, MA: Harvard University Press.

Sapp, Allen D., and Michael S. Vaughn 1990. 'The Social Status of Adult and Juvenile Sex Offenders in Prison: An Analysis of the Importation Model'. *Journal of Police and Criminal Psychology* 6 (2): 2–7.

Saunders, Kate. 1996. *Eighteen Layers of Hell: Stories from the Chinese Gulag*. London: Cassell.

Scheff, Thomas J., Suzanne M. Retzinger, and Michael T. Ryan. 1989. 'Crime, Violence, and Self Esteem: Review and Proposals'. In *The Social Importance of Self-Esteem*, edited by Andrew M. Mecca, Neil J. Smelser, and John Vasconcellos, 165–99. Berkeley: University of California Press.

Schrag, Clarence. 1954. 'Leadership among Prison Inmates'. *American Sociological Review* 19: 37–42.

Scott, James. 1985. *Weapons of the Weak: Everyday Forms of Peasant Resistance*. New Haven, NJ: Yale University Press.

Scott, James. 1990. *Domination and the Arts of Resistance: Hidden Transcripts*. New Haven, NJ: Yale University Press.

Seymour, James D. 2005. 'Sizing Up China's Prisons'. In *Crime, Punishment, and Policing in China*, edited by Børge Bakken, 140–70. Lanham, MD: Rowman & Littlefield.

Seymour, James D. 2006. 'Profit and Loss in China's Contemporary Prison System'. In *Remolding and Resistance among Writers of the Chinese Prison Camp: Disciplined and Published*, edited by Philip Williams and Yenna Wu, 157–73. London: Routledge.

Seymour, James D., and Richard Anderson. 1998. *New Ghosts, Old Ghosts: Prisons and Labor Reform Camps in China*. London: M. E. Sharpe.

Shanxi Prison Administration Bureau. 2010. *Nüzi jianyu juxing fuxing renyuan guoxue jingdian yuanwen beisong, guifan duilie bisai* [Female prison organized inmate competition on classic text recitations and foot drill]. Shanxi Prison. 3 June. http://www.sxjyj.gov.cn/Item/650.aspx.

Shaw, Clifford Robe. 1968. *The Jack-Roller: A Delinquent Boy's Own Story*. Chicago: University of Chicago Press.

Shaw, Victor. 1998. 'Productive Labor and Thought Reform in Chinese Corrections: A Historical and Comparative Analysis'. *Prison Journal* 78 (2): 186–211.

Sherman, Lawrence. 1993. 'Defiance, Deterrence, and Irrelevance: A Theory of the Criminal Sanction'. *Journal of Research in Crime and Delinquency* 30 (4): 445–73.

Shi, Naian. 2010. *The Water Margin: The Outlaws of the Marsh*. North Clarendon, VT: Tuttle.

Sichuan Prison Administration Bureau. 2011. 'Guangyuan jianyu juxing "qiang guifan yan lüji" duilie bisai' [Guangyuan Prison organized 'strengthening rules and reinforcing self-discipline' marching tournament]. Accessed 2 July 2013. http://www.jybj.gov.cn/2011-11/3/660-4701-4508.htm.

Sinha, Rajita. 2001. 'How Does Stress Increase Risk of Drugs Abuse and Relapse?' *Psychopharmacology* 158 (4): 343–59.

Smith, Adam (1973). *An Inquiry into the Nature and Causes of the Wealth of Nations*. New York: Modern Library.

Smith, Catrin. 2002. 'Punishment and Pleasure: Women, Food and the Imprisoned Body'. *Sociological Review* 50 (2): 197–214.

Solomon, Joan. 2013. *Science of the People: Understanding and Using Science in Everyday Contexts*. New York: Routledge.

Song, Bin, and Ding Xu. 2011. 'Qiangzhi geli jiedu gongzuo renyuan zhuanye hua zhi biaozhun' [The standard of the professionalization of Compulsory Isolation for Drug Rehabilitation staffs]. *Journal of Shanghai University of Political Science & Law (The Rule of Law Forum)* 26 (1): 103–107.

South, Catherine R., and Jane Wood. 2006. 'Bullying in Prisons: The Importance of Perceived Social Status, Prisonization, and Moral Disengagement'. *Aggressive Behavior* 32 (5): 490–501.

Spohn, Cassia, and David Holleran. 2002. 'The Effect of Imprisonment on Recidivism Rates of Felony Offenders: A Focus on Drugs Offenders'. *Criminology* 40 (2): 329–58.

State Council. 1982. *Zhonghua renmin gongheguo laodong jiaoyang shixing banfa* [Trial measures for re-education through labour].

State Council. 1990. 'Kanshou suo tiaoli' [Law on detention centre].

State Council. 1995. 'Qiangzhi jiedu banfa' [Compulsory drugs rehabilitation methods].

State Council. 2011. 'Jiedu tiaoli' [Drugs treatment regulations].

Sun, Guang. 2007. 'Xidu renyuan dongtai guankong jizhi de goucheng' [The structure of the drugs user's dynamic control system]. *Jiangsu jingguan xueyuan xuebao* [Journal of Jiangsu Police Officer College] 22: 22–31.

Sun, Zhi. 2007. 'Jianyu shixing liangji guanli de sikao yu shijian' [Thoughts and practices on the use of the 'two level management' in the prison]. *China Prison Journal* 22(1): 95–96.

Surette, Ray. 2011. *Media, Crime, and Criminal Justice: Images, Realities, and Policies*. Belmont, CA: Wadsworth.

Sutherland, Edwin H. 1955. *Principles of Criminology*. Chicago: Lippincott.

Sykes, Gresham M. 1958. *The Society of Captives: A Study of a Maximum-Security Prison*. Princeton, NJ: Princeton University Press.

Sykes, Gresham M., and David Matza. 1957. 'Techniques of Neutralization: A Theory of Delinquency'. *American Sociological Review* 22 (6): 664–70.

Sykes, Gresham M., and Sheldon L. Messinger. 1960. 'The Inmate Social System'. In *Theoretical Studies in the Social Organization of the Prison*, edited by Richard A. Cloward, 5–19. New York: Social Science Research Council.

Tang, Feng. 2014. 'Xidu fandu you taren xidu beipan sannian ban zhuihui moji' [Drugs dealer felt regret after being sentenced for three years because of seducing others to take drugs]. *Dalian wanbao*, 29 June.
Tanner, Harold M. 1994. 'China's "Gulag" Reconsidered: Labor Reform in the 1980s and 1990s'. *China Information* 9 (1): 40–71.
Tasca, Melinda, Marie L. Griffin, and Nancy Rodriguez. 2010. 'The Effect of Importation and Deprivation Factors on Violent Misconduct: An Examination of Black and Latino Youth in Prison. *Youth Violence and Juvenile Justice* 8 (3): 234–49.
Thomas, Charles W. 1977. 'Theoretical Perspectives on Prisonization: A Comparison of the Importation and Deprivation Models'. *Journal of Criminal Law and Criminology* 68 (1): 135–45.
Tian, Doudou. 2012. 'Shenbian de gandong: chiqiang dufan zai zai jiaojing shoushang' [Touching things by your side: Armed drug dealers arrested by traffic police officers]. *People's Daily*. 19 March. Accessed 15 April 2013. http://cpc.people.com.cn/GB/64093/64104/17420568.html.
Tomás-Rosselló, Juana, and Anne Bergenstrom. 2013. 'Policies and Approaches to Drugs Use and Dependence in East and Southeast Asia: From Compulsion to Evidence Base?' *Drugs and Alcohol Review* 32 (3): 229–31.
Tong, Changli. 2011. 'Maguan xian xuanpin "zhian ermu" weihu chengqu zhian wending' [Maguan County employs 'security ears and eyes' to protect local security and stability]. Maguan County: Maguan County People's Government. Accessed 20 February 2013. http://www.ynmg.gov.cn/news/2011/201111/20111108091742_9930.html.
Trammell, Rebecca. 2012. *Enforcing the Convict Code: Violence and Prison Culture*. Boulder, CO: Lynne Rienner.
Tran, Thi Tuyet. 2013. 'Is the Learning Approach of Students from the Confucian Heritage Culture Problematic?' *Educational Research for Policy and Practice* 12 (1): 57–65.
Trevaskes, Susan. 2003. 'Public Sentencing Rallies in China: The Symbolizing of Punishment and Justice in a Socialist State'. *Crime, Law and Social Change* 39 (4): 359–82.
Trevaskes, Susan. 2007. *Courts and Criminal Justice in Contemporary China*. Lanham, MD: Lexington Books.
Tucker, John. 2014. 'Durham Police Bonus Payments to Informants Could Violate Defendants' Rights: Civil Rights Group Questions Legality of Offering Financial Incentives to Drugs Informants Without Disclosure'. *Indy Week*, 12 March. Accessed 25 June 2018. http://www.indyweek.com/indyweek/durham-police-bonus-payments-to-informants-could-violate-defendants-rights/Content?oid=3927386.
Turner, Victor W. 1987. 'Betwixt and Between: The Liminal Period in *Rites de Passage*'. In *Betwixt & Between: Patterns of Masculine and Feminine Initiation*, edited by Louise Carus Mahdi, Steven Foster, and Meredith Little, 3–22. La Salle, IL: Open Court.
UN. 2004. 'Istanbul Protocol Manual on the Effective Investigation and Documentation of Torture and Other Cruel, Inhuman or Degrading Treatment or Punishment, New York and Geneva'. Accessed 29 December 2017. http://www.ohchr.org/documents/publications/training8rev1en.pdf.
UN General Assembly. 1984. 'Convention against Torture and Other Cruel, Inhuman or Degrading Treatment or Punishment'. 10 December, United Nations, Treaty Series, vol. 1465, p. 85. Accessed 29 December 2017. http://www.refworld.org/docid/3ae6b3a94.html.

Visher, Christy, Nancy G. La Vigne, and Jill Farrell. 2003. *Illinois Prisoners' Reflections on Returning Home*. Urban Institute Report. Washington, DC: Urban Institute Justice Policy Center.

Walder, Andrew. 1986. *Communist Neo-traditionalism: Works and Authority in Chinese Industry*. Berkeley: University of California Press.

Wang, Feiling. 2004. 'Reformed Migration Control and New Targeted People: China's Hukou System in the 2000s'. *The China Quarterly* 177: 115–32.

Wang, Haiguang. 2011. 'Zhuangui he chanbian: Zhongguo dangdai hukou zhidu xingcheng de zhidu yuanyuan tanxi' [Changing and mutation: The formation of contemporary *hukou* system in China]. *Zhanlue yu guanli*. Accessed 10 January 2012. http://www.cssm.gov.cn/view.php?id=31890.

Wang, Lin. 2006. 'Wanglin: qizongzui jueding zhian zhibiao dang fei' [Wanglin: 'Seven sins' show that security quota should be abolished]. Xinjingbao/Sinanews. Accessed 13 April 2013. http://news.sina.com.cn/c/pl/2006-08-01/054010591065.shtml.

Wang, Shun'an. 1999. 'Lun Mao Zedong gaizao zuifan de sixiang' [On Mao Zedong's ideology on criminal reform]. *Zhongguo renmin daxue xuebao* [Journal of the Renmin University of China] 8 (1): 75–79.

Wang, Xiudong. 2011. 'Sha wei bang mian qian, hequ you hecong' [In front of the killing-might-rods, from where to where?]. *Yuedu yu xiezuo* [Reading and writing] 5: 37–38.

Wang, Yuechuan. 2007. 'Rujia jingdian chongyi de dangdai yiyi' [Contemporary significance of the reinterpretation of Confucian classics]. *Xinan minzhu daxue xuebao (renwen sheke ban)* [Journal of Southwest University for Nationalities (humanities and social science)] 10: 60–76.

Wanyan, L. 2013. 'Wang Jie: The Hero Who Was Nearly Forgotten'. *Hongyan chunqiu* 1: 76–79.

Weitzer, R., and S. A. Tuch. 2005. 'Determinants of Public Satisfaction with the Police.' *Police Quarterly* 8(3): 279–97.

Welch, Michael. 2011. *Corrections: A Critical Approach*. New York: Routledge.

Wellford, Charles. 1967. 'Factors Associated with Adoption of the Inmate Code: A Study of Normative Socialization'. *Journal of Criminal Law, Criminology and Police Science* 58 (2): 197–203.

Williams, Philip, and Yenna Wu. 2004. *The Great Wall of Confinement: The Chinese Prison Camp through Contemporary Fiction and Reportage*. Berkeley: University of California Press.

Wolf, René. 2007. 'Judgement in the Grey Zone: The Third Auschwitz (*Kapo*) Trial in Frankfurt 1968'. *Journal of Genocide Research* 9 (4): 617–35.

Wong, K. C. 2004. 'Govern Police by Law (Yifa Zhijing) in China'. Supplement. *The Australian and New Zealand Journal of Criminology* 37 (S1): 90–106.

Wu, Danhong, and Xiaofu Sun. 2001. 'Lun youhuo zhencha' [On enticement detection]. *Fa shang yanjiu—Zhongnan caijing daxue xuebao faxue ban* [Studies in law and business]: 23–31.

Wu, Guilong. 2009. 'Waibiao shouruo yeshi zuiguo? Zhian zhibiao gai quxiao le ba' [Looking weak is a crime? Security quota should be abolished]. *Haixia dushi bao*, 4 June. Accessed 13 April 2013. http://news.163.com/09/0604/19/5B03FBD3000120GR.html.

Wu, Hongda Harry. 1992. *Laogai: The Chinese Gulag*. Boulder, CO: Westview.

Wu, Hongda Harry. 1993. *Bitter Winds: A Memoir of My Years in China's Gulag*. New York: John Wiley & Sons.

Wu, Y. 2012. 'Tisheng zhengfu gonggong guanxi shuiping yanjiu' [Study on how to improve the government-public relationship]. *Shehui kexue yanjiu* [Social science research] 2: 38–43.

Xia, Guomei, Xiushi Yang, Jun Li, and Jia Miu. 2009. 'Xinxing dupin lanyong de chengyin yu jieguo' [The reason and effects of the rise of new drugs]. *Shehui kexue* [Social science] 3: 73–81.

Xu, Bin. 2012. 'Grandpa Wen: Scene and Political Performance'. *Sociological Theory* 30 (2): 114–29.

Xu, Jianhua. 2010. 'Motorcycle Taxi Drivers and Motorcycle Ban Policy in the Pearl River Delta'. PhD thesis, University of Hong Kong.

Xu, Jingcun 2011. 'Youhuo zhencha de yingyong yu kongzhi' [The use of enticement detection]. *Renmin jiancha* [People's procuratorial semimonthly] 14: 6–9.

Xue, Haoming, Zhi Luo, Lin Duo, Xue Ji, Ling Deng, Yang Lihua, Junrui Zhong, Yuan Ruan, Yun Lin, and Jiarui Zheng. 2010. 'Reports on the Possibility for Former Drug Users to Quit the Dynamic Control System'. Yunnan: Yunnan jianshao shanghai wangluo [Yunnan Harm Reduction Network].

Xue, Haoming, Zhi Luo, Lin Duo, Xue Ji, Ling Deng, Yang Lihua, Junrui Zhong, Yuan Ruan, Yun Lin, and Jiarui Zheng. 2011. 'Jiwang xidu renyuan dui xidu renyuan dongtai guankong xitong de taidu ji pingjia fenxi' [Analysis on ex-drug users' attitude and evaluation to the IDU Dynamic management and control]. *Zhongguo yaowu lanyong zazhi* [Chinese journal of drug dependence] 6: 447–50.

Yan, Dengshan. 2009. 'Jiedu moshi tansuo yu sikao' [Reflection and discussion on the drug treatment model]. *Zhongguo sifa* [Justice of China] 5: 53–56.

Yan, R. 2004. *Xiandai zhengfu xingxiang guanli* [Modern government image management]. Sichuan: Sichuan University Press.

Yang, Dan. 2010. 'Study of the Informers of Criminal Investigation'. Master's dissertation, Southwestern University of Finance and Economics.

Yang, Jie. 2006. 'Shi lun xidu laojiao renyuan zhong de renge quexian ji qi jiaozhi' [On the personality defects of drug users in re-education through labour]. *Fanzui yu gaizao yanjiu* 10: 46–48.

Yang, Jun, Yujun Mao, and Qiwu Hou. 2008. 'Qianyi jianyu ganjing zhiwu fanzui de tedian, yuanyin ji duice' [On the characteristics, reasons and solutions to crimes committed by prison officers]. *Jingguan wenyuan* 4: 73–76.

Yang, Tao, and Jianzhon Cheng. 2012. 'Qianlun jianyu de jingli peizhi' [On police force allocation in the prison]. *China Prison Journal* 2: 133–36.

Yang, Zhigang. 2008. *Youhuo zhencha yanjiu* [Studies on enticement detection]. Beijing: Zhongguo fazhi chuban.

Yao, H. 2012. 'Yunei zuifan jiaocha ganran yu chongxin fanzui' [Cross-infection in the prison and recidivism]. *Hubei jingguan xueyuan xuebao* [Journal of Hubei University of Police] 2: 63–65.

Yao, Tianyong, and Yong Wang. 2012. 'Diaoyu zhifa de xingzheng weifa xing ji qi guize' [The administrative illegality and regulations on 'fishing enforcement']. *Zhengzhi yu falü* [Political science and law] 6: 73–78.

Yu, Jianrong. 2004. 'One Interpreting Framework of Rural Migrants' Right Protection Activities'. *Shehui xue yanjiu* [Sociological research] 2: 49–55.

Yu, N. 2007. 'Establishing an Honest Image of the Government'. *Fazhi yu shehui* 9: 528.

Zhang, J. 2011. 'On Human Resources Management in the New Prison Enterprise under the New System'. *Jingguan wenyuan* 3: 37–41.

Zhang, Keke. 2012. 'Xingshi zhencha zhong de xianren zhidu tantao' [On 'lines' in criminal investigation]. *Fazhi yu jingji* [Law and economy] 2: 39–40.

Zhang, Lianghong, and Enlin Yao. 2005. 'Baduan' jiedu kangfu moshi' [Eight steps towards drugs rehabilitation]. *Zhongguo yaowu yilai xing zazhi* 14: 237–39.

Zhang, Yang. 2012. 'Nanmen lijian zhan dumo' [The sword of the south slays the drug devil]. *People's Daily*, 13 June.

Zhang, Yonghai, and Huan Qi. 2006. 'Affection in Law, from "Stubborn and Dangerous Offender" to "Active Reform Element"'. *Falü yu shenghuo* [Law and life] 22: 50–51.

Zhang, Zhongxiang. 2006. Zhiwu fan jia gaofen de yuanyin fenxi ji guifan tujing' [Analysis on the reasons for the phenomenon of high scores for inmates providing daily services in the prison and ways to regulate it]. *Zhongguo sifa* [Justice of China]: 20–21.

Zhao, Xiaogeng, and Xiaoli Ma. 2005. 'Cong chiru xing dao xiuchixin: mantan zai jianyu jiaozheng zhong huanqi fuxing ren de xiuchi zhi xin' [From shaming penalty to the sense of shame: How to arouse the sense of shame among prisoners]. *Zhengfa luncong* 5: 75–79.

Zhejiang Province. 2008. 'Zhejiang sheng "shequ jiedu (shequkangfu) gongzuo guifan" shixing' [Zhejiang Province regulations on community drug rehabilitations and recovery].

Zheng, Min. 2006. 'Wanshan laodong jiaoyang zhidu youguan wenti de sikao' [On perfecting the related regulations of labour education and rehabilitation]. *Journal of Anhui Vocational College of Police Officers* 5 (3): 23–35.

Zhi, Zhengfa. 2013. 'Xianren zhencha de hefaxing ji guize tansuo' [Discussion on the legality and regulation of informant investigation]. *Journal of Yunnan Police Officer Academy* 5: 70–75.

Zhou, G., L. Ma, and W. Xie. 2013. 'Jianyu qiye ganlan moshi yanjiu' [Studies on the 'olive' model of the prison enterprise]. *China Prison Journal* 2: 111–15.

Zhou, Nan. 2009. 'Jingli buzu shi laotou yuba chansheng de keguan yuanyin' [The lack of police manpower is the main reason that contributes to the formation of 'prison bullies']. Xinhua News Agency, 31 May. Accessed 8 November 2013. http://big5.xinhuanet.com/gate/big5/news.xinhuanet.com/local/2009-05/31/content_11460673.htm.

Zhou, Qian, and Yiwen Wan. 2008. 'Dui queli zonghe jingli guan jiejue jingli ziyuan buzu wenti de sikao' [Thoughts on solving the problem of a lack of resources in the police force from a comprehensive police force perspective]. *China Prison Journal*: 131–34.

Zhou, Yuezhi. 2000. 'Watchdogs on Party Leashes: Contexts and Implications of Investigative Journalism in Post-Deng China'. *Journalism Studies* 1 (4): 577–97.

Zhou, Z., and Y. Zhou. 2006. 'Major Problems Exist in Contemporary Prison Work'. *Fanzui yu gaizao yanjiu* 11: 14–20.

Zhu, Quangen, Guiyong Chen, and Yanping Deng. 2010. 'Jidong che jiashi yu yaowu lanyong wenti' [Motor vehicle driving and drug abuse]. *Zhongguo yaowu lanyong zazhi* [Chinese journal of drug dependence] 19: 438.

Zhu, Weixing, Jiaqiang Dong, and Therese Hesketh. 2009. 'Preventing Relapse in Incarcerated Drug Users in Yunnan Province, China'. *Drug and Alcohol Review* 28 (6): 641–47.

Zhu, Yuchen. 2005. 'Teqing: Jingfei zhijian de huise renqun' [Special agents: Grey area between the police and the criminals]. *Zhongguo xinwen zhoukan* [China newsweek], 6 June.

Zijderveld, A. C. 1982. *Reality in a Looking-Glass: Rationality through an Analysis of Traditional Folly*. London; Boston: Routledge Kegan & Paul.

Zimbardo, Philip. 2007. *The Lucifer Effect: Understanding How Good People Turn Evil*. New York: Random House.

Index

The letter *t* following a page number denotes a table, the letter *f* a figure.

activists, 93
administrative detention penalty, 52
administrative system of punishments, 2. *See* re-education-through-labour centres (*laojiao*)
administratively detained, 51
administrators, prison: and strategy of control, 81
'administrators', prisoner: in cells, 89, 100; in factories, 91
admission training, 57–58. *See also* 'autobiography writing', marching drill, quiet sitting, studying
Analects, 61, 64
anti-drug day, 107
anti-drug education, 64
Anti-drug Law of 2008, 51
anti-drug propaganda, 19, 20, 22, 100, 107
arrest, 51, 52, 64, 75
arrest quotas, 7, 30, 44, 45, 46, 123; and hooking, 42–43
'ascetic monk', 26
authority among inmates. *See* inmate authority
autobiographies, 61–63, 120

background information investigation, 105–8
backstage reality versus front-stage ideal, examples of, 5, 6, 8, 46, 102, 124, 125; prisoner witness to, 7, 16, 30, 76, 112
'bad' police practices. *See* police practices
betrayal: acts of, 36; feelings about, 41–42, 121; refusal to commit, 37, 39

biaoxian, 59, 61, 94
'big account', 96
'big crime-cracking rate'. *See* crime-cracking rate
Bakken, Borge, 1, 29, 39, 84, 122; on exemplary norms, 5–6, 16, 18; on model figures, 7, 17; on sacrifice, 26; on self-criticism, 62; on ways of lying, 5–6, 61, 74
'boundless loyalty', 23
Brady, Anne-Marie, 17, 124, 125
Braithwaite, John, 3–4, 120
bureaucratic system, 116; criteria set by, 30; pressures created by, 7; routine in, 107

cash bonuses, 43
cell bosses. *See* prison bullies
cellmates, 54, 66
cells, 54, 58, 64, 65, 71, 84; arrival in, 8; compulsory isolation for drug rehabilitation centres, 66; in detention centres, 51, 66; initiations inside, 66–73; as a 'living area', 66; in re-education-through-labour centres (*laojiao*), 52, 66; social organization within, 66–67, 76–78, 84, 88–89, 99, 100; underground market in, 86; violence within, 66–69, 76, 77, 86, 88. *See also* cellmates; initiations; inmate elites; marching drills; underground market
censorship, 125
children: as a metaphor for drug users, 55; ex-inmate's wariness of, 106
Churchill, Winston, 118

cigarettes, 81, 96; access to, 70; in prison economy, 86–87, 95, 98; and prison status, 97. *See also* underground market
'civilized' behaviour, 65; as an ideal, 77, 87; in prison jargon, 87; versus 'uncivilized', 66. *See also* 'uncivilized' treatment
code of conduct among inmates, 65; contrast with official code, 66, 81; enforcement, 86–87. *See also* 'inmates' code of conduct'
cold baths, 69–70, 76
commonness, as a Chinese concept, 39–40
Communist Party, 7; and cultural norms, 122; as models in 'front-stage ideal', 18, 23, 26, 124; as an object of blame, 115–16; as a term for police, 45, 123–24; use of informants, 32
community-based drug treatment. *See* drug treatment programmes: community-based 'compulsory education and treatment measure', 51
compulsory drug rehabilitation centres (*qiangjie*), 2, 49, 51, 52, 66, 110; change from re-education from labour legal education in, 53, 64; definition of, 75; prisoner-guard ratio, 85; relationship to *qiangge*, 52; song sung in, 62; violence in, 67–69, 71. *See also* administrative system of punishments; re-education through labour
compulsory labour, 8, 74, 78; education through, 100–101; idealization of, 8, 102; as punishment, 129; in rehabilitation strategy, 82–84
compulsory isolation for drug rehabilitation centres (*qiangge*), 1, 2, 32, 49, 51, 74, 113, 120; change from re-education from labour, 50, 52–53, 83; conditions, 56; definition of, 2; dorm heads, 85; education in, factories, 84, 89–91, 100–101; goods in, 96; legal education in, 64, 83; power relations, 79; sentence reduction in, 94–95; relationship to *qiangjie*, 52; staff-to-inmate ratio,

85. *See also* administrative system of punishments; compulsory isolation for drug rehabilitation centres; prisonization; re-education through labour
'comrades-in-arms', 21
concentration camps, 81
'correction of acts', 57–58
'correction of thoughts', 61. *See also* autobiographies, 'studying'
corruption, 87, 100–101
'courtesy', 13
Crewe, Ben, 80, 87, 96
crime-cracking rate, 34
Cultural Revolution, 32, 104

deculturation, 54
danwei. *See* work unit
deprivation model, 49
detainees. *See* prisoners
detention, 40; administrative, 2, 50; experience in 3, 55–73, 76, 94. *See also* merit points
detention centres, 1, 40, 51, 55, 66, 85, 99, 110; coercion in, 67, 71, 72, 76; inmate bureaucracy within, 99
detention facility officers, 1, 79
dignity: deprivation during detention, 54, 55, 57, 72, 76, 78, 120; deprivation post-release, 107, 113; efforts to regain, 99, 100*t*
'dirty work', 87, 88
discipline, 50, 58, 85; through hunger, 72; power to, 8; and violence, 69
'discipline administrator'. *See* 'administrators', prisoner: in cells
discreditable stigma. *See* stigma: discreditable
discredited stigma. *See* stigma: discredited
district police, 32–33, 44
dorm head, 66–67, 68, 86; authority of, 68, 69–70, 72; as enforcer, 85; 'followers', 85; responsibilities, 67–68, 99
drivers' license, loss of, 114–16, 123, 124
drug addicts, 9, 44, 123; in post-release 'control system', 110–11; in detention centres, 51–52; in front-stage ideal,

20, 24; in law and regulation, 44, 51; and police, 44; withdrawal in prison, 52. *See also* prison experience; former drug users; hooking: among drug users; labelling
drug dealer 'hooks'. *See* 'hooks': drug dealer
drug dealers, 2, 17, 19, 44; collusion with police, 38, 42–43, 123; contrast with users, 24; in front-stage ideal, 19–22, 27, 28, 31. *See also* hooking: among drug dealers
'drug reform', 52
drug tests, 108–9, 111–13; in the control system, 108, 110; effects, 113; surprise, 116, 120; as harassment, 111, 112. *See also* drug user control system; harassment
drug treatment programmes: community-based, 51; missionary-run, 50
drug user control system, 108, 110–13, 116–17, 120, 123
drug user 'hooks'. *See* 'hooks', drug user
drug user information database, 110, 114
drug-driving, 114
Drug-Rehab Three-Character Classic, 64
drugs used, 1n1
dynamic management and control system, 110, 116

early release, 94–95
'education administrator', 89, 100–101. *See also* 'administrators', prisoner: in cells
education, 50, 73, 82, 100; among inmates, 85, 89; in Chinese social control policy, 75–77; ideal, 8; improved, 101; inmate response to 3; through model learning, 17, 27; through studying', 63–67; prison, 73, 74; 'transitional', 57; unrealized promises of, 5, 6, 8, 47, 58, 78. *See also* studying
educational effect of violence and shame, 76, 78
'education training', 54, 55
educational activities, 100–101
Eight Honours and Eight Disgraces, 63–64
'enemy-and-me', 50
enticement detection, 32, 34–35, 38, 39, 46; use of informants in, 34–35. *See also* hooking; 'hooks'; informants, use of
'essential regulations for inmates', 65
'exchange of favours', 86
exemplary norms, 1, 16, 18–19, 122
exemplary tales, 27–28, 122

factories, prison, 8, 83–84, 88, 101, 123; inmate elites and, 83, 89, 92; management of, 79, 82, 84, 90, 91; in Maoist theory, 102; punishment in, 91; replicating 'real world', 90–91; smuggling in, 98. *See also* compulsory labour
family, 10, 13, 26, 98; as background informants, 105, 106; in exemplary tales, 27
feeling betrayed. *See* betrayal, feelings of
'five regularities', 58
food deprivation, 71–72, 101. *See* initiation ceremony
former drug detainees, 1, 13, 47; breaking into the world of: *see* methodology: gaining social access; propaganda about, 2, 9–10
former drug users. *See* former drug detainees
former prisoners, 3–8, 29; and control system, 110, 112; fear of social stigma, 107; firings, 113; social isolation, 112–13; social world, 9–15; stories told by, 27–28; views of the Communist Party, 116. *See also* drug tests; drivers' license, loss of; former drug detainees, 'hooks', stigma
Freud, Sigmund, 125
front-stage ideal. *See* back-stage reality and front-stage ideal

Garfinkel, 118, 119
Goffman, Erving, 5, 9–10, 54, 55, 71, 78, 104. *See also* backstage reality versus front-stage ideal
'good' police practices. *See* police practices
government public relations, 18

'great wall', 2
'green eyes and ears', 33
greeting to officer, compulsory, 59
'grey eyes and ears', 33
guanxi, 86–87, 94
Guomindang, 104

'happy diary entry', 74
happy pill, 1n2
health centres, 50
'heart-to-heart talk', 11, 105
help education, 105, 115; and shame, 111
helplessness, feelings of, 116
'heroes', police as, 27, 29, 122, 123; clash with detainees' experiences, 16, 31, 121; detainees' internalization of ideal, 125; examples, 19–22; fighting 'evil' drug dealers, 19–22; Maoist precedent, 17–18; in propaganda, 7–8, 16–22; and the state, 22–23. *See also* exemplary norm; self-sacrifice, spirit of; 'saviours', police as
Heroic Civilians (*Pingmin yingxiong* 平民英雄), 27
'hideous reality', 122–124
hierarchy of goods, 94, 96–97
hierarchy of power, inmates', 80–82; 92f; within cells, 88–89, 93f; eating and, 72; new and old, 70–71
home visits, 105; and shame, 106–8
hooking, 30, 31–32; among drug dealers, 34, 35, 38, 39–40; circulating information about, 39–41; to meet arrest quotas, 123; as proof of police immorality, 41–43, 44–45, 46; three types, 35–38. *See* enticement detection; lines; 'uncivilized' treatment
'hooks', 31; 'double agents' 39, 79; drug dealers, 38, 79; drug users, 37–38; one-off, 36, 37. *See also* 'being hooked'; informants: use of
Howard, John, 118–19
'housekeeping administrator'. *See* 'administrators', prisoner: in cells
Hu Yaobang, 17

humiliation: of prison life, 5, 6, 57, 99, 119, 120–21; efforts to avoid, 113; in initiation ceremony, 66, 75, 76; in re-integration, 103–4, 106, 111–12, 116, 118, 120, 123; rule enforcement and, 72
hypocrisy as a system, 3, 5, 6, 7, 54, 108, 113, 119, 125–26; definition of, 5–7; detainee experience of, 16, 29, 45–46, 63, 66, 102, 115; participation in, 61; and play-acting, 4–7; in post-discharge life, 103; the production of, 30, 31, 47, 73–78, 108; roles of officials and inmate elites, 99–101. *See also* 'official hypocrisy'; play-acting; propaganda: and moral expectations
hypocritical system. *See* hypocrisy as a system

identity card, 110–12
importation model, 48–49
impression management, 5, 6, 18, 46. *See also* backstage reality versus front-stage ideal, examples of
'informal force', 88–89
informants, 39; use of, 32–33; monetary rewards, 43; normalization, 46. *See also* enticement detection: informants in; hooking; 'hooks'; lines; snitch
informers. *See* informant
initiation ceremony, 6, 47–48, 53–54, 75; in compulsory drug-rehabilitation centres, 52–53; in detention centres, 51; effect on prisoners, 76–77, 102; and prison culture, 48–49; by officers, 54–66; by prisoners, 66–73; in re-education-through-labour centres (*laojiao*), 52–53
inmate authority, 47–48, 66–67, 92, 100t; and dignity, 99; in enforcing officer authority, 87–89; formation of, 84–85; purpose, 78, 81–82; in self-regulation, 86–87. *See also* inmate elites
inmate elites, 79, 98, 123; as 'activists', 93; formation of, 80–82; role in prison system, 84–92; relations with officers,

100t; rewarding, 92–93, 94, 96–98. *See also* inmate authority; organized dependence; principled particularism
inmates' code of conduct, 64, 65, 73, 76; and prisonization, 48. *See also* code of conduct among inmates
inmates' trials, 67, 70–71, 76, 120
immorality of police, perceived. *See also* 'uncivilized' treatment
'inside-regulation', 67. *See also* code of conduct among inmates; hierarchy of power, inmates'; inmate authority
institutional change, 2
'instructors' (inmate enforcers), 53–54, 91; of the prison factory, 98
'investigative line', 33
Istanbul Protocol, 75

Jiao Yulu, 17
job-placement centre, 111
jokes, 125–26

Kapos, 81, 101

labelling of former drug users, 2, 106–7, 108, 113
labour. *See* compulsory labour
'labour rehabilitation'. *See* compulsory labour
laojiao. See re-education-through-labour centres (*laojiao*)
'law breakers', 104
Lei Feng, 17, 135
'liaison personnel', 33. *See also* informants
life opportunities, post-detention, impact of police on, 111–13
'life-and-death battle', 20. *See also* 'heroes', police as
life-history approach, 9
liminal *persona*, 53
lines, 33–34
'lip service', 13
liu (流), effect of word, 110
'living area', 66
local police station, 24, 32, 33, 44, 112

making profits. *See* profit generation, prison
'manager', 89, 97, 111
'management and control system'. *See* drug user control system
Maoist thought, influence of, 104
Mao Zedong, 82, 102
march-drilling. *See* marching drill
marching drill, 58–59, 76, 119
market, prison, 80, 87, 95–96, 100t. *See also* 'prison supermarket'; underground market
Marxist-Leninist ideology, 82–83
media, 33, 35; joke about, 125–26; and moral legitimacy, 117–18; negative report on police, 44; portrayal of drugs, 42–43; portrayals of police and prison officers, 19–28, 41–42, 105, 115; portrayal of prisons, 75; propaganda function, 7, 16, 30, 125
mental torture. *See* torture: mental and physical
merit points, 94–95
methodology: gaining social access, 9, 10
Mills, C. Wright, 6
missionary drug-treatment centres. *See* drug treatment programmes: missionary-run
'model figures', 7, 16, 17–19; in Party propaganda, 14. *See also* in drug dealers: front-stage ideal; drug users: front-stage ideal; 'heroes', police as; media: portrayals of police and prison officers; 'selfless' 'models'
modi paicha. See background information investigation
moral expectations: creating, 28–29; propaganda and, 121–22
moral legitimacy, Communist Party, 7, 29, 124; role of media, 19–26; and propaganda, 122
Motai, 1, 68, 70, 76, 86, 99
'mouthpiece of the party', 17, 28. *See also* media; moral legitimacy, Communist Party
mythology, Chinese, 59

myths, social, 26; confrontation with reality, 123

National News Broadcast, 125–26
'natural therapy', 52
neutralization theory, 4, 118
'newcomers' district', 57–58
'new drugs', 112
'new men', 83
'noble quality', 23
norms: enforcement in cells, 77; in Party strategy, 122; police and prison, 1, 6; in prison, 48; prisonization and, 49; traditional: *see* exemplary norms

officer-inmate collusion. *See also* 'turning a blind eye'
officers' initiation ceremony. *See* admission ceremony
'official hypocrisy', 49
'official languages', 13
one-off 'hooks'. *See* 'hooks': one-off
One-to-One (television show), 22
organized dependence, 92–94
'outsiders', 96

pain. *See also* torture; pains of imprisonment
pains of imprisonment, 47–48, 77–78
'palace', the, 2
panopticon, 97
paramilitary training, 58–59
party propaganda, 1, 27, 74; based on 'exemplary norms', 16; contrast with prison realities, 3, 75, 78, 102, 115, 119, 121, 123, 125; and hypocrisy, 28; as impression management, 6; models in, 14, 18; police in, 7, 31, 109; prisoners in, 46. *See also* exemplary norms; impression management; 'political performances'
'people at the top', 85
'people in the front', 85
People's Police, 23, 26, 45
physical torture. *See* torture: mental and physical

play-acting and hypocrisy, 4–7. *See also* impression management
'police and criminals come from the same family', 31
police-drug dealer collusion. *See* drug dealers: collusion with police
police officers: backstage reality of, 44; in home visits, 105–6; treatment of post-detainees, 109–10, 112. *See also* district police; drug deals: and police; drug users: and police; heroes: police as 'model figures'; police practices; portrayals of police and prison officers; 'saviours', police as; shame: and police
police performance, in criminology, 121
police practices, 'good' versus 'bad', 108, 111
police station. *See* local police station
'political performances', 122
'political stability', 32
principled particularism, 84, 92–95, 97–98
prison: definition of, 1; nicknames, 2. *See also* compulsory drug rehabilitation centres (*qiangjie*); compulsory isolation for drug rehabilitation centres (*qiangge*); factories, prison; prison culture; prison economy; prison experience, prison food; re-education-through-labour centres (*laojiao*)
'prison bullies', 79, 99; hypocrisy of, 76
'prison canteen'. *See* 'prison supermarket'
prison culture, 3, 47; concept of, 47–49
prison economy. *See* market, prison
'prison enterprise group', 90
prison experience, 11, 49, 51–53, 57, 60, 74, 83, 95. *See also* administrative training; food deprivation; paramilitary training; quiet sitting; 'shock-and-awe' ceremony; stripping
prison factory. *See* factories, prison
prison food, 83, 95, 96, 101. *See also* food denial
prison gangs. *See* inmate elites
prison officers: enforcing authority, 87–88; ideal of, 26; and inmate elites, 79, 81; and prisoners, 74, 82, 84, 98

Index

prison rules, 8, 64–65, 72, 87, 88, 98, 100t; informal, 70, 73
'prison supermarket', 96f
prisoners, 54, 59, 80, 84, 85. *See also* former prisoners; hierarchy of power, inmates; initiation ceremony
prisonization, 3, 48–49; forms of, 54–77. *See also* admission training
'production administrator', 89
production lines, factory, 91–92
production quotas, factory, 91, 96, 100
profit generation, prison, 8, 101–2; and compulsory labour, 83; increasing pressure on, 88, 89–92, 100; as officer responsibility, 82
propaganda. *See* party propaganda
propagandizing. *See* party propaganda
Public Security Bureau, 110, 114

qiangge. *See* compulsory isolation for drug rehabilitation centres
qiangjie. *See* compulsory drug rehabilitation centre
QQ chat group, 13, 115
quiet-sitting, 59–61, 63, 73, 74; in Chinese tradition, 75

radio calisthenics, 58
recidivism, 3–4, 51
recidivists, 62–63
'red and ears', 33
re-education camps. *See* re-education-through-labour centres (*laojiao*)
re-education-through-labour centres (*laojiao*), 8, 49, 50, 83, 104, 119; authority in, 79; change to *qiangjie*, 51, 52–53; compulsory isolation, 52–53; compulsory labour, 83; coercion in centres, 63; definition, 2, 52, 75; effects of, 46; paramilitary training in, 58; profiting from, 86, 88–89; recidivists, 51; study, 63; termination, 2, 83; under administrative system, 50. *See also* compulsory isolation for drug rehabilitation centres (*qiangge*)
'reform through labour', 1; camp, 2

'regulations governing inmates' daily lives', 64
reintegration, 3–4, 103; ideal, 2; perceived failure, 123. *See also* 'background information'; drivers' licenses, loss of; drug tests; drug user management and control system; 'help education'; home visits; shame; 'targeted populations'
rejecting the rejector, 118
'remorse letter', 61
resolving conflict, 86–87
revenge, 38; 'taking violent revenge', 104
revocation of driver's licences. *See* driver's licences, loss of
'rule breakers', 104
rules and regulations, 1, 8, 72, 86
rules governing inmates' behavioural manners, 64

sacrifice. *See* self-sacrifice, spirit of
'salvation', 64
'saviours', police as, 23–24. *See also* 'heroes', police as
'security eyes and ears', 32
self-criticism, 62, 120
self-cultivation, 29–60
self-interested, 100: image of 'evil' dealers as, 20; image of 'bad' officers as, 31, 43, 45, 109
selfishness, 45, 81, 122
'selfless models', 5, 125
self-sacrifice, spirit of, 26–27, 122; as a concept, 26. *See also* heroes, police as; 'saviours', police as
'serious criminal offences', 104
'seven things that are not to be talked about', 17
shame, 4–6, 53, 55, 57, 62, 103, 120, 123; in Chinese philosophy, 75–77; among former detainees, 104; avoiding, 113; and police, 41–42; in prison cells, 69–70. *See also* background information investigation; help education: and shame; home visits: and shame; initiation ceremony
shaming, of police officers, 44

Sherman, Lawrence, 30, 118
'shock-and-awe' ceremony, 68–69, 76
sinner, 22
Smith, Adam, 121
snitch, 31, 34; prison, 81–82. *See also* 'hooks'
'social reform', 52
'social stability', 32–33, 104
'special agent', 34. *See* 'hooks', lines
'special residents', 104
spies, 32. *See also* informants
'spirit-breaking beating', 67, 69
'Standards for Being a Good Pupil and Child', 63
stigma, 9–10, 95, 102, 104–9, 113; discreditable versus discredited, 104–5; effect on fieldwork, 11. *See also* stigmatized identities
stigmatized identities, 109, 113, 116, 123
'strict-control period', 57
strip-searches, 76, 99, 119
'stripping', 54–57
'studying', 63*f*
surveillance, 32, 60; cameras, 85; post-release, 103–5; and stigma, 102

'taking violent revenge', 104
'targeted populations', 103–4, 116
the press. *See* mouthpiece of the party, media
theatrical performance, 5, 122
'threatening state security', 104
'three empties, six halves', 72

'to-be-a-newbie', 68
'tofu blankets', 58–59
torture, mental and physical, 8, 36, 50, 73, 119; reduction in, 88
'transitional education', 57
trash collectors, 97–98
'Treat the People as Family Members', 24
turning a blind eye, 66–67. *See also* officer-inmate collusion

'ultimate good', 60
'uncivilized' treatment, 66, 111–12. *See also* 'civilized' behaviour
US Convention against Torture, 75
underground markets, 86, 87, 100*t*
unlicensed taxis, 114
urine test. *See* drug test

violence: *See also* cells: violence within; compulsory drug rehabilitation centres (*qiangjie*): violence in; educational effect of violence and shame
vocational training, 8, 84, 86, 87, 102

Water Margin, 68, 69
ways of lying, 5–6, 61, 74, 120
'wise' people, 10
work target. *See also* production quotas, factory
work unit, 93

Zhiyang, 1, 69, 70, 89, 91, 95, 96, 101